IMAGES
of America

OAKBORO

I0799427

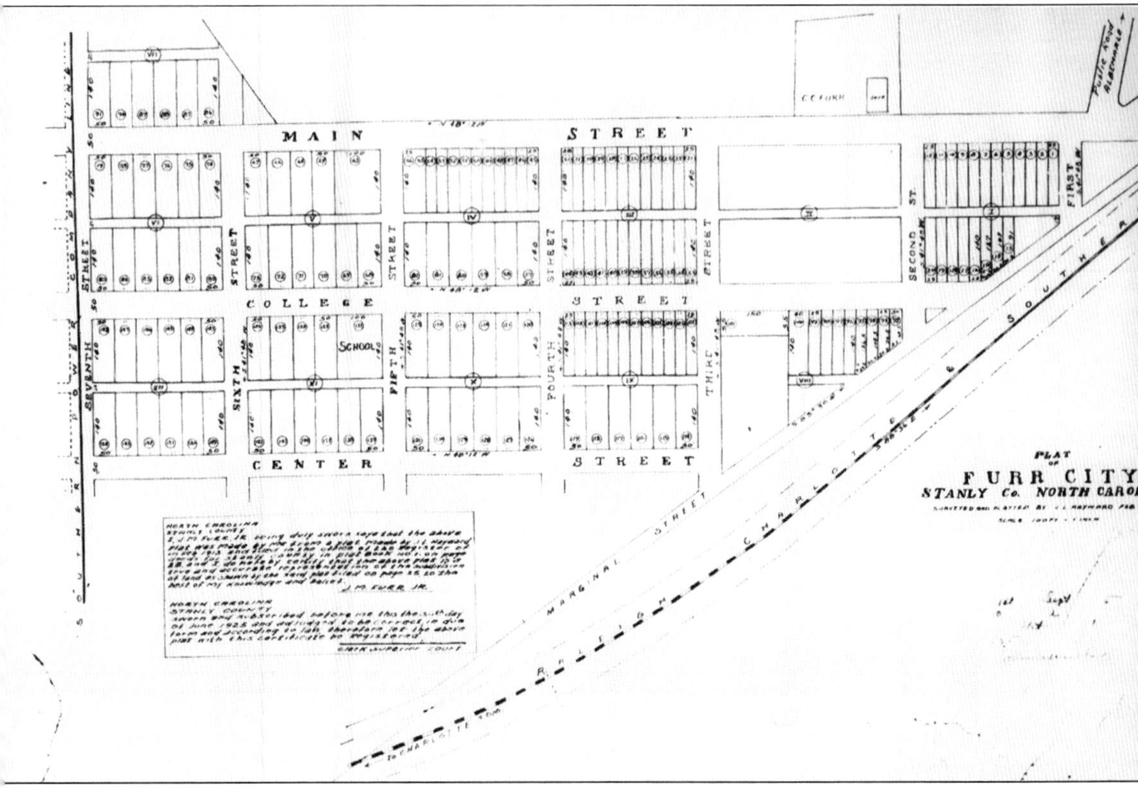

C.C. Furr hired surveyor J.L. Hayward to plat the town of Furr City in Stanly County, North Carolina, in 1913. This map shows the boundaries from the Southern Power Company line on the north to the intersection of Main Street, with public roads to Albemarle, Norwood, and Wadesboro. First through Seventh Streets were named, as were Main, College, and Center Streets. Marginal Street separates the town from the route of the Raleigh, Charlotte & Southern Railway. When the railroad became established, the name of the town was changed to Oakboro. (Courtesy of Oakboro Regional Museum of History.)

On the Cover: Oakboro area residents enjoy dinner on the grounds during the homecoming at Barbee's Grove Baptist Church in 1929. (Courtesy of Oakboro Regional Museum of History.)

IMAGES
of America

OAKBORO

Dr. Annabelle P. Morgan
Foreword by Dr. Charles Coble

ARCADIA
PUBLISHING

Copyright © 2012 by Dr. Annabelle P. Morgan
ISBN 978-0-7385-9284-8

Published by Arcadia Publishing
Charleston, South Carolina

Printed in the United States of America

Library of Congress Control Number: 2012933880

For all general information, please contact Arcadia Publishing:
Telephone 843-853-2070
Fax 843-853-0044
E-mail sales@arcadiapublishing.com
For customer service and orders:
Toll-Free 1-888-313-2665

Visit us on the Internet at www.arcadiapublishing.com

To all the people of Oakboro who pulled together to form the Oakboro Regional Historical Foundation—your dedication and perseverance have brought a remarkable organization into fruition.

Contents

FOREWORD

What is it about Oakboro?

Oakboro has the look and the feel of a special place. It has grown and changed, but not so rapidly and not so dramatically that it does not still feel like home to the many generations who have grown up, lived, and worked in and around Oakboro since it was founded along the railroad line built south of Red Cross and Big Lick.

Growing up in the 1940s and 1950s, when Main Street was the only paved road in town, I recall my grandfather Lee Coble's three-story flour mill and pigpen just off Main Street. That spot is now the lot behind the current Oakboro Methodist Church, which was built in the 1950s, as was the First Baptist Church—with its steeple just a little higher!

Walking down the street at that time, one would pass by Davis Self Serve Grocery, where you could buy on credit; R.C. and John Hatley's Electrical and Plumbing Supply, which sold the first black-and-white televisions in Oakboro; Security Bank & Trust; Drye's Furniture; J.P. Efird's & Son Texaco; Clark's Barber Shop; Pickett's Department Store; Barger's (then Tollison's) Pharmacy; Medlin's Watch Repair; Huneycutt Shell and Bus Line, which transported workers to Cannon Mills; the theater, which burned down; and Dr. McLendon's office. Just off Main Street were Vann Coble's smithery, Helms & Sons' Garage, and the Oakboro Mill & Farm Supply. At the end of town past the post office and Teeter's was the old train depot, T.W. Coble's Rocky River Lumber Company (the sawmill), the Granite & Marble Company, and J.E. Little's cotton gin. There were many others, which space prohibits my mentioning, but are captured in this publication.

Reflecting on the experience of growing up in and around Oakboro and seeing the many faces of the town over time, as this photographic history allows, we can all cherish the memories of the many wonderful individuals and families—white and black—who were such an intimate part of shaping our values and providing us a solid foundation on which to build our lives.

—Charles R. Coble
Oakboro High School, 1959

Acknowledgments

The author gratefully acknowledges the following people and organizations who shared their original photographs for this project: Donald Aldridge, Brooks and Jane Barnhardt, Mitzi Caddell, Jim Cameron, Jerry Carpenter, the Greater Oakboro Business Association, Heath Hahn, Jackie Hahn, Eva Ann Howard, Irene Kennedy, Pam Medlin, Oakboro Fire and Rescue, the Oakboro Police Department, Paul Reynolds of Stanly County Geographic Information Systems, the Stanly County Historic Properties Museum (SCHPM), Jack Thomas, Ruby Thomas, and Mildred Thomas.

A special thank you goes to the faithful volunteers who assisted in bringing the project to its conclusion. They are Robert Barbee, Jane and Brooks Barnhardt, Charles Coble, Debbie Edwards, Peggy Little, Claudette Love, Anabel and James Speight, the Town of Oakboro, and Judy and Larry Tucker.

The author thanks the members of the Oakboro Regional Historical Foundation for graciously sharing their knowledge of the events, places, and people of the Oakboro region.

Materials related to the history of architecture were gleaned from the pages of *Stanly County: The Architectural Legacy of a Rural North Carolina County* by Donna Dodenhoff, published by the Stanly County Historic Properties Commission in 1992.

Unless otherwise noted, all photographs in this volume appear courtesy of the Oakboro Regional Museum of History.

Introduction

Oakboro, North Carolina, is a great example of the small towns that began to appear throughout the southeastern countryside in the late 1800s and early 1900s. Many were located along rivers or streams, frequently traveled roads, trading trails, or railroad tracks.

Located in western Stanly County, the area has a rich history, with Native American settlements traced as far back as 10,000 BC. When the European settlers came, they formed small communities, which usually contained a country store providing items not grown on the farm, a church, and a one-room schoolhouse.

The coming of the Norfolk Southern Railroad in 1913, which carried both passengers and freight, brought profound changes. It provided connections to many places, near and far. Farmers brought their produce, cotton, corn, lumber, and other products to ship to buyers. In return, merchandise was received to help make life on the farms more livable and productive.

Electricity became available as early as 1909, and once the railroad line was established, people from the town of Big Lick began to move their businesses and homes to Furr City. C.C. Furr and other property owners crafted a map of possible building sites, and people began to purchase plots for homes and businesses. These included cotton gins, roller mills, and general mercantile stores, as well as a blacksmith shop, livery stable, and other concerns necessary to the agricultural life of the area. In 1923, Oakboro Cotton Mill was built, beginning the textile industry that continued into the early 2000s.

Another period of significant growth occurred in the early 1930s and 1940s when hardware stores, dry goods stores, grocery stores, and gasoline service stations began to flourish. A few of these continue to serve the public today, although perhaps in different ways. Notable among the buildings no longer standing were those designed to serve early agricultural needs.

This collection of photographs provides a peek into the past; however, a small volume such as this cannot contain images of every important event or person. As you reflect on the memories conjured up with these images of days gone by, imagine how many more treasures may be hidden in the old boxes in grandma's attic or in your uncle's trunk in the basement. Let these glimpses into the past inspire you to share your own stories and photographs with your local historical organization or library.

One

Early History and the Coming of the Railroad

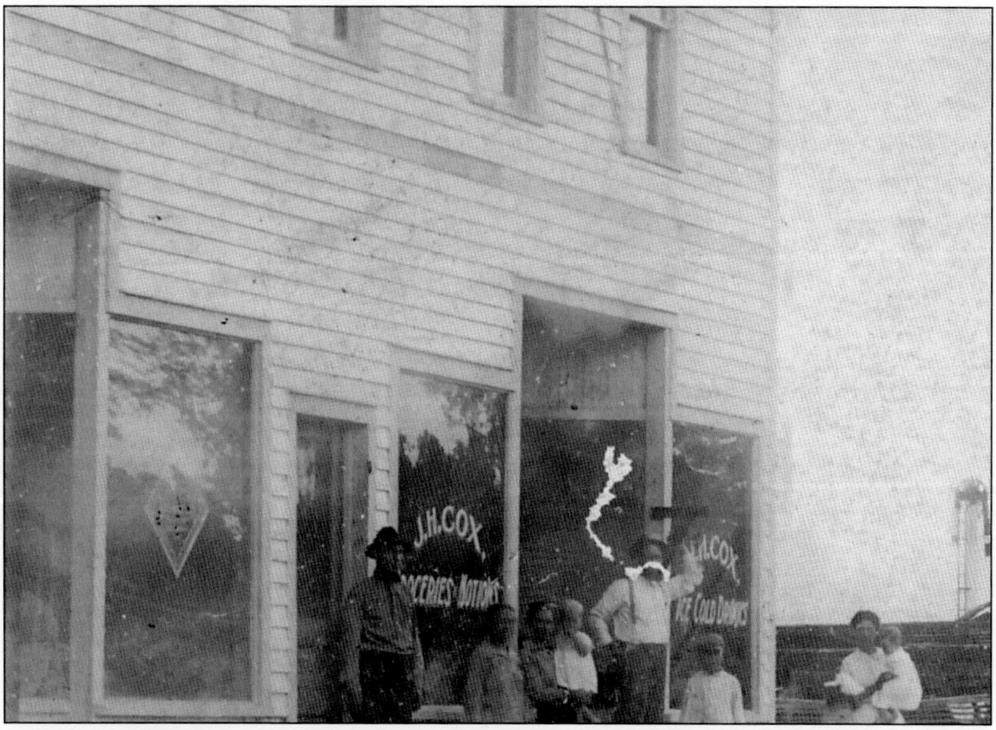

In the early 1900s, photographer Will Hatley traveled around the area capturing likenesses of people and places for printing postcards. Much of his work involved the use of glass negatives, some of which have survived. Many of the street scenes depicted are attributed to him. The J.H. Cox general store was a popular place for families to shop. The Cox brothers came to Oakboro soon after the Norfolk & Southern Railroad was completed. The store burned in 1915, and all the merchandise was lost. Shown here are unidentified members of the Cox, Austin, Hartsell, and Kennedy families.

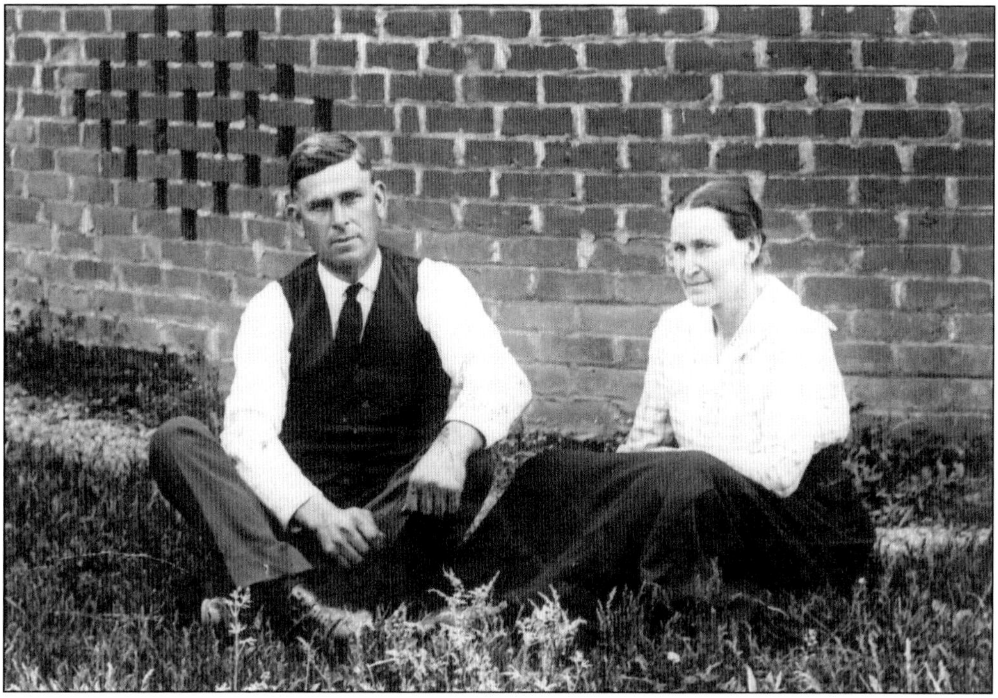

Croson C. Furr married Maude Hartsell, the daughter of a major landowner in the Five Roads community. Furr was able to capitalize on the development of the area by purchasing additional land and surveying it off into lots. These were then sold to businesses and people looking to settle in the new community. The coming of the railroad made the community an attractive place to work and live. Furr and his wife built the home below on the corner of North Main and West Ninth Streets.

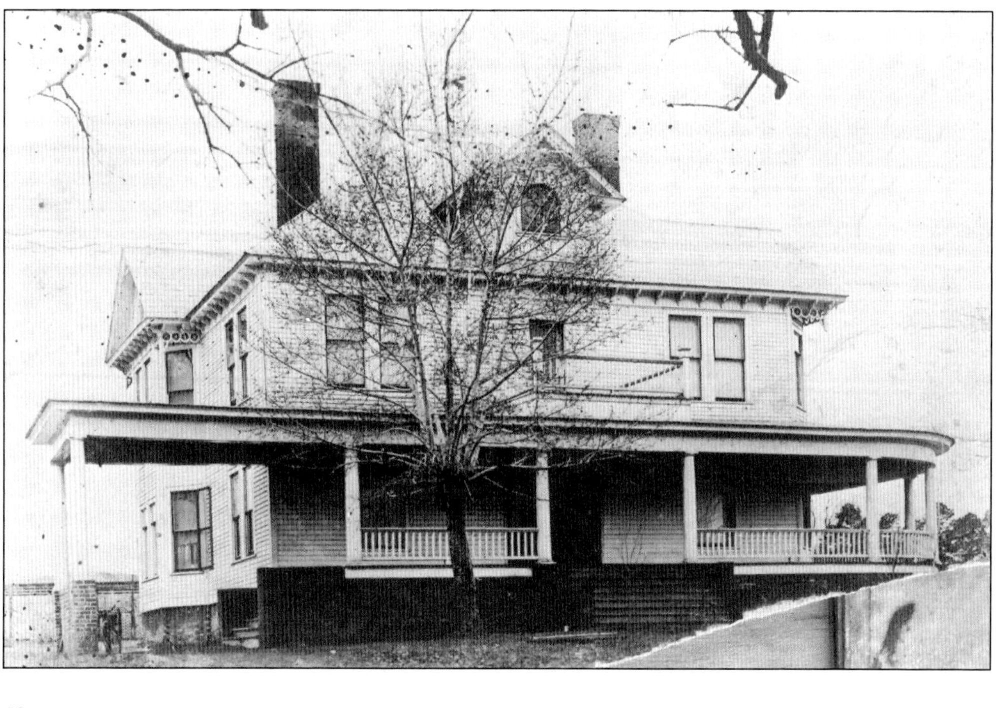

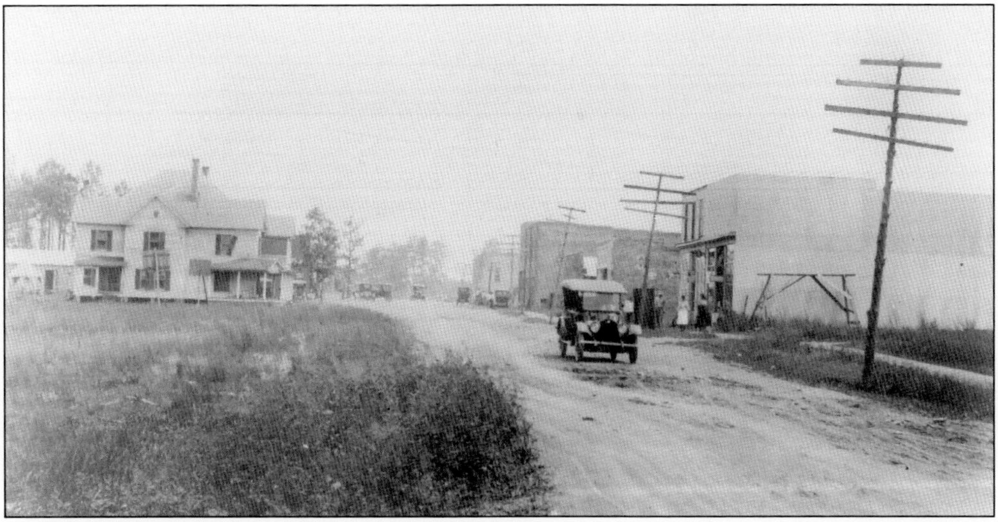

The above image looks south from Fourth Street showing Jason Coble's residence with the well house in the left background and stores and offices in the right foreground. The white, two-story C.C. Furr store housed the upstairs law offices of Craig Richardson. The below image looks north through the center of town, and the first two buildings on the left would eventually house Barger's Drugs and Western Auto. None of the buildings on the right still stand, but the first structure was Oakboro Drug Company, operated by John Welch of Monroe. (Both, courtesy of SCHPM.)

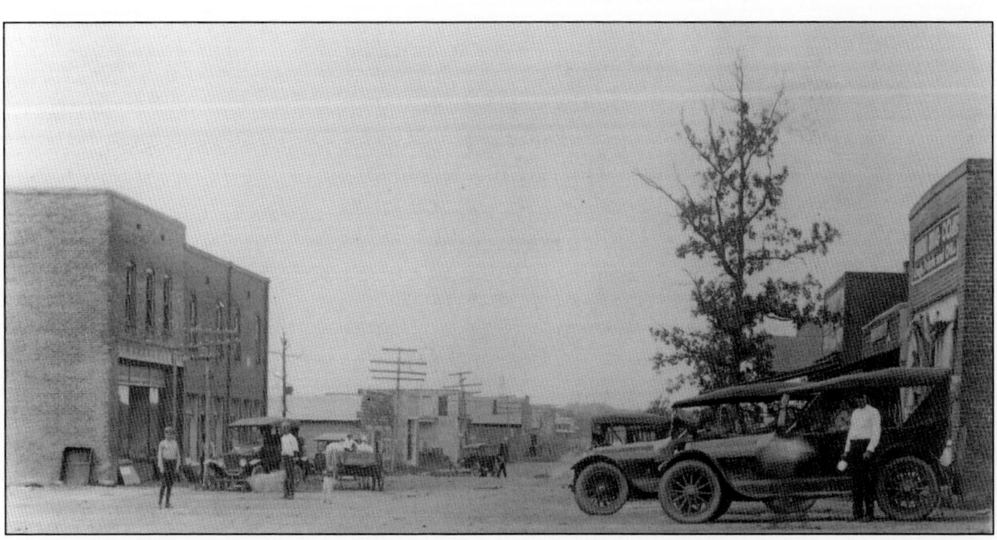

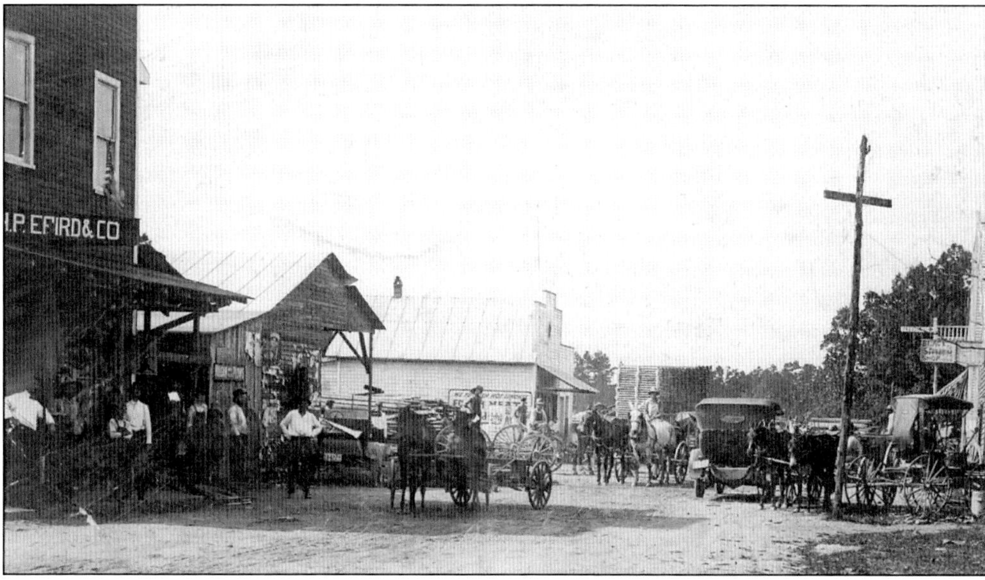

This early-1920s photograph shows cars, wagons, and buggies on the unpaved streets lined with wooden buildings. From the white shirts and the number of people congregated in the town, it may have been a celebration, such as the Fourth of July. Notice the H.P. Efird store and the lone light pole. (Courtesy of Jane Barnhardt.)

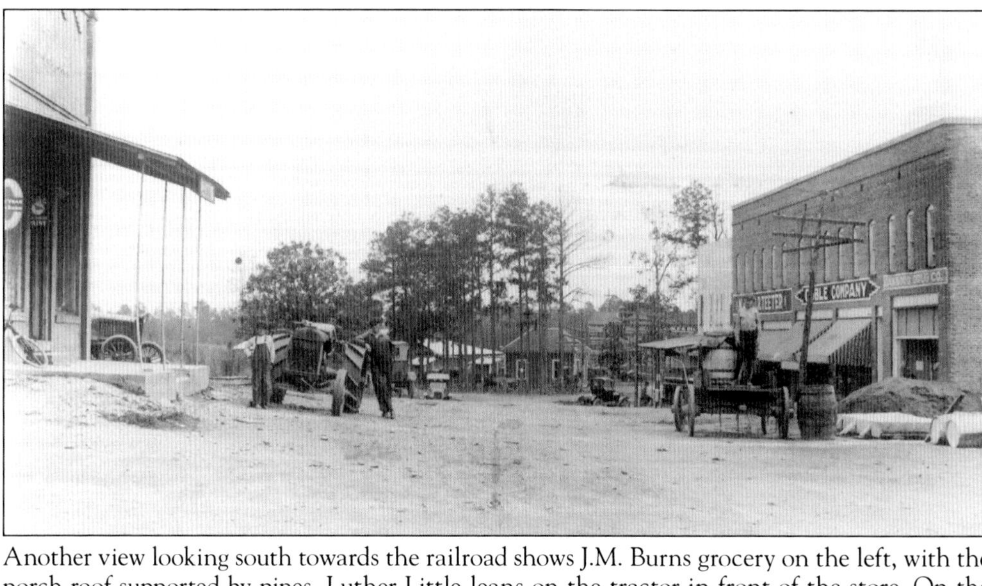

Another view looking south towards the railroad shows J.M. Burns grocery on the left, with the porch roof supported by pipes. Luther Little leans on the tractor in front of the store. On the right are Rayvon Teeter's Oakboro Drug Store, the Coble Company, the N.A. Teeter store, and Dee Huneycutt's general store. The Norfolk & Southern Railroad owned the small building across the street.

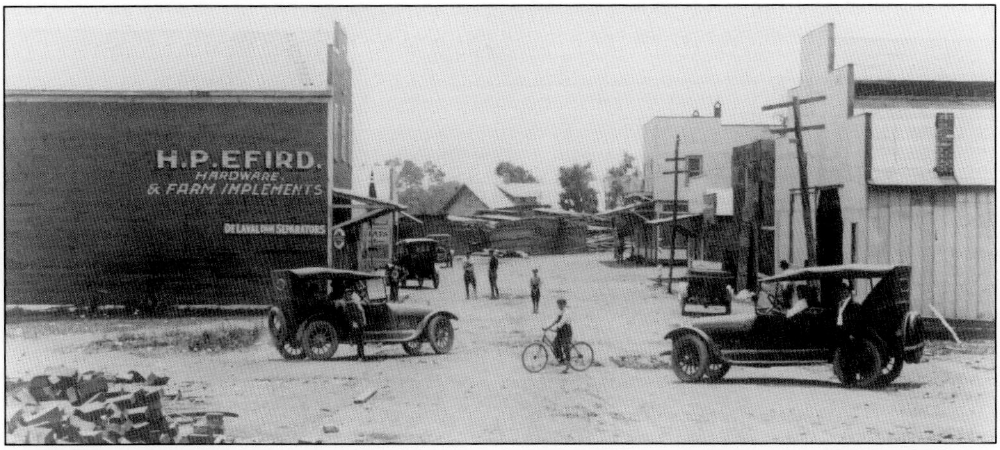

Beside the H.P. Efird store stands the Huneycutt meat market, which was operated by Phillip S. Huneycutt from 1925 into the 1930s. Mutton, beef, and pork, all raised and butchered by the Huneycutt family, were for sale. The market also sold soup and sandwiches all day. (Courtesy of SCHPM.)

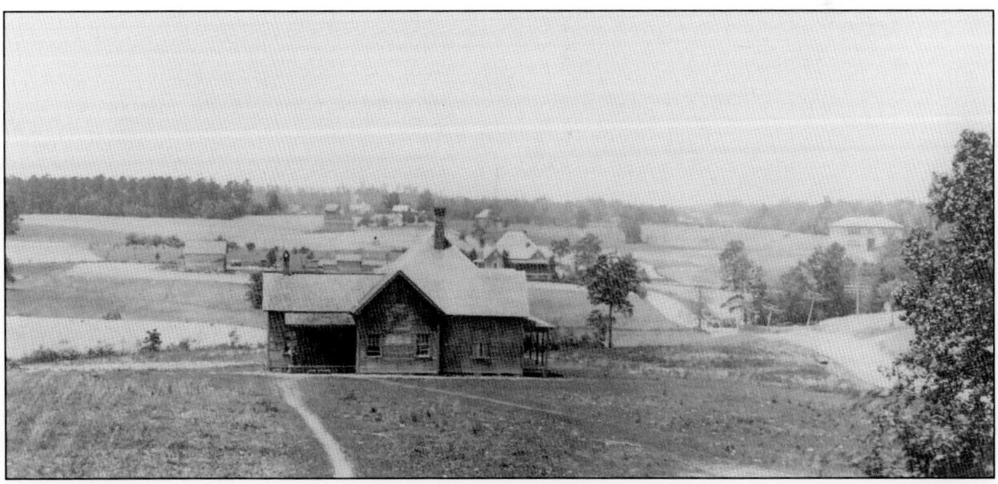

This photograph looks down North Main Street toward Big Lick with the Charlie Curlee residence in the center and the home of Sid Howard in the distance. On the right in the background is the original Oakboro–Big Lick School. (Courtesy of SCHPM.)

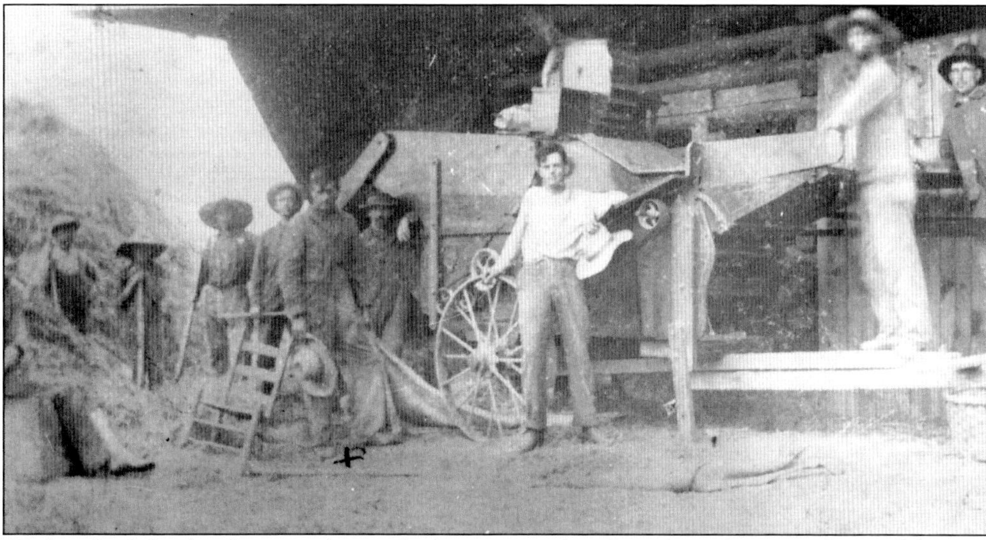

Workers load the threshing machine, which separates the wheat from the straw. Some of the men on the left hold pitchforks while others have sacks to load the grain in. It is believed that one of the men was U.S. Whitley, the grandfather of Marshall Whitley.

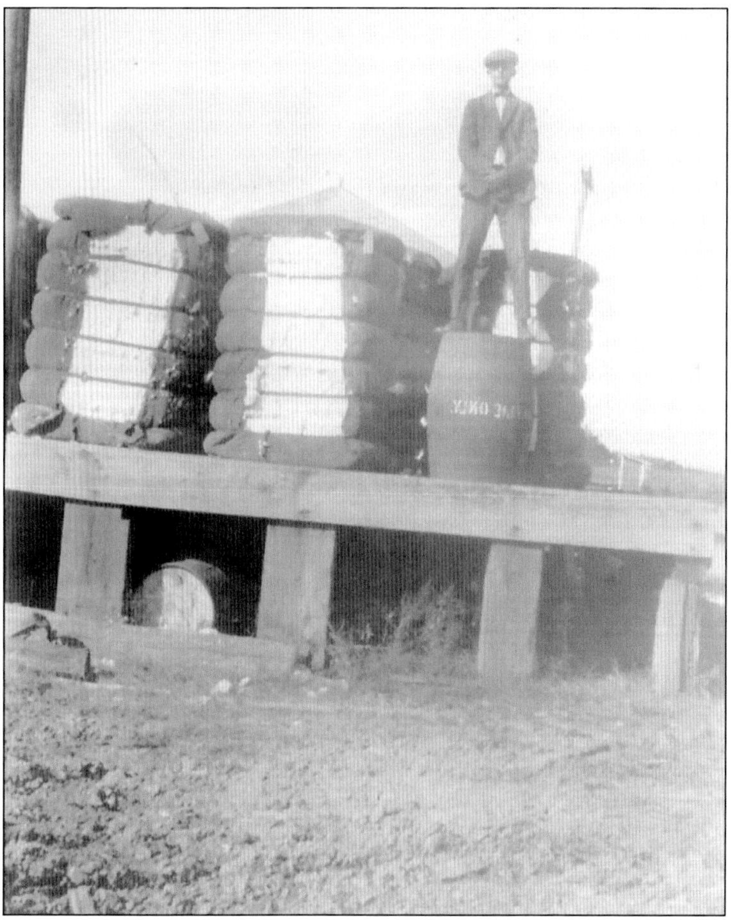

Cotton gins were abundant in the Oakboro area. Fields were plowed with mules, and the cotton was hoed and picked by hand before being transported by wagon for baling at local gins. Wagons loaded with cotton lined up before dawn and sometimes sat over half a day waiting to get the cotton ginned.

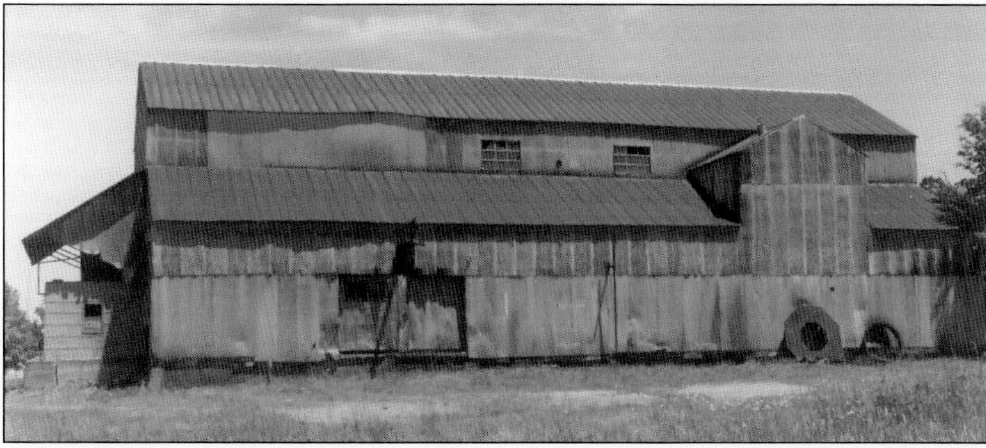

Johnny Little's cotton gin, pictured above, has since been torn down to make way for a modern doctor's office. C.E. and J.R. Teeter's gin, situated at the corner of Haywood and East First Streets, is seen below in 1975. (Courtesy of SCHPM.)

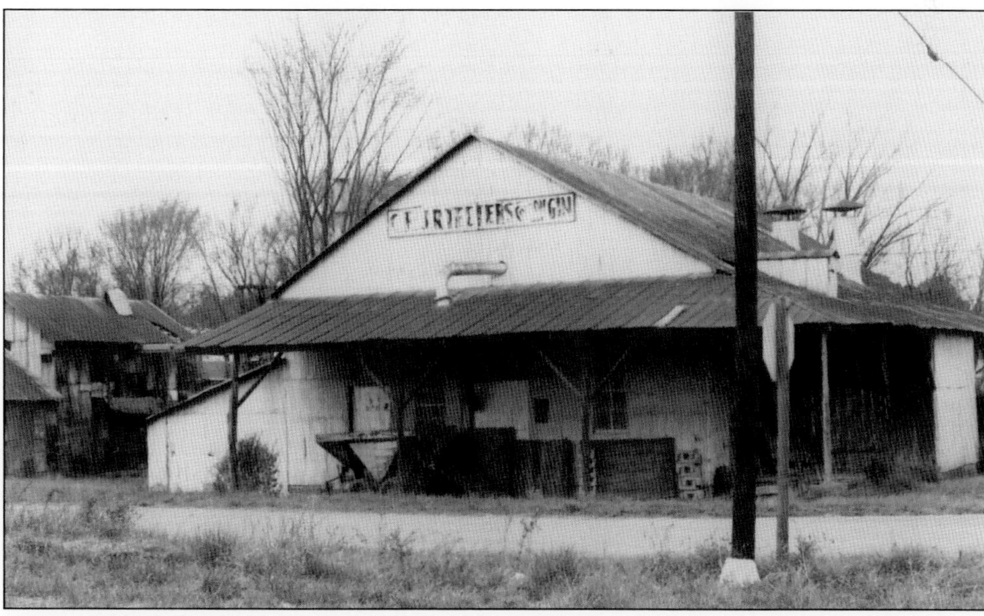

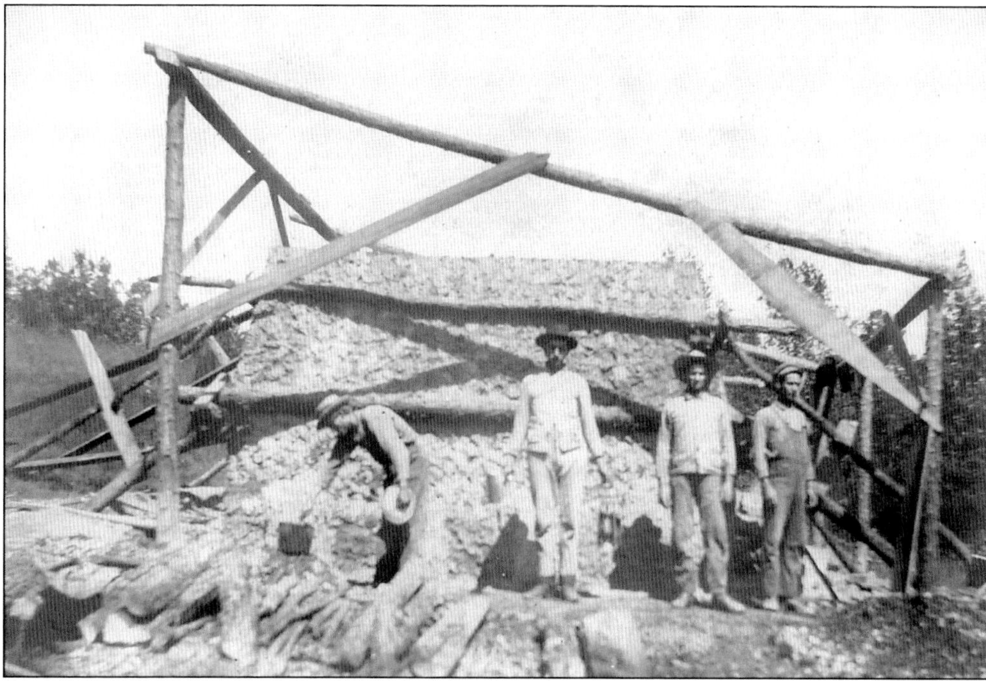

Big Lick boasted a large and prosperous brickyard in the early 1920s. Most of the bricks used to build stores, houses, and churches in Oakboro were made here. The facility was possibly owned by a man named John Goodale, who used horses or mules to tamp out mud for the bricks. (Courtesy of Mildred Thomas.)

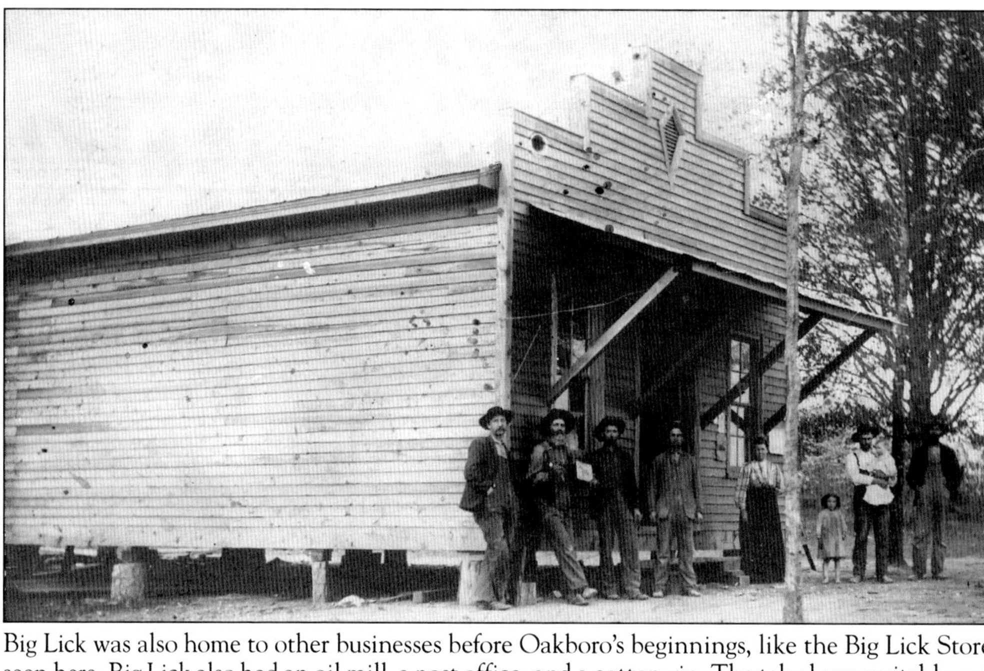

Big Lick was also home to other businesses before Oakboro's beginnings, like the Big Lick Store seen here. Big Lick also had an oil mill, a post office, and a cotton gin. The telephone switchboard was located there until it was moved to Oakboro. (Courtesy of Jane Barnhardt.)

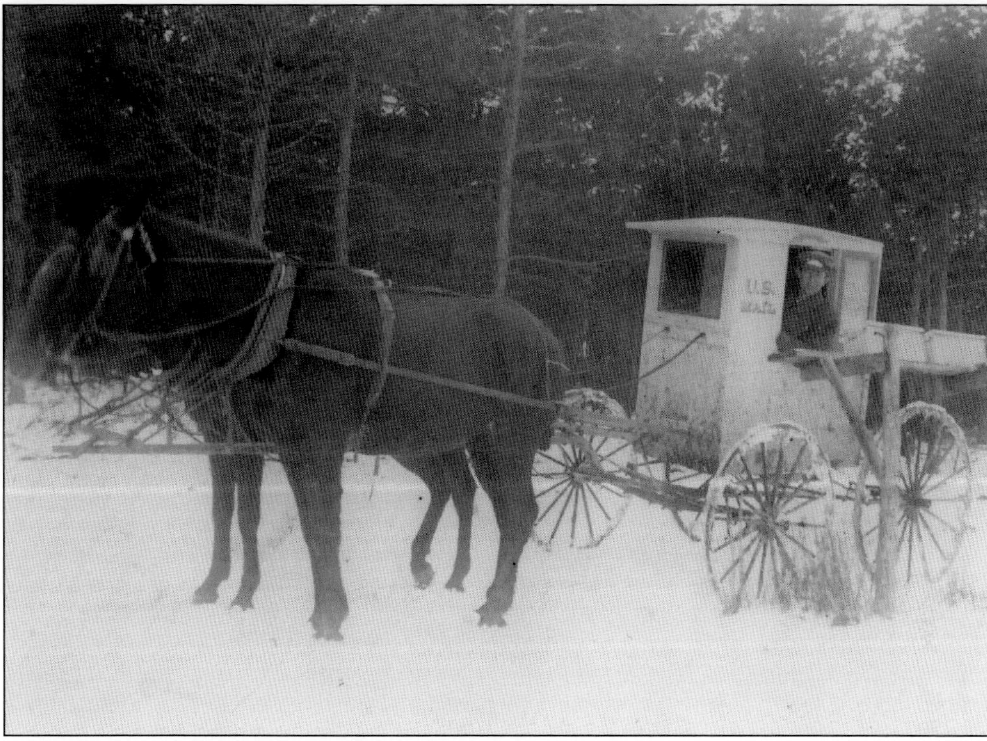

Rural mail carrier Martin James places mail in a box on his snowy route. James began carrying mail for the post office at Big Lick and continued when it was moved to Oakboro in 1911. This photograph was taken after it had moved, as the name of Oakboro is on the cab.

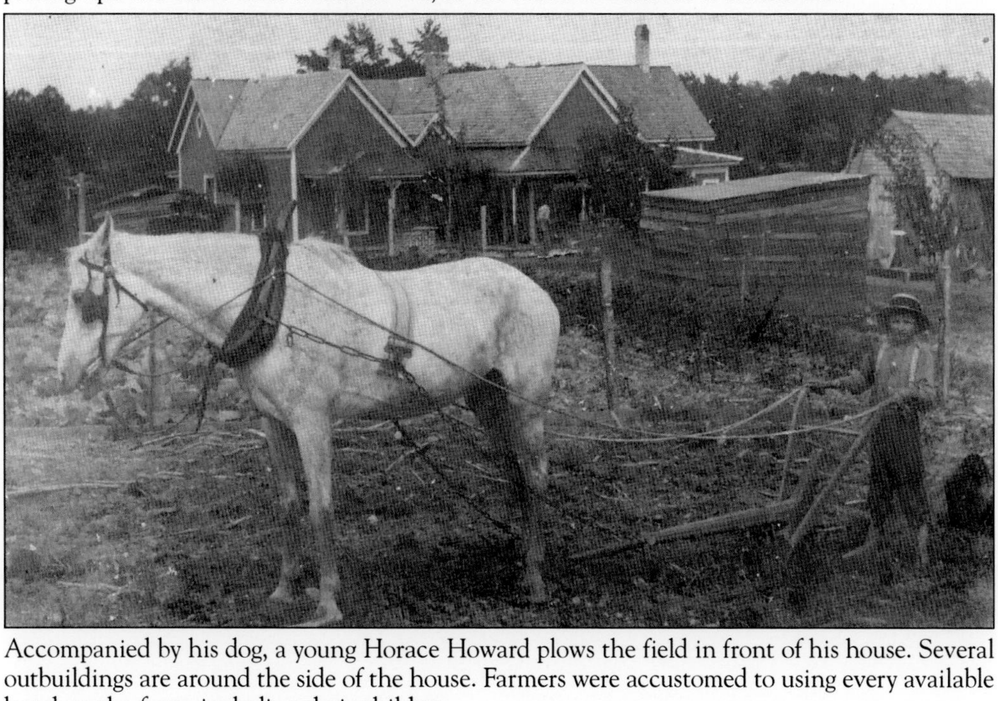

Accompanied by his dog, a young Horace Howard plows the field in front of his house. Several outbuildings are around the side of the house. Farmers were accustomed to using every available hand on the farm, including their children.

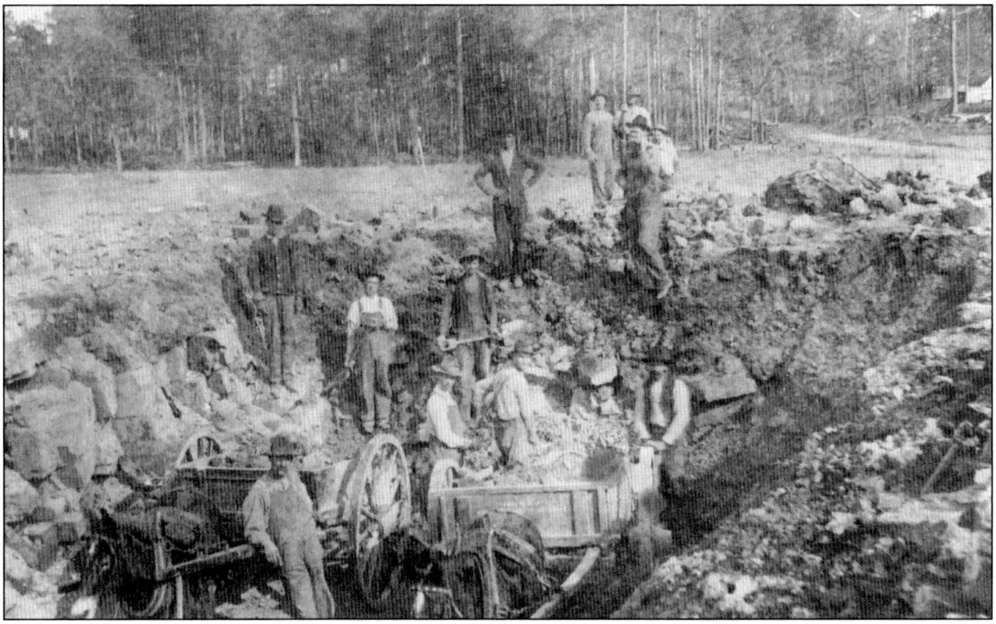

When the Norfolk & Southern Railroad decided to expand their tracks from Montgomery County to Charlotte, it selected a site in what would become Oakboro. The company used local workers, as well as their own crews, to build the base and lay the tracks. The first trains hauled freight, but in December 1913, the first passenger train stopped at Oakboro to the delight of the crowd gathered there. Shown here are two of the crews responsible for completing the tracks. The men below from left to right are L.D. Blackwelder, George Huneycutt, Lawson Hill, Doug Turner, Henry Hill, Silas Taylor, Shepard Taylor, and Fred Hill. (Both, courtesy of SCHPM.)

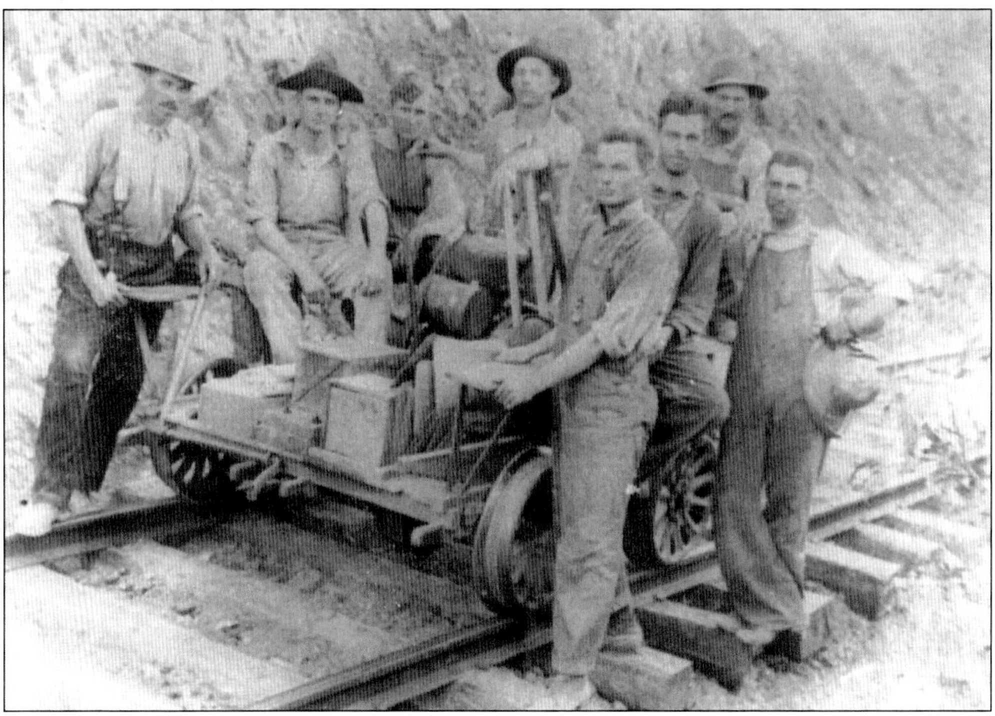

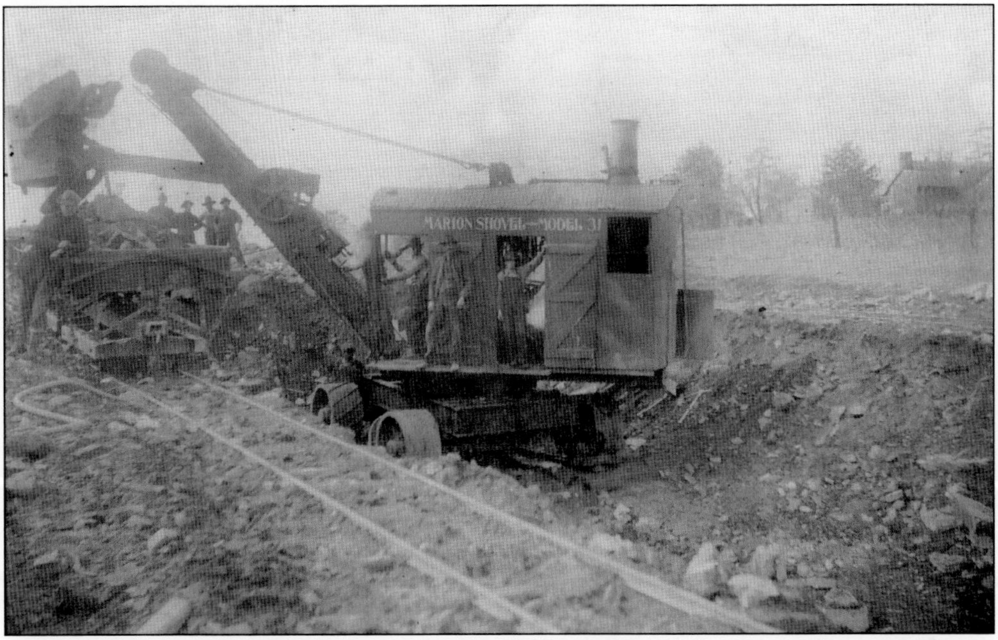

A Marion Shovel Model 31 was used to dig through the rocky soil along the rail line. The shovel was originally built as a rail-mounted shovel with the option of steel traction wheels, and it could be configured to run on steam, gasoline, or diesel fuel. Three men are on the deck, four men are on the far left, and one man on the left props against a railcar.

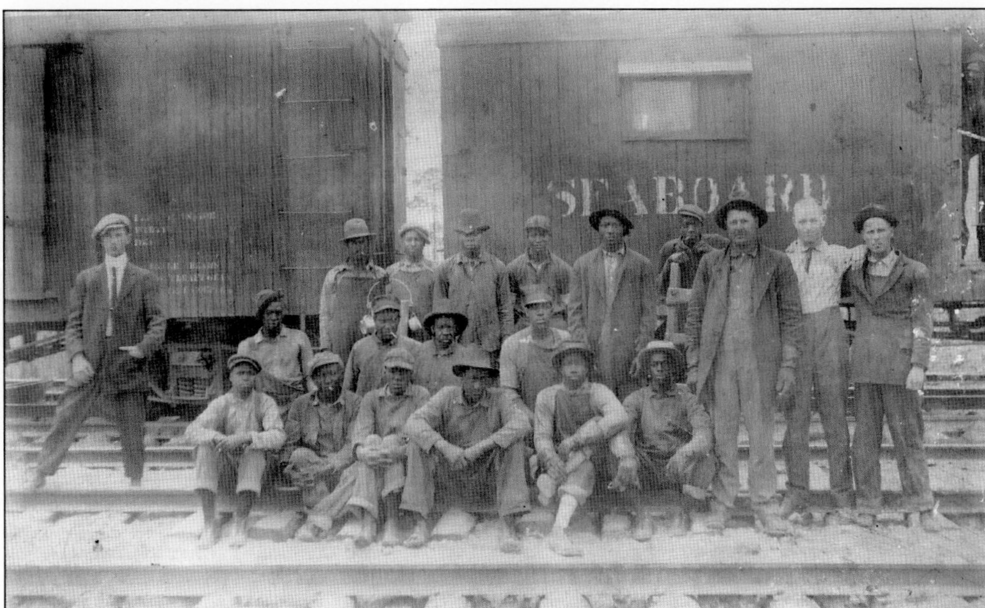

This is believed to be a photograph of the men who completed the railroad through Oakboro in 1913. Some of the men seem to have dressed in their best clothes for the photograph, especially the gentleman to the left. On the left in the back row, a man holds a water bucket with two dippers.

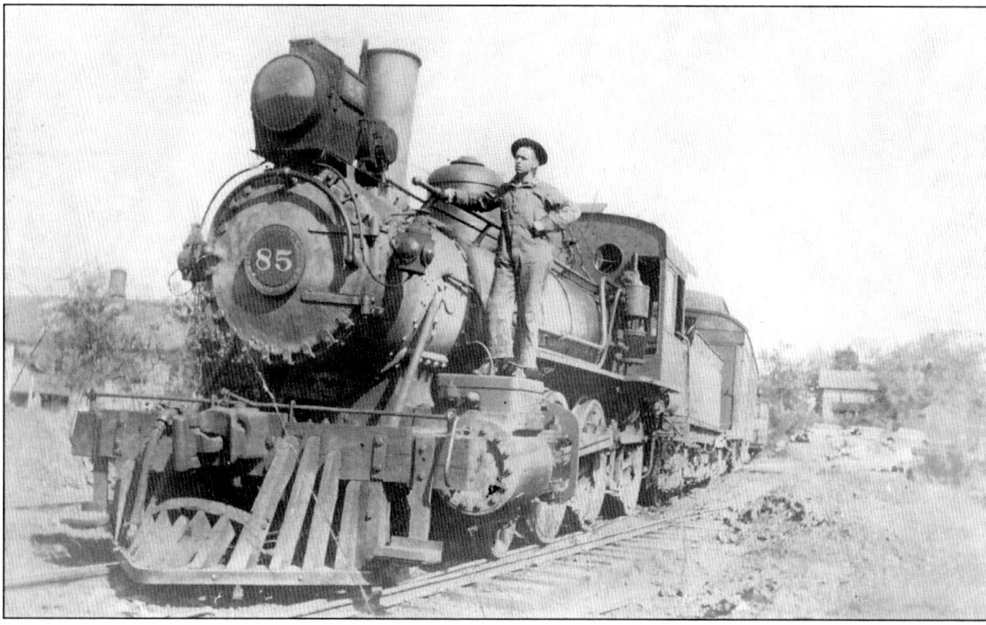

Frelon A. Hahn is seen above on the side of Norfolk Southern engine no. 85. This engine traveled from Oakboro to Carthage on a somewhat regular schedule. Hahn, an Oakboro resident, worked for the railroad and was away from home for long periods of time. At one time, Oakboro was noted for moving the most freight between Charlotte and Raleigh. Trains stopped at the depot pictured below.

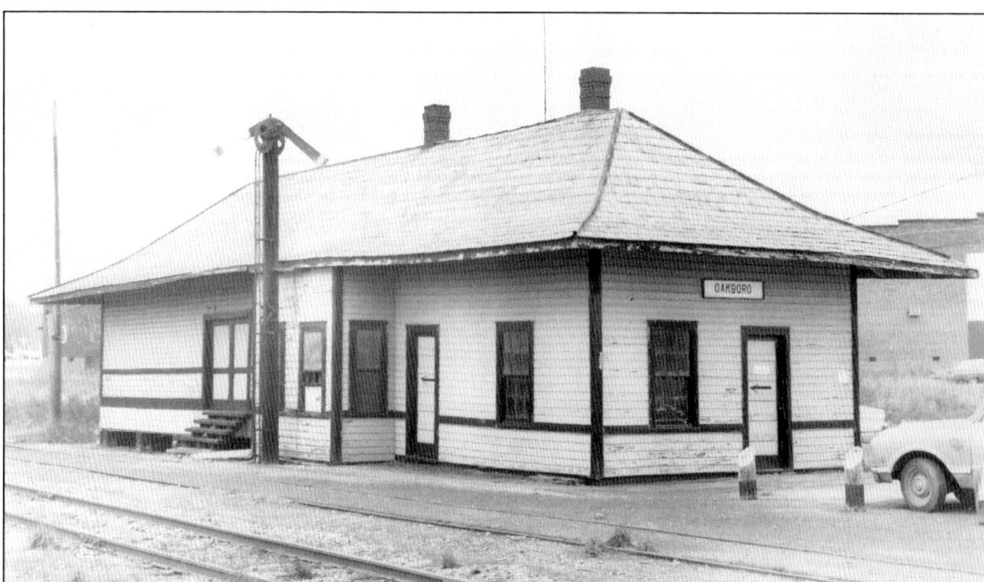

Two

Growth and Development

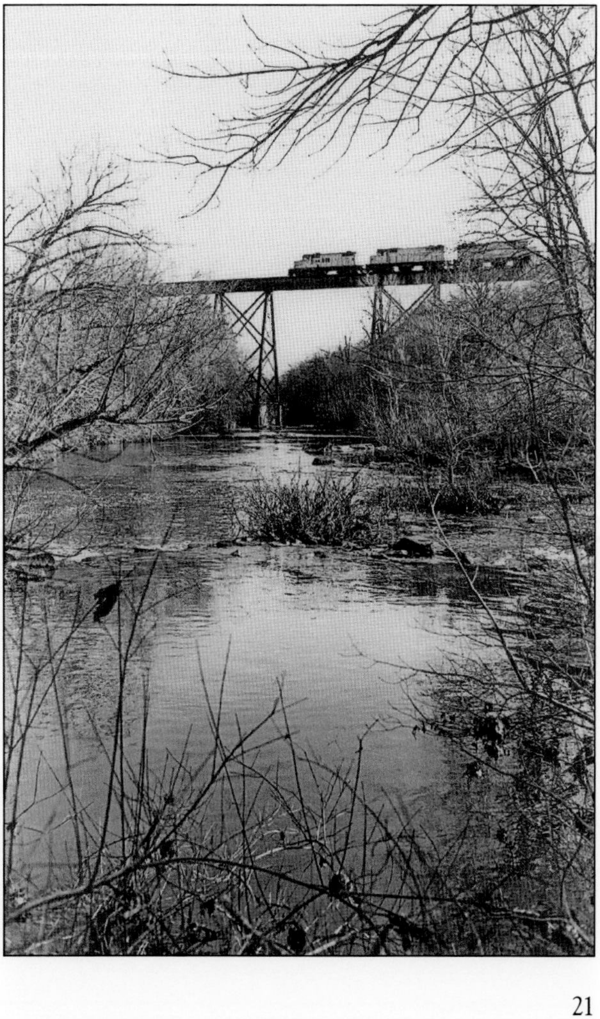

Beginning in 1963, photographer Donald Aldridge captured images of trains crossing the trestle across Long Creek. One of the highest in North Carolina, the trestle was part of the construction of the original line in 1911–1913. Although it has been refitted many times through the years, it is a symbol bridging the past with the present. Today, the Aberdeen, Carolina & Western Railroad operates on the same line. (Courtesy of Donald Aldridge.)

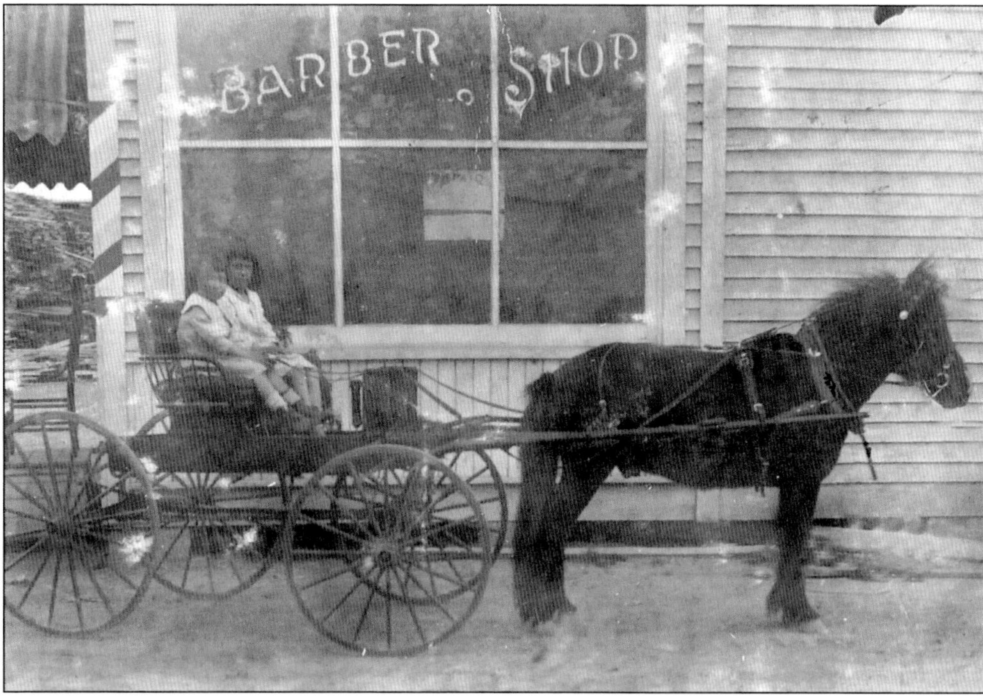

Sisters Nellie "Bill" (Hartsell) Church and Virginia (Hartsell) Hartsell ride in a buggy pulled by their horse Star in front of the Findley Hinson barbershop on West Second Street around 1919.

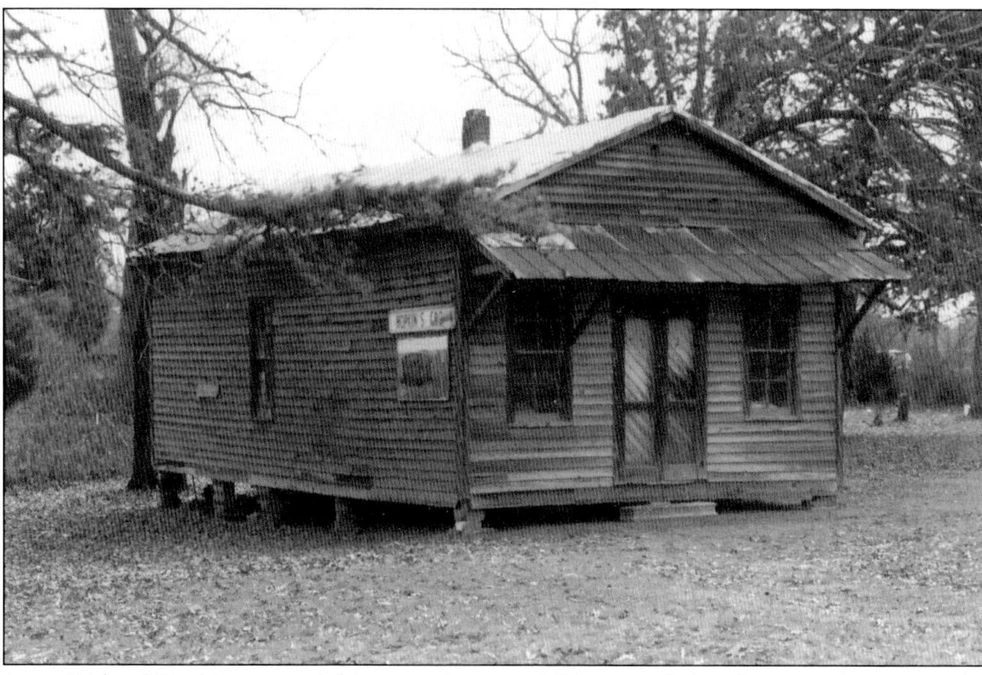

James Richard Hopkins opened this general store at 7:00 a.m. and closed it at sundown every day from 1914 to 1981. He served the rural community along Silver Road with a variety of dry goods and grocery items. Hopkins and other rural merchants went by wagon to Charlotte for wares to restock their stores, often sleeping under the wagons to return the next day.

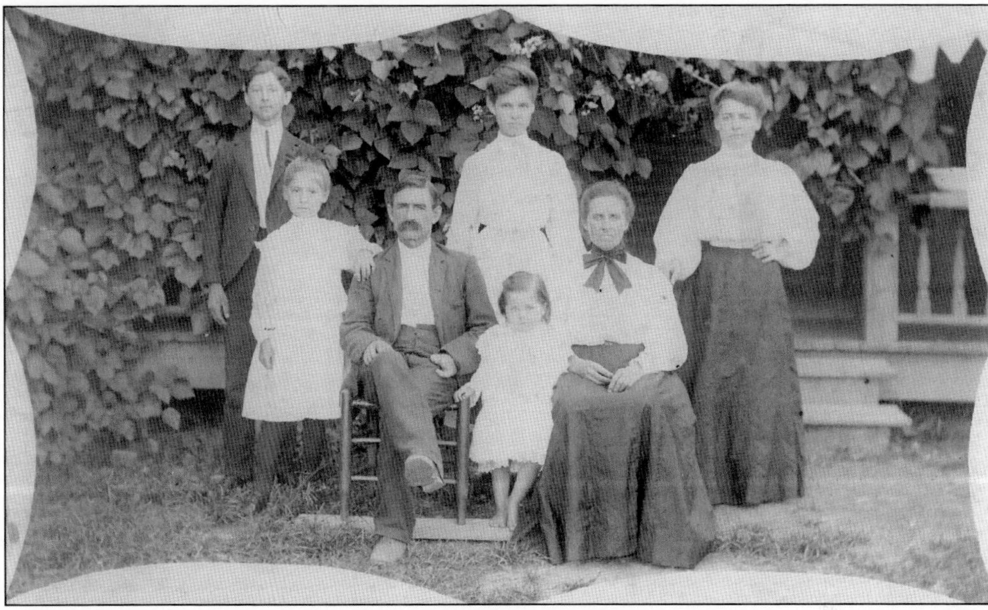

N. Arthur Teeter and his wife, Malinda, are seen above surrounded by their children, from left to right, Ralph Teeter, Annie (Teeter) Newsome, Ina (Teeter) Hatley, young Croppsie (Teeter) Furr, and Lena (Teeter) Hartsell. Arthur ran a general store in the building below for many years. Ralph and his younger brother Claud operated the store after their father died.

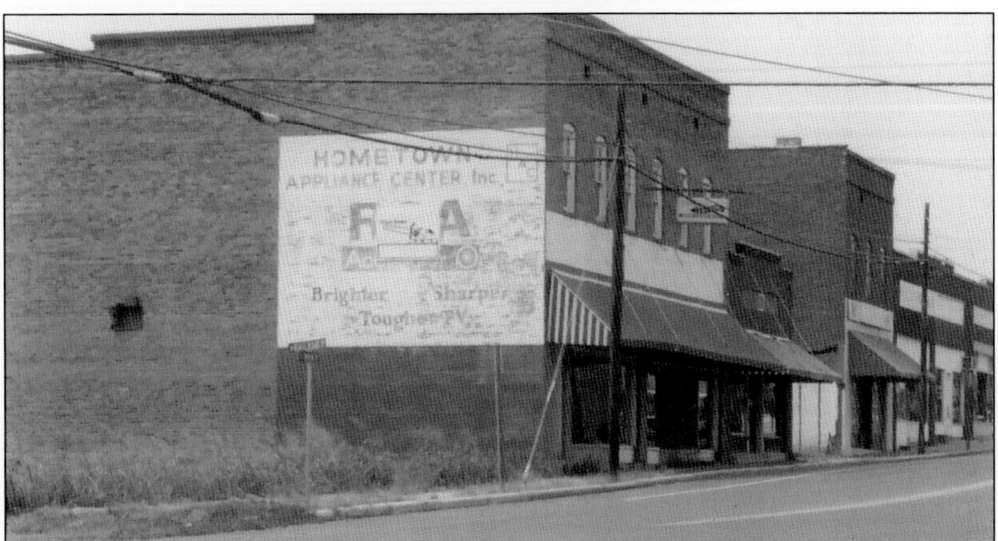

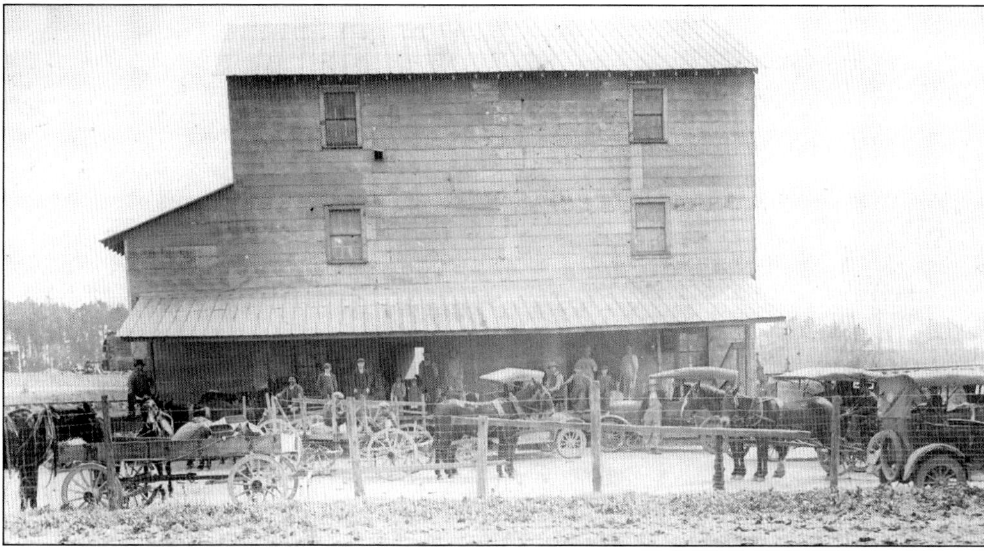

Henry Houston Little owned this flour, meal, and feed mill known as the Oakboro Milling Company. This building burned in the early 1930s and was replaced by another structure. Automobiles and horse-drawn wagons are both seen in this image.

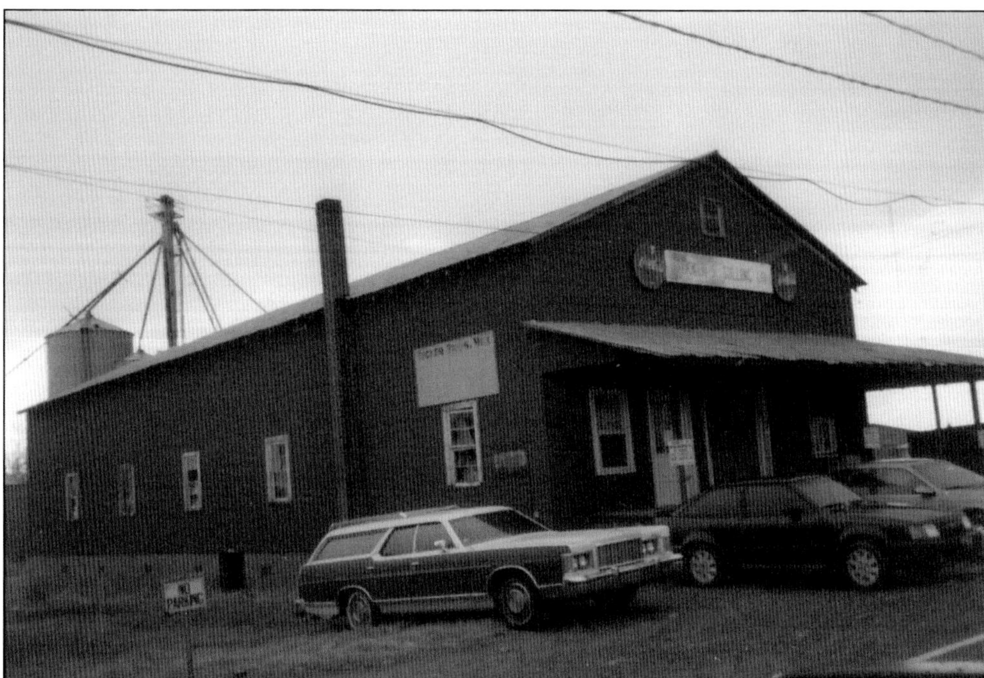

The Tucker Brothers Milling Company building still stands in the first block of Highway 205 south. The company was operated by brothers J.D. "Jake" and Curtis Tucker.

World War I veteran Dee Huneycutt returned to Oakboro to operate Huneycutt's cash store on the corner of Highway 205 and Main Street. A second store was located at the corner of Railroad Street and Main, and a third on Main Street below Teeter's store housed a boarding room.

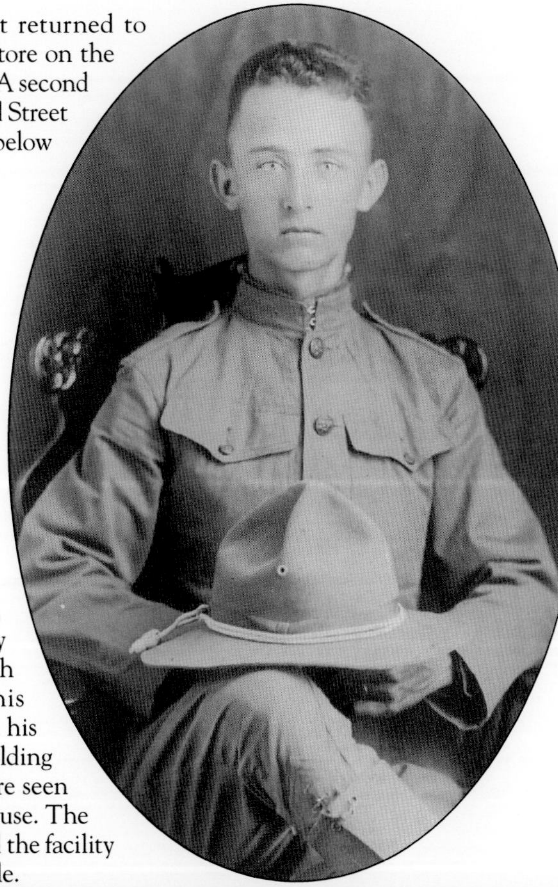

Lemuel "Lem" Little and his wife, Rosie, operated the rural general store previously operated by Silas Smith in the Smith Grove Church community. After this structure burned, Little built a store on his farm. Soon after, he converted that building into a granary and constructed the store seen below on the roadside in front of his house. The current owners of the farm have retained the facility in as close to its original form as possible.

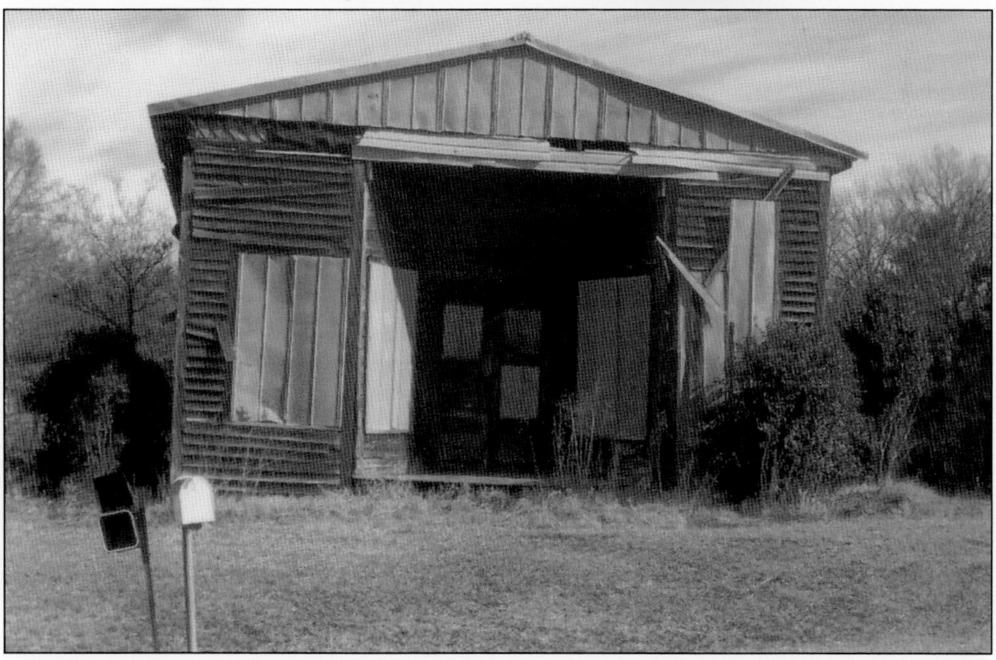

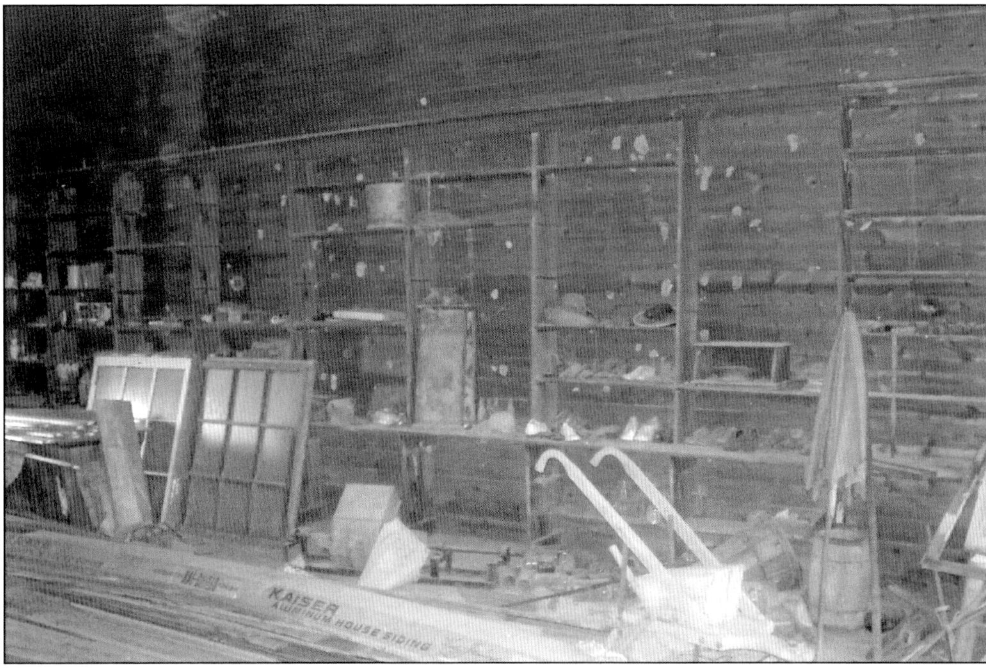

Merchandise fills the shelves of the Lem Little store today on Old School Road, much as it did when the store was open in the 1920s. Farm implements, canning jars, shoes, clothing, and other necessities were stocked for customers. Tin signs advertising tobacco and snuff still hang on the walls.

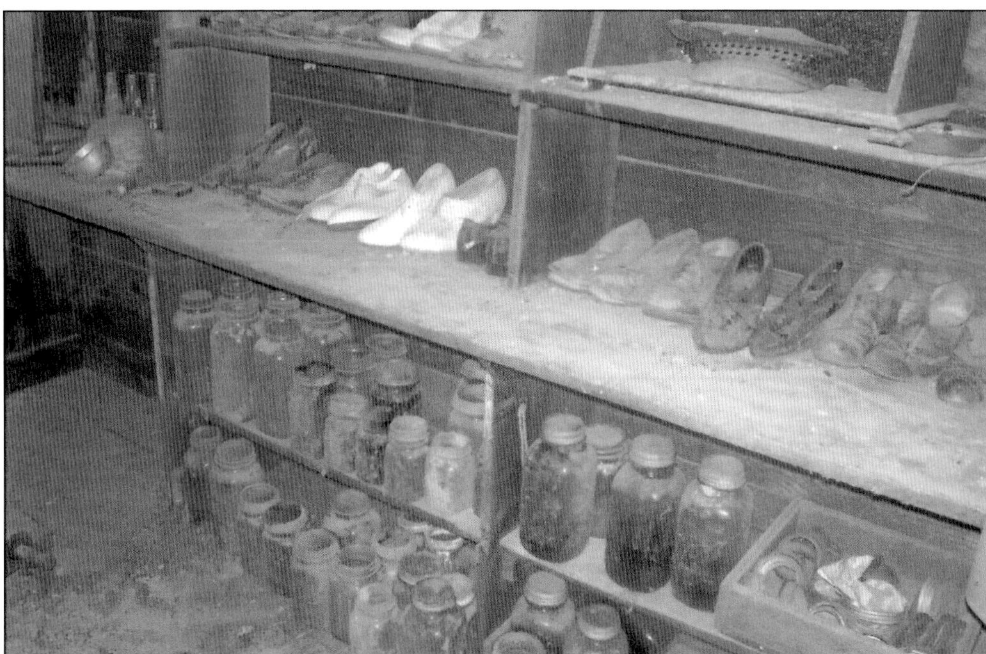

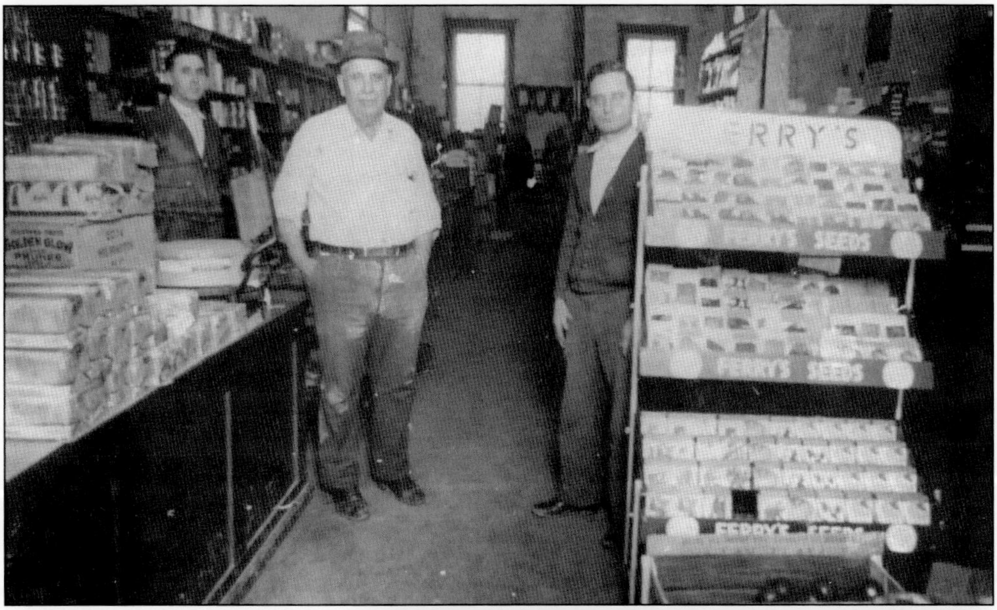

Lem Little and his son Johnny later moved the general store to Main Street. Johnny operated the store and stocked much of the same merchandise his father did at the farm, but he added more up-to-date items as people requested them. Shown here from left to right are Claude Coble with Lem and Johnny Little.

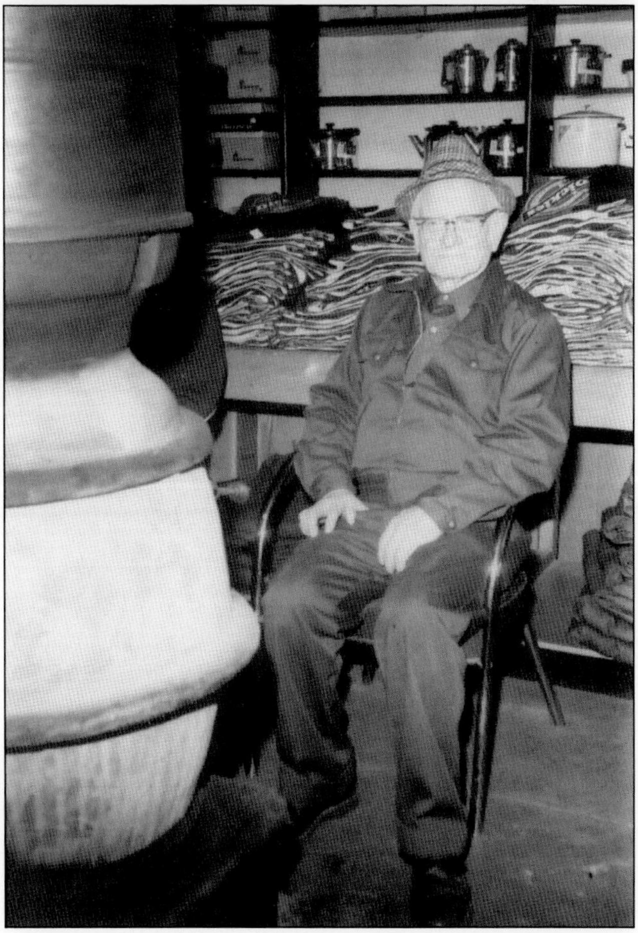

Johnny Little, seen here sitting by the wood-burning stove, ran the store after his father died in the 1940s. The store was a gathering place for farmers who came to purchase goods and learn the news of the town. The store closed in the 1980s.

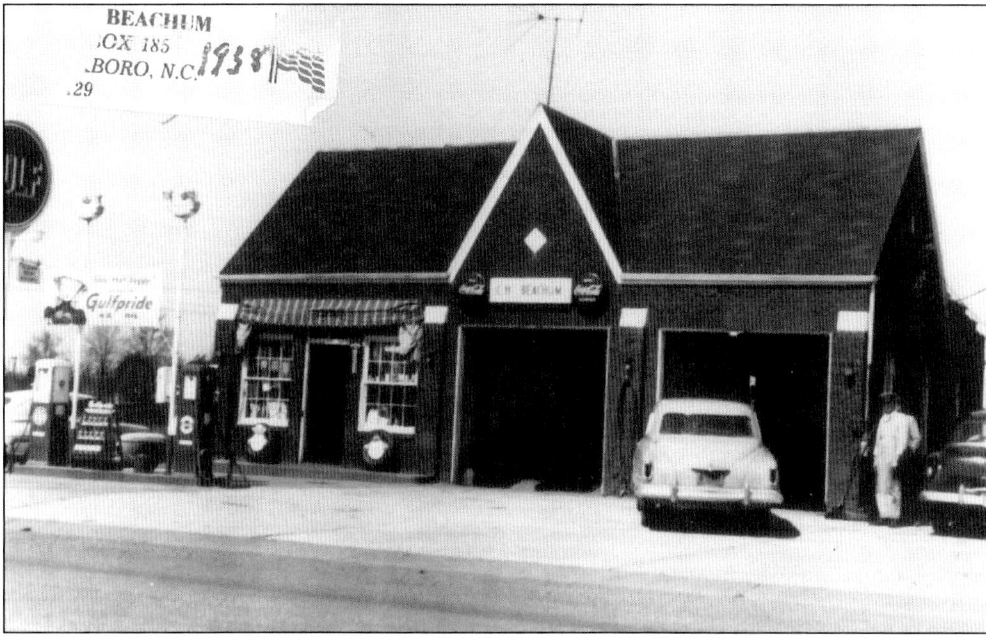

Hayes Beachum operated a service station on the corner of East Third and Main Streets. Beachum studied automobile mechanics in Michigan for a year and returned to Oakboro to spend his life as owner and operator of the business. The building, seen here in 1958, is no longer standing.

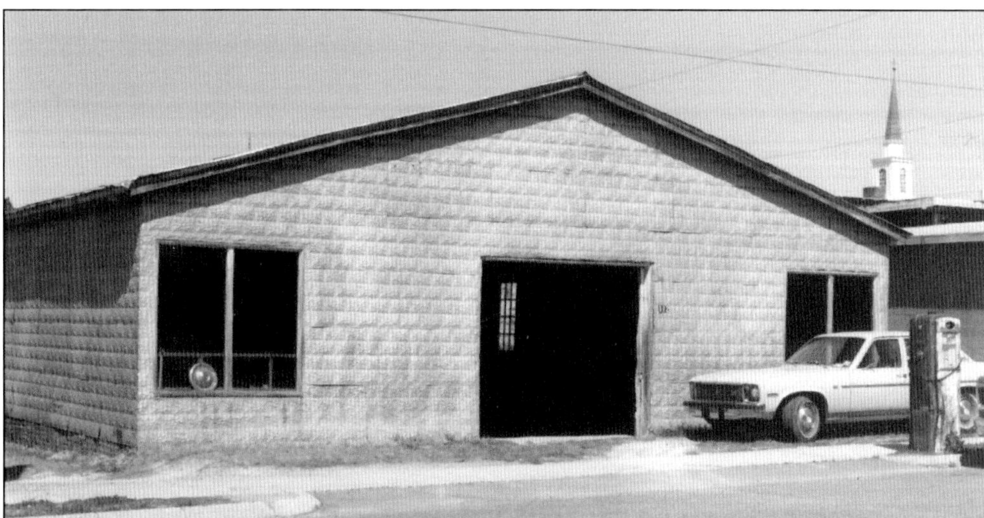

Coble brothers Vann and Burt built this blacksmith shop around 1925. In addition to blacksmithing, they also did general mechanical work on Model T Fords, made farm implements, and sold car parts and tools. Vann bought out his brother's interest in 1935 and operated the business until his death in 1988. Much of the original equipment remains in the building.

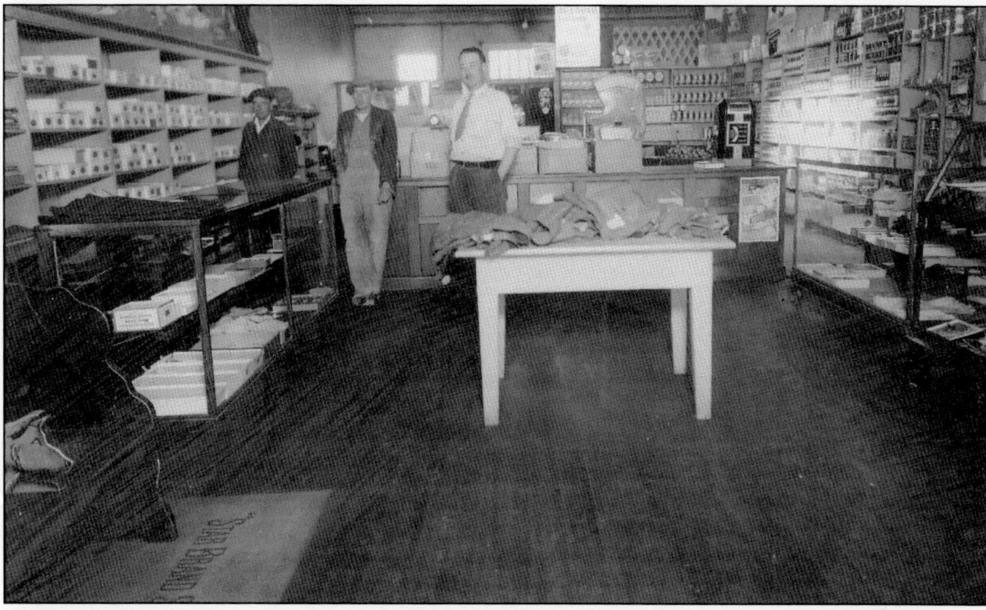

Oakboro Clothing Store offered customers a variety of items. Here, boxes line the shelves and display racks as two shoppers browse through the store.

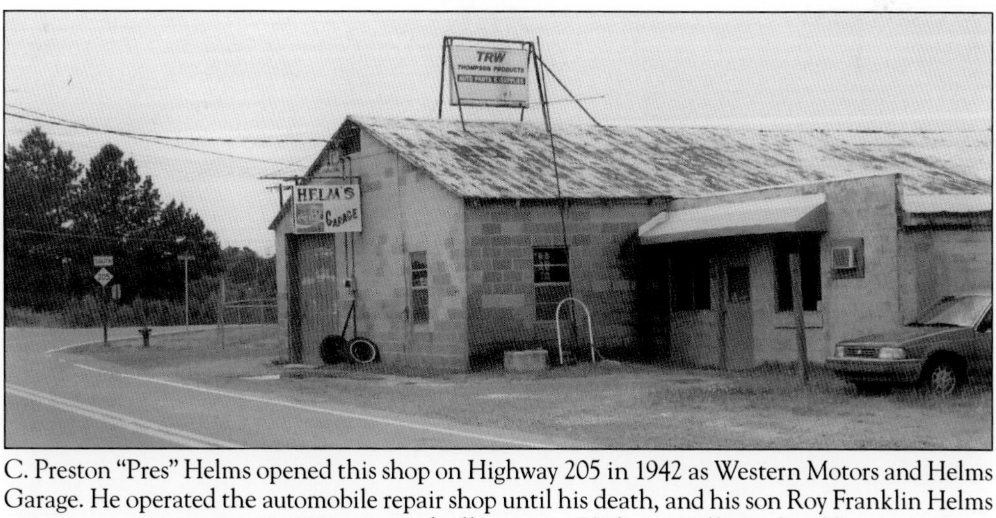

C. Preston "Pres" Helms opened this shop on Highway 205 in 1942 as Western Motors and Helms Garage. He operated the automobile repair shop until his death, and his son Roy Franklin Helms continues to operate it, repairing cars and selling parts. He has an affinity for older cars and can often be found performing restoration jobs on classics.

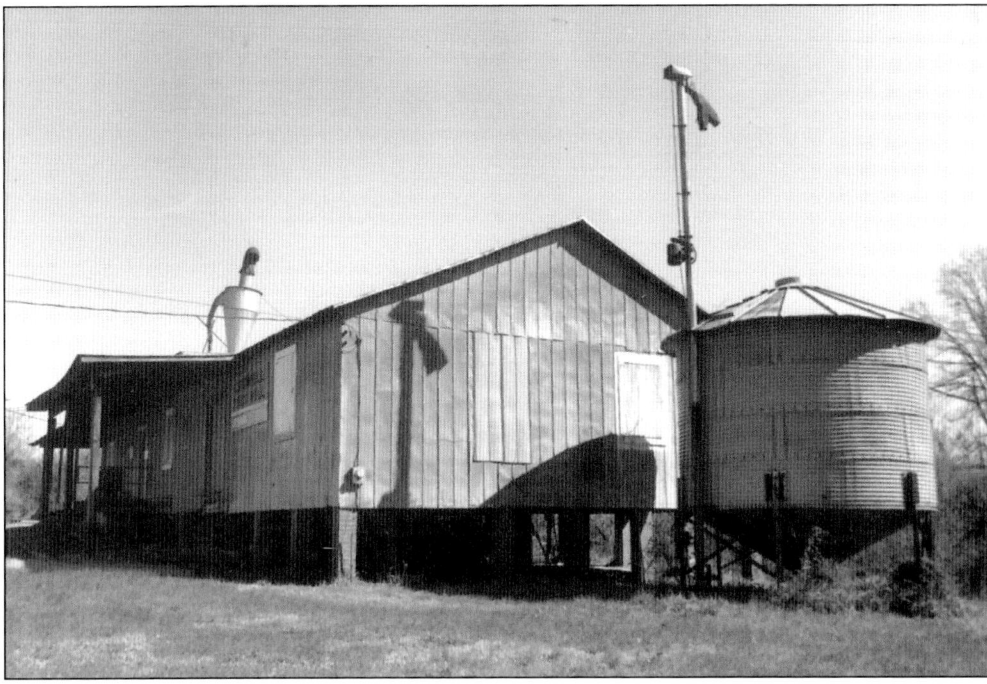

The Crowell-Burris seed grader began as a mill operated by H.H. Little. When the first structure burned, a second was built with help from local business owner Ed Crowell, who became the sole owner until his death. The mill was purchased by Reggie Burris, who still operates it today. Below, in 1982, Crowell is seen inside the business with a hopper and grinder, part of the milling machinery required to grind grain.

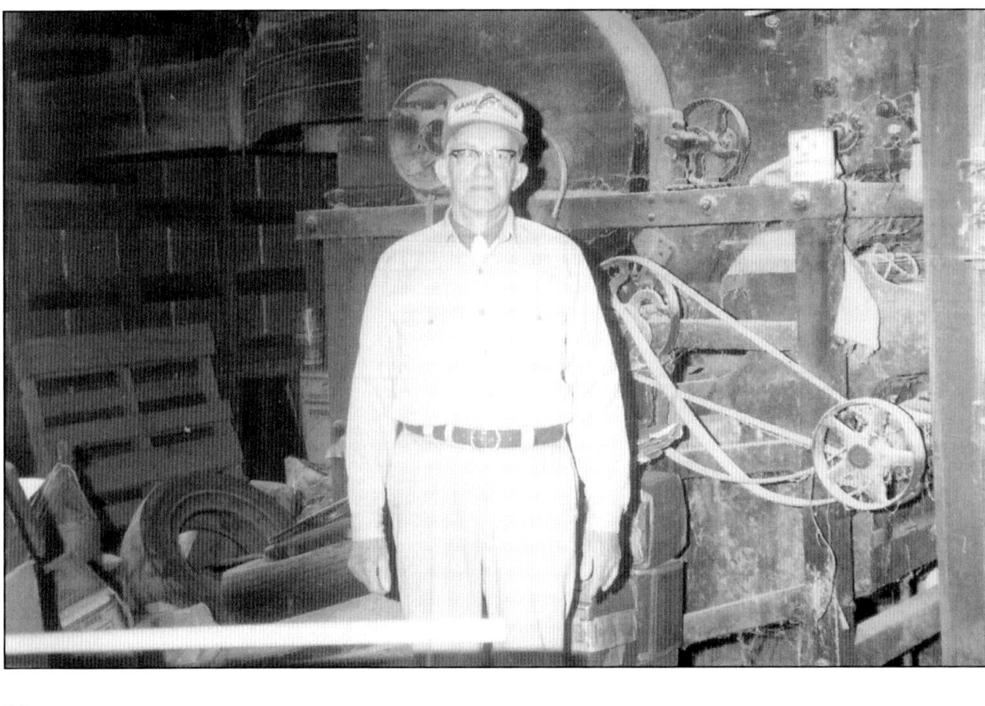

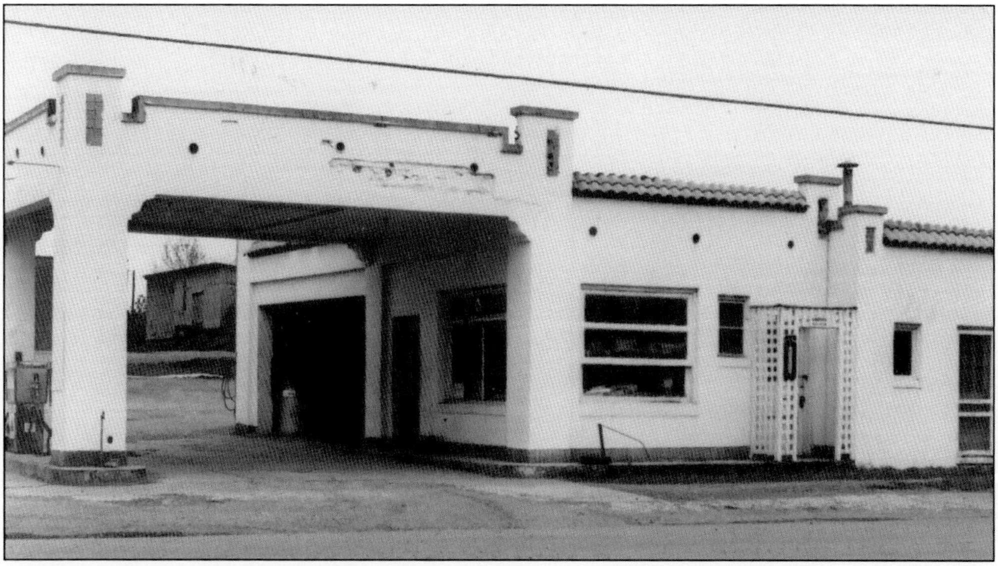

Earl Crowell also operated a service station on the corner of North Main and East First Streets. Now known as Variety Pickup, it is run by Crowell's daughter Dr. Margaret Stewart and her daughter and son-in-law, Betsy and David Heath.

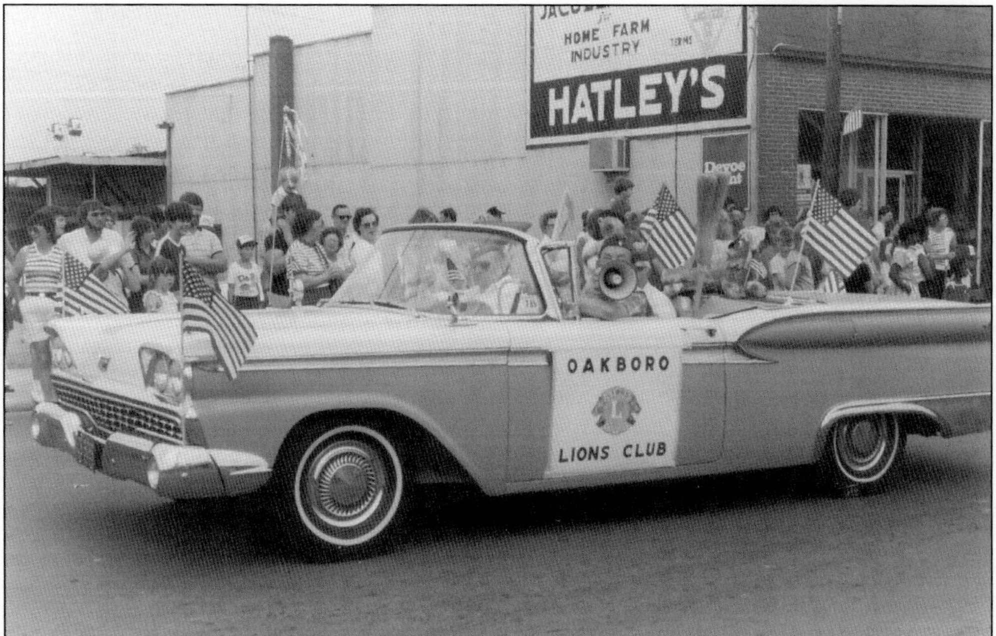

This 1959 Skyliner passes in front of Hatley's Hardware in the 1984 Fourth of July parade. Raymon C. Hatley started the business in 1937, and his brother John joined as a partner after World War II. The company remained in business until 1982.

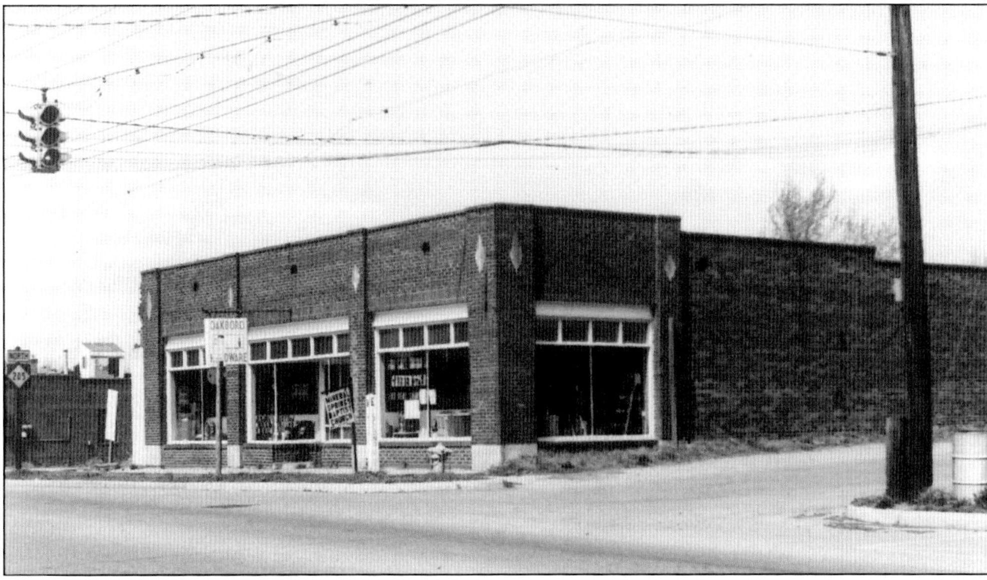

The Oakboro Hardware Store, seen here in 1975, was operated by Bryce Whitley and Rayvon Foreman. Ann Austin also worked in the office, which was located on the northeast corner of East Second and North Main Streets. The building is currently occupied by Penny's Restaurant.

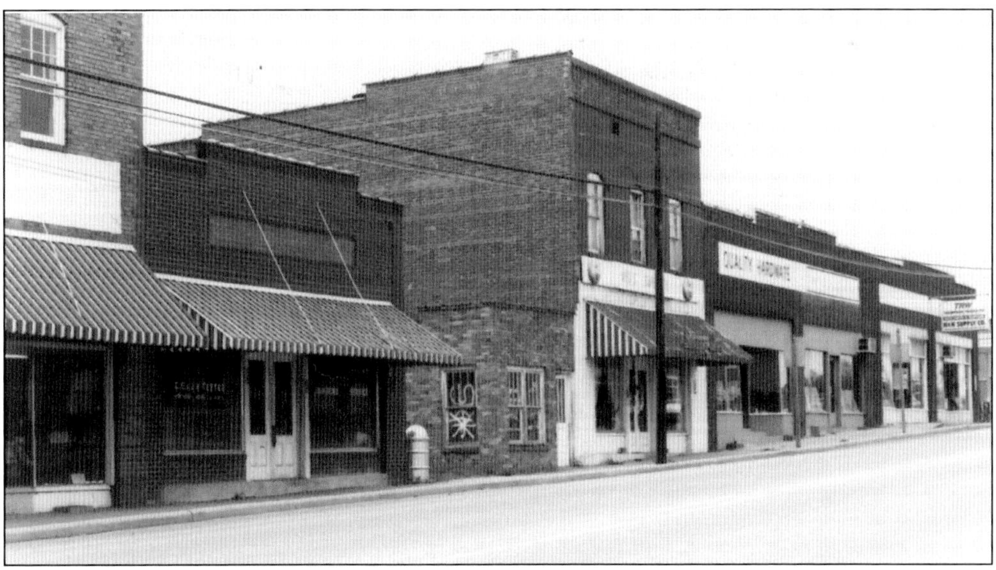

This 1975 photograph shows the west side of North Main Street between First and Second Streets. The first two buildings on the left are C.E. and J.R. Teeter's general merchandise, feed, and fertilizer stores, and next to them are a shoe repair shop and B.B. Medlin's grocery store. The fifth building has Quality Hardware written on its front, and the last store is Roscoe Hatley's H and H Supply Company.

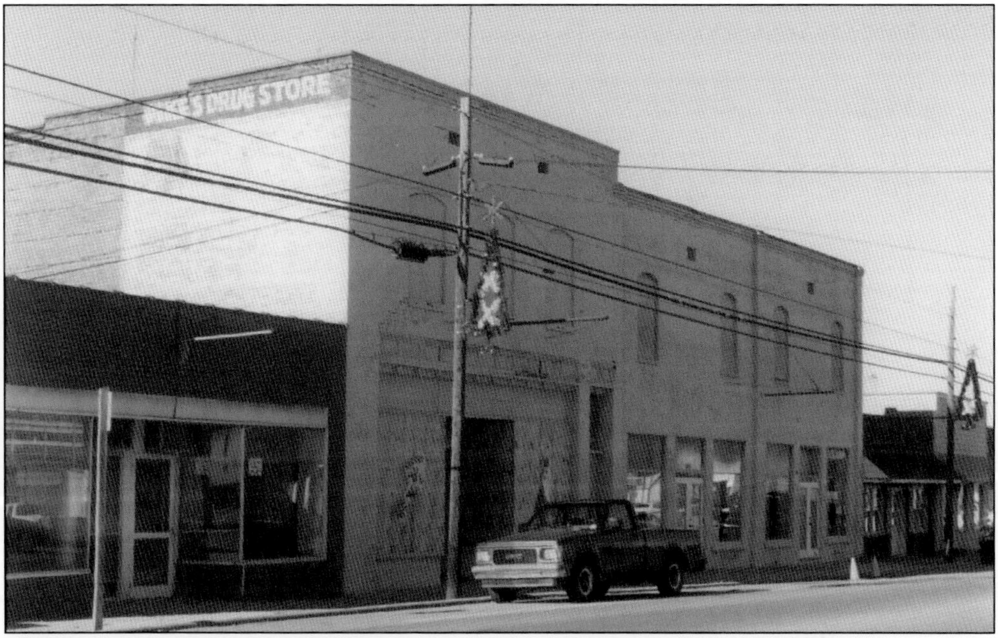

Another view of the west side of Main Street shows the James Coble barbershop, Lee Medlin's jewelry and watch repair, Pikes Drug Store, and Pickets Department Store. The street scene also shows the town's Christmas decorations on the light pole. (Courtesy of SCHPM.)

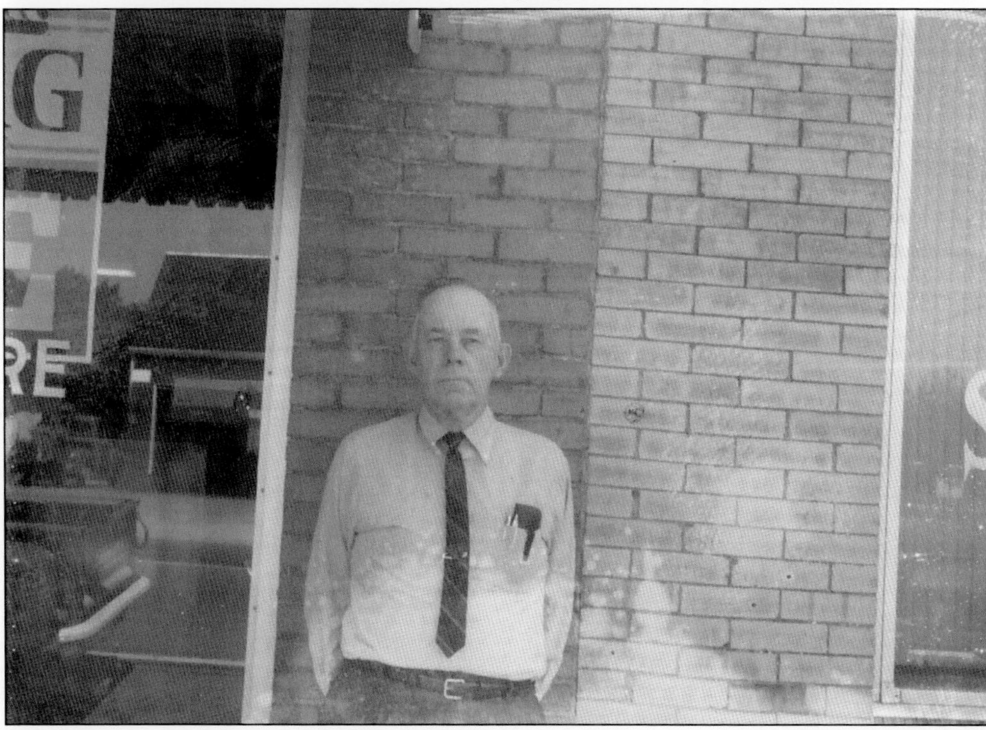

Roy Drye is seen here on the day he closed Drye's Furniture Store in 1975, after operating it for 30 years next to the Security Bank on Main Street. The Drye building is now the home of the Oakboro Regional Museum of History.

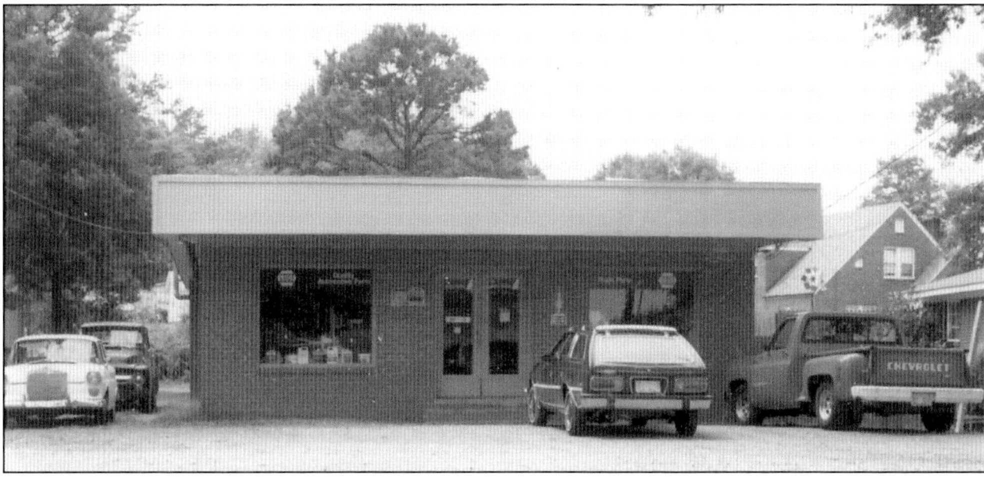

Roy Brooks built and operated a furniture store next to his home on North Main Street. Brooks capitalized on his knowledge of the townspeople and the rural farmers. After his death, the building became Butch's Auto Parts.

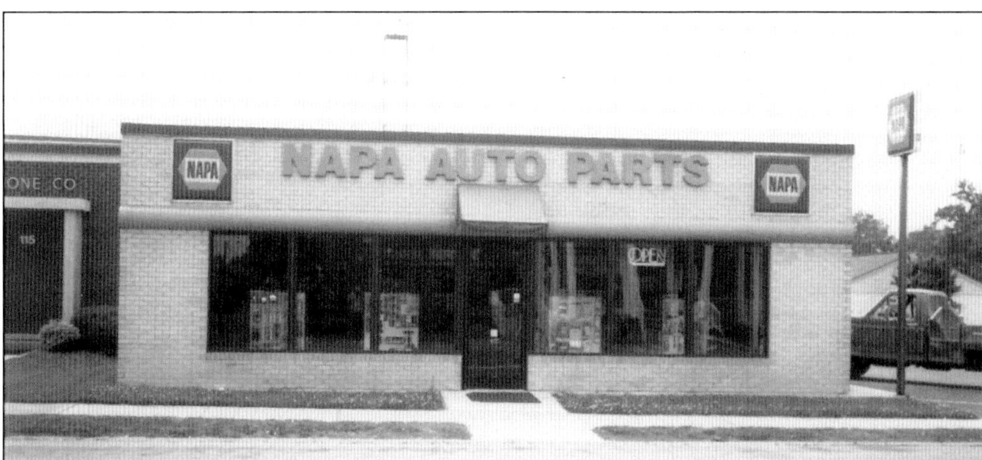

NAPA Auto Parts began as Butch's Auto Parts in the Brooks building and later moved to a facility at 319 North Main Street. Charles "Butch" Preslar continues to operate the store at this location.

In this recent photograph, the marble yard and monument sales office, originally erected by Roy Wolfe Sr., is seen across the street from the foundation for the railroad museum. The tall monument to the left of the tree is now on the grounds of the museum. The medical office of Dr. Harrell Royer was built on the former site of Little's cotton gin, and Casio's Auto Sales now occupies the sales office.

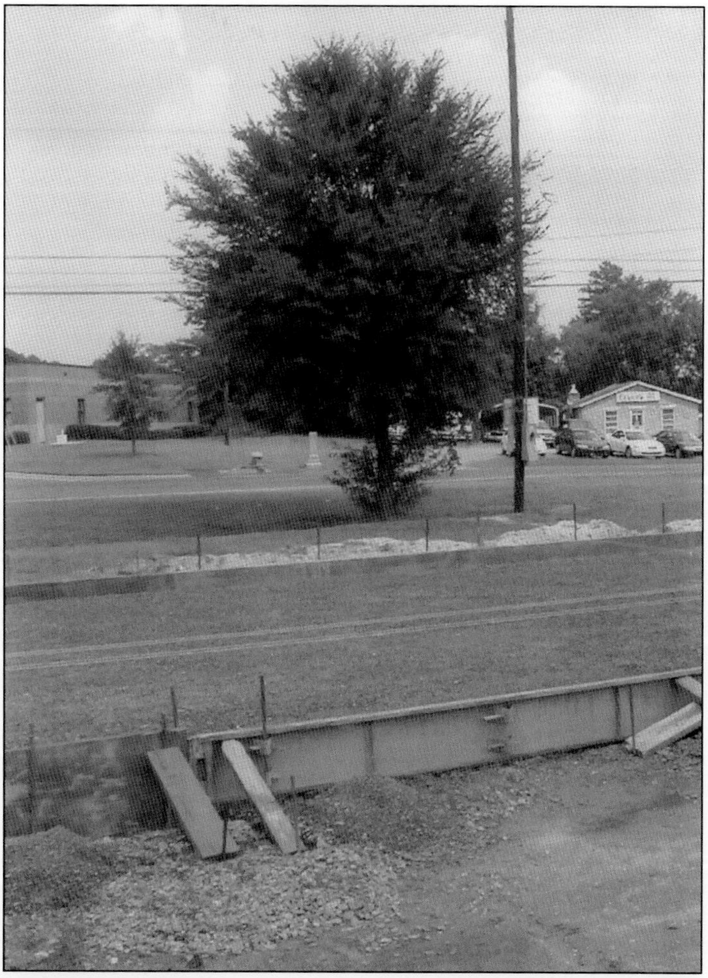

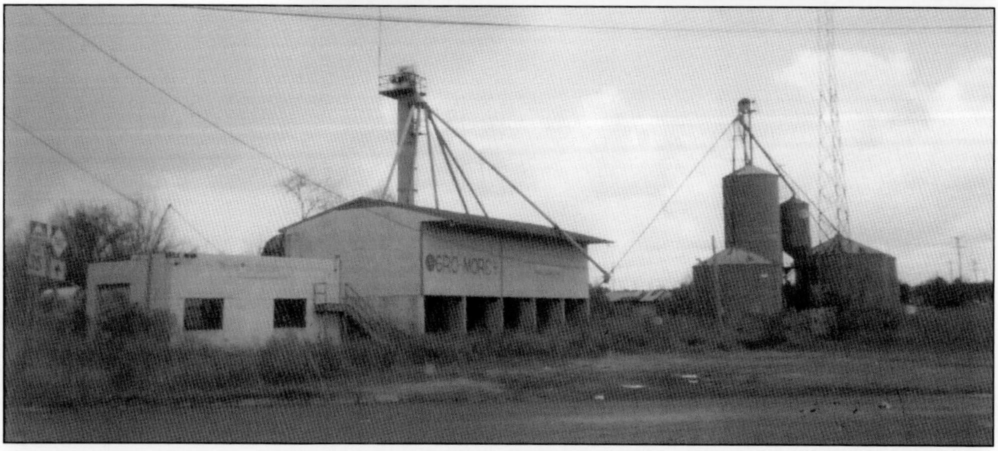

The Gro-More Company operated a seed and grain distribution center next to the railroad tracks. Several silos were used for bulk storage, and a grain elevator allowed easy loading to the railcars. The silos have been removed, and the building now stands empty. The last operators were Kevin and Peggy Baucom.

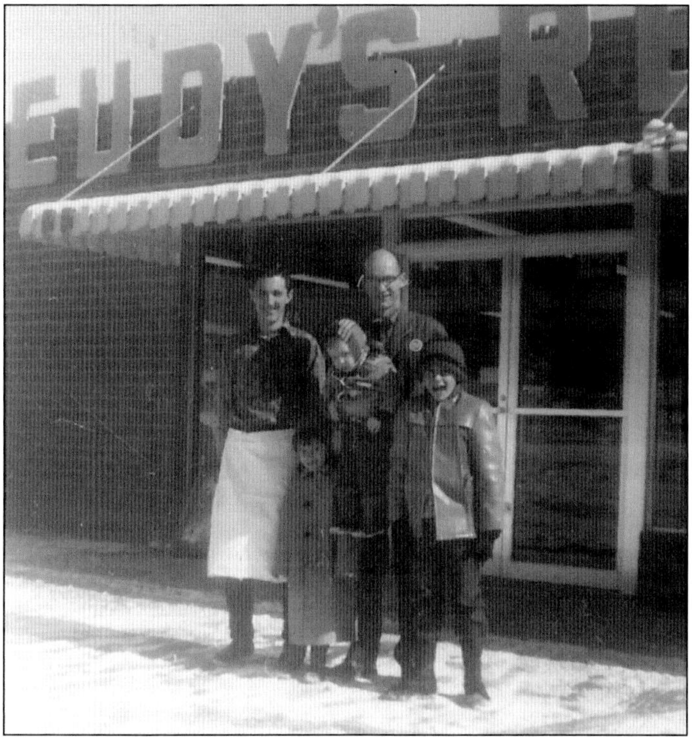

Kenneth Eudy operated Eudy's Red and White, a grocery store situated at the north end of Oakboro. Shown here from left to right are clerk Ronnie Drye, Amy Eudy, Kenneth Eudy (holding an unidentified child), and young Brad Love. Uncharacteristically, there is snow on the ground in this March 1963 picture.

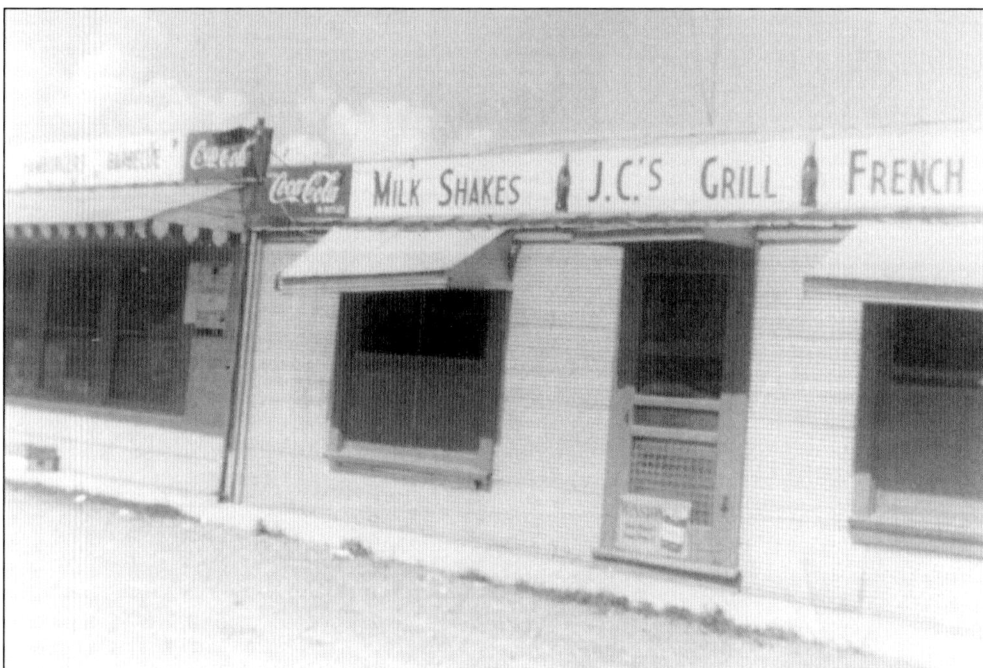

J.C. Furr owned J.C.'s Grill, located beside Oakboro School, from 1954 to 1961. Students were allowed to leave campus to eat there, and J.C. made hot dogs and hamburgers ahead of time since students only had 30 minutes for lunch. After ball games and other activities, the older students enjoyed the curb service at the grill.

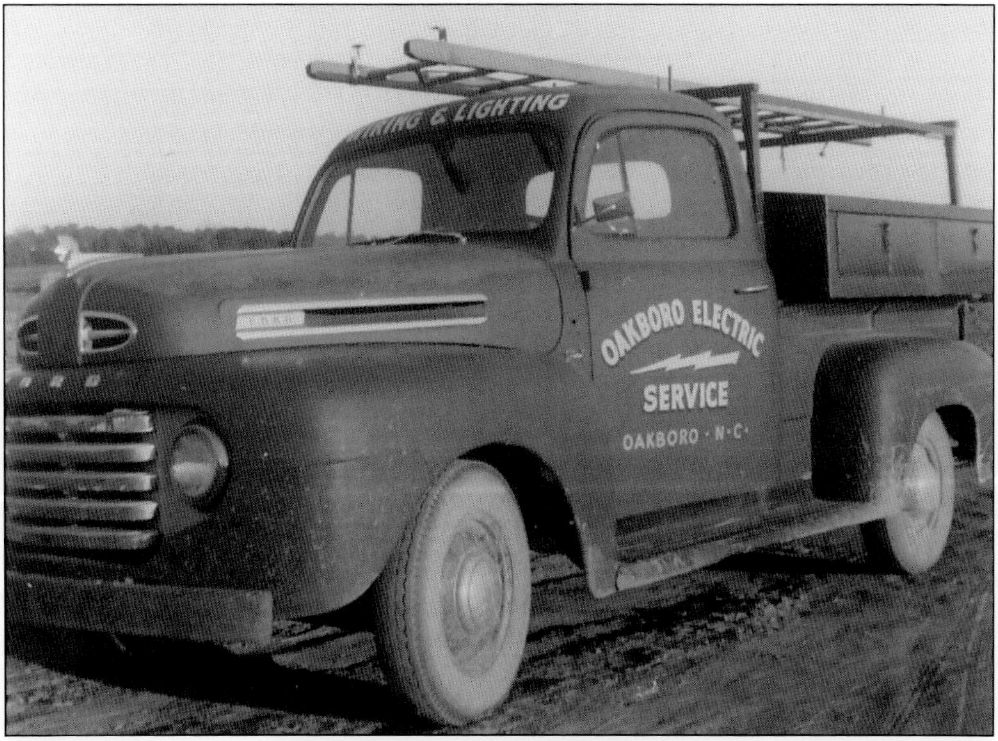

Oakboro had electricity as early as 1909. The Southern Power Company of Monroe built the service and eventually became Duke Power Company. Oakboro Electric Service was another company formed to provide for the needs of the community, installing electric lines in homes and businesses.

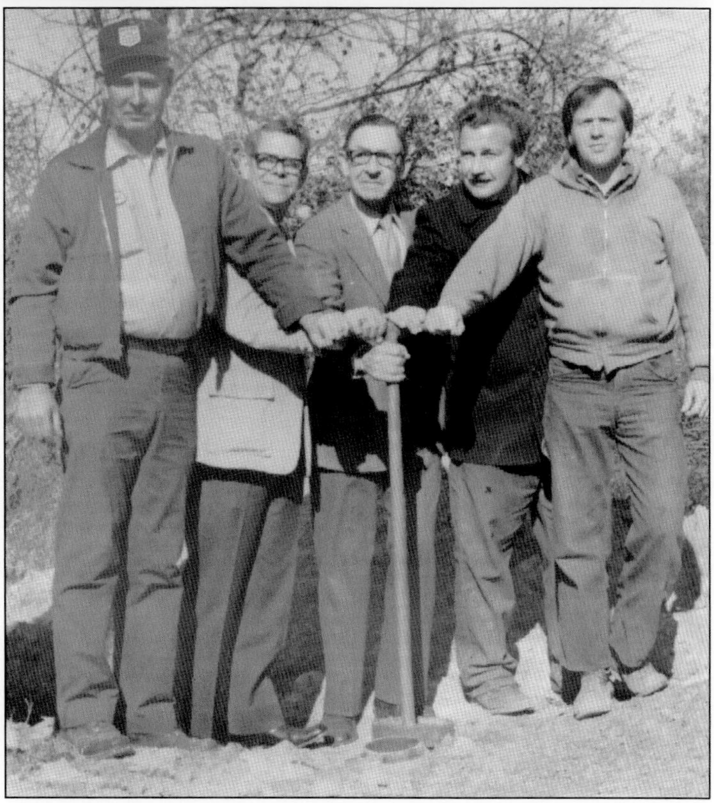

In this undated picture, Oakboro mayor Claude Teeter (center) and the crew that installed the first water line through Oakboro turn the valve, permitting water to flow through for the first time. Town employee Rayvon Foreman is on the far left.

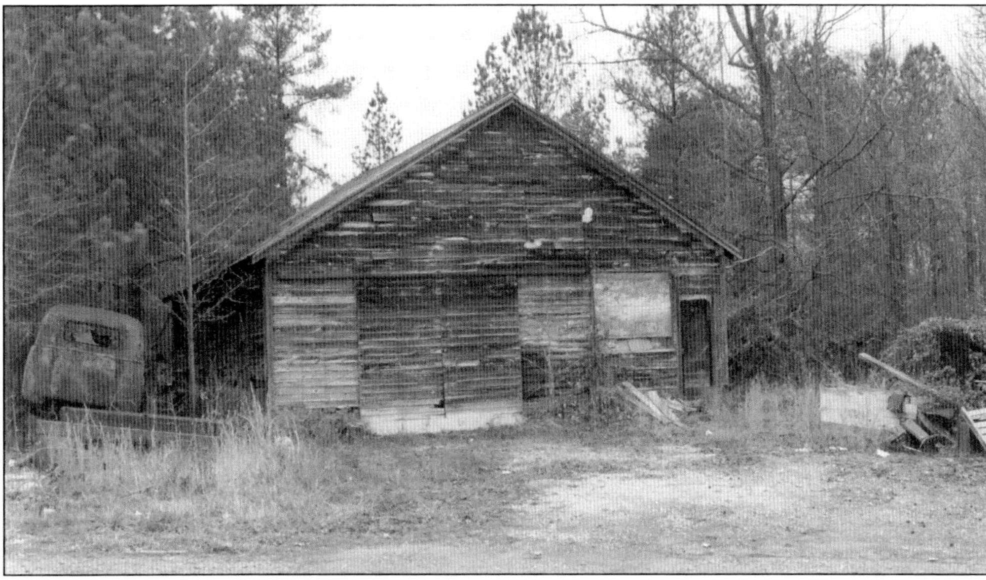

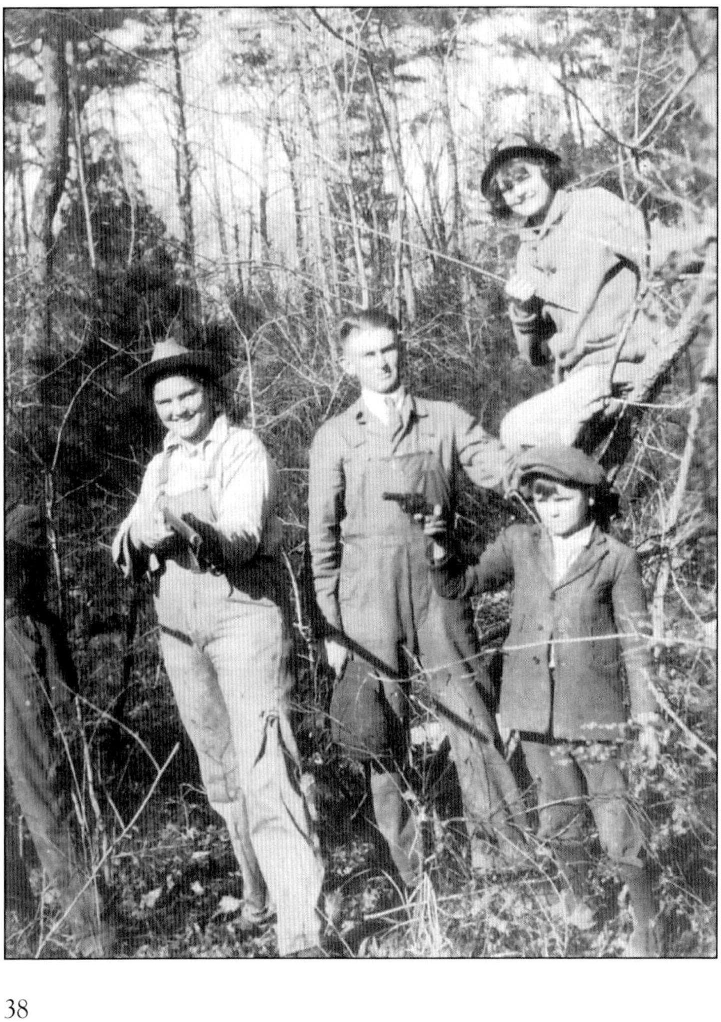

Henry Smith owned and operated this automobile repair shop on Highway 205 south. A well-known mechanic, Smith was also a collector of folktales and stories of days gone by. His poetry was published in local and national magazines and has been collected in a volume available from the Oakboro Regional Historical Foundation. Seen in the lower right of this image as a small boy, Smith is learning to shoot. Also pictured from left to right are Numa Smith, Claude Crisco, and Kermot Smith.

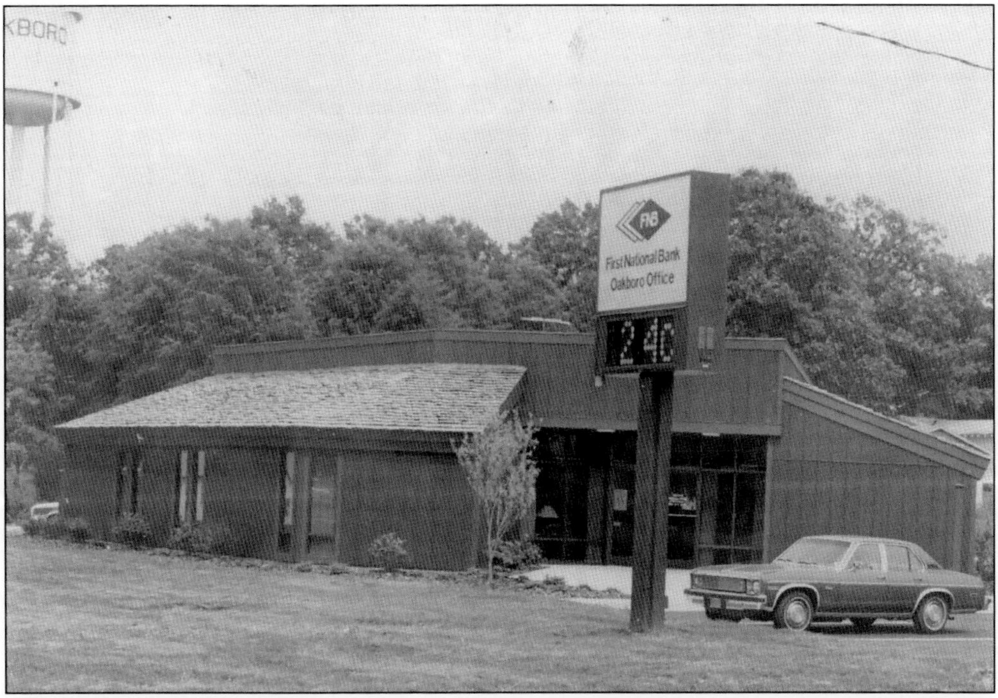

The Oakboro branch of the First National Bank opened on the corner of Seventh and Main Streets. Oakboro's water tower is prominent in this photograph, as is the time and temperature sign, an innovation for the town. Oakboro has been home to a number of banks over the years and currently has three: the Bank of Stanly, Home Savings Bank, and SunTrust.

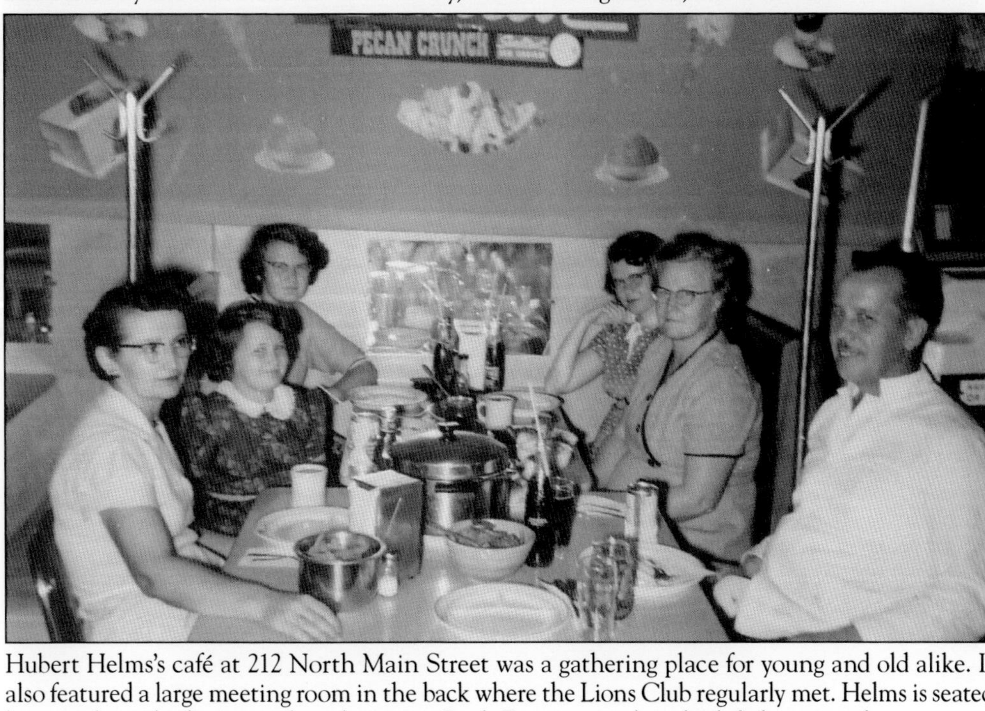

Hubert Helms's café at 212 North Main Street was a gathering place for young and old alike. It also featured a large meeting room in the back where the Lions Club regularly met. Helms is seated here in the right foreground, and waitress Ruth Furr is seated in the left foreground.

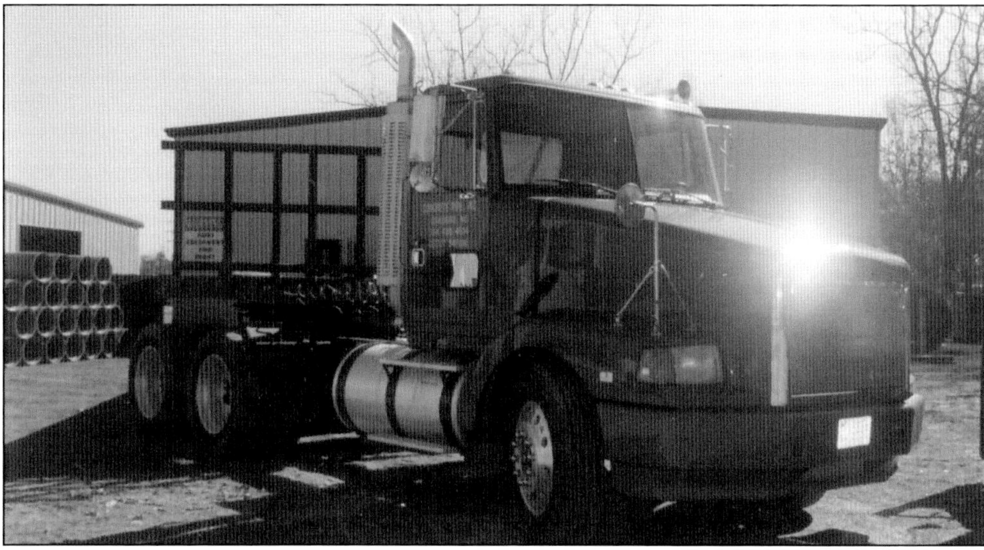

Oakboro Concrete Company was operated by Bennett Kennedy. The company moved to its present site in 1990 and used a dry-cast machine to form pipe. New machinery was purchased in 1996 to meet the market demand for more construction materials, and trucks, such as the one seen here, were used to haul both raw and finished materials from the plant.

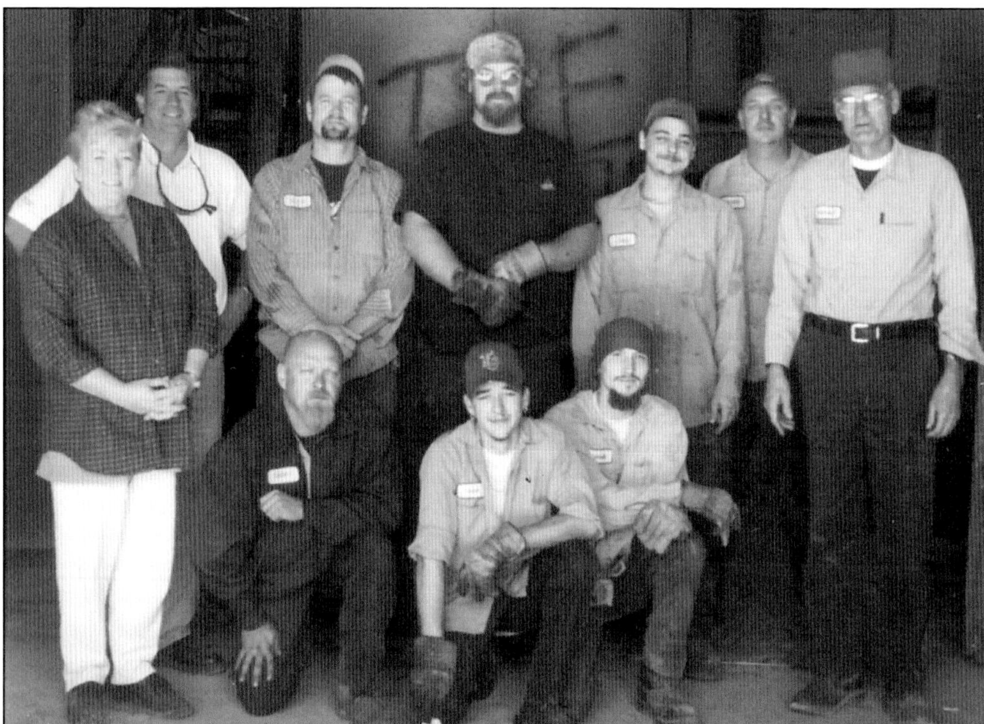

At the time of Bennett Kennedy's retirement, the company enjoyed a worldwide reputation. These employees from left to right are (kneeling) Danny Earnhardt, Michael Lowder, and Mark Lowder; (standing) Irene Kennedy, Danny Matthews, Scott Kennedy, Trent Taylor, Chip Knowling, Jimmy Wilson, and Bennett Kennedy.

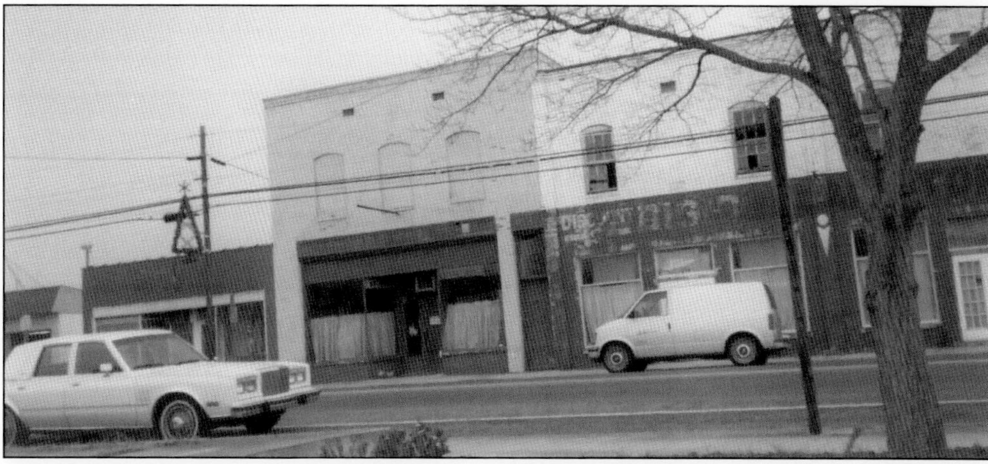

This 1986 photograph indicates the decline in business on Main Street. From left to right, the four structures, looking desolate and unused, once housed the James Coble barbershop and Medlin's Jewelry, the Barger drugstore, Picket's Department Store, and Nance TV shop. In the late 1990s, a group of developers changed the nature of the buildings and restored them to use.

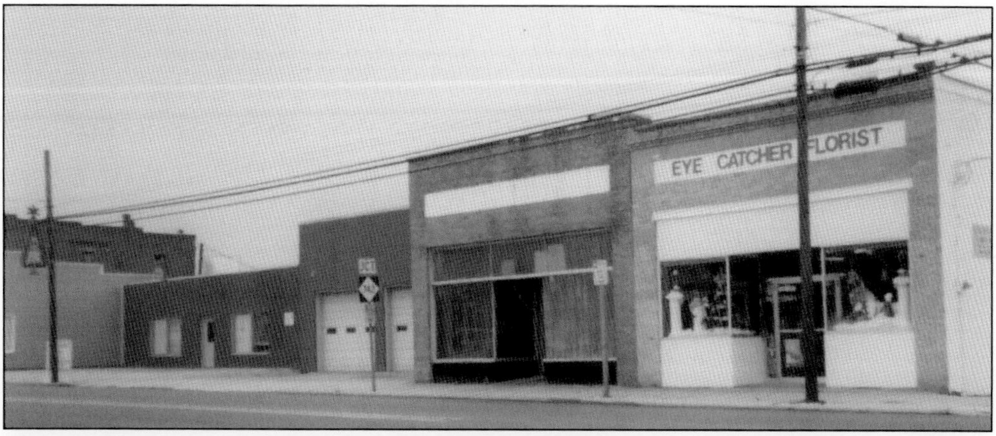

These buildings are just to the right of those above. They are, from left to right, Harward Efird's auto parts store, Efird's garage, Roy Drye's furniture store, and Eye Catcher Florist. All four buildings are currently in use after the revitalization of downtown in the late 1990s and early 2000s.

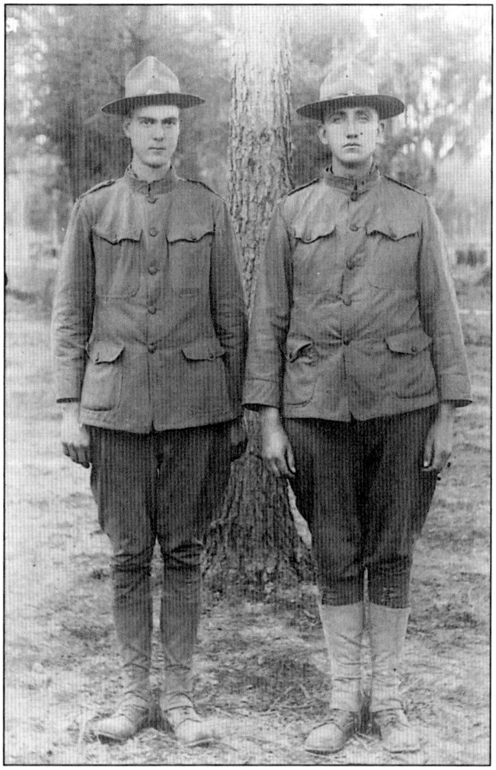

World War I veterans Seymore Hatley (left) and Eli Thomas Drye pose in full uniform. The men grew up close to each other and remained friends their entire lives. They served together in Florida in the medical division.

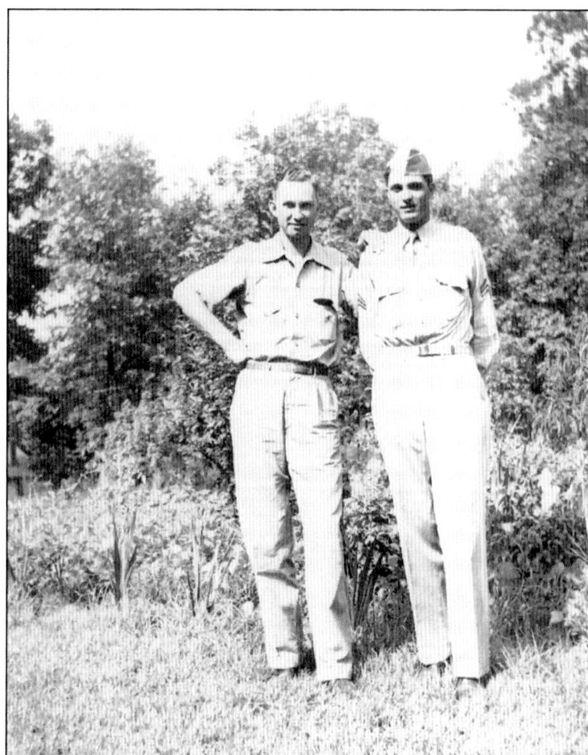

World War II veteran John Wiley Hatley is seen here with his brother Raymon C. Hatley in 1942 at their home place near Oakboro. Raymon started Hatley Hardware in 1937. John was wounded in the war and returned to become business partners with Raymon. Both men were influential leaders in town. The business operated until 1982.

Three

Emergence of Textile Mills

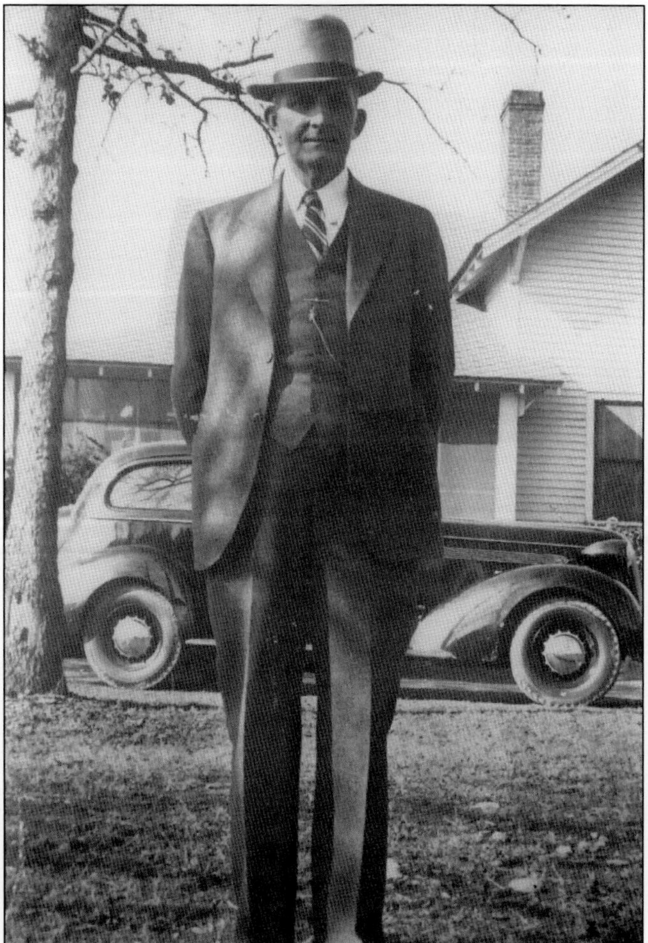

Benjamin M. Rogers was the plant superintendent at the Oakboro Cotton Mill on the corner of Pine and West Eighth Street. The Rogers family was prominent in the textile business in Oakboro, as well as elsewhere in the state, and several generations have been active throughout the history of the mills.

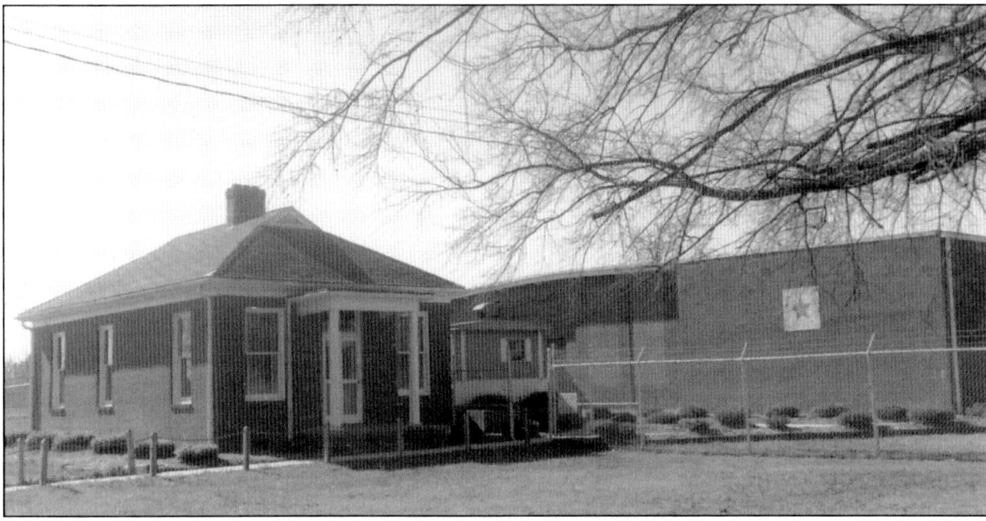

Oakboro Cotton Mill, built in 1923, was bought by Tuscarora Cotton Mill in 1960 and converted to a novelty spinning mill in 1967. The offices of the mill are in the small square building beside the plant. By the early 1930s, the company had constructed a mill village with 12 Craftsman-style houses. This mill house shown below is one of the remaining few that have not been covered with vinyl siding. (Courtesy of SCHPM.)

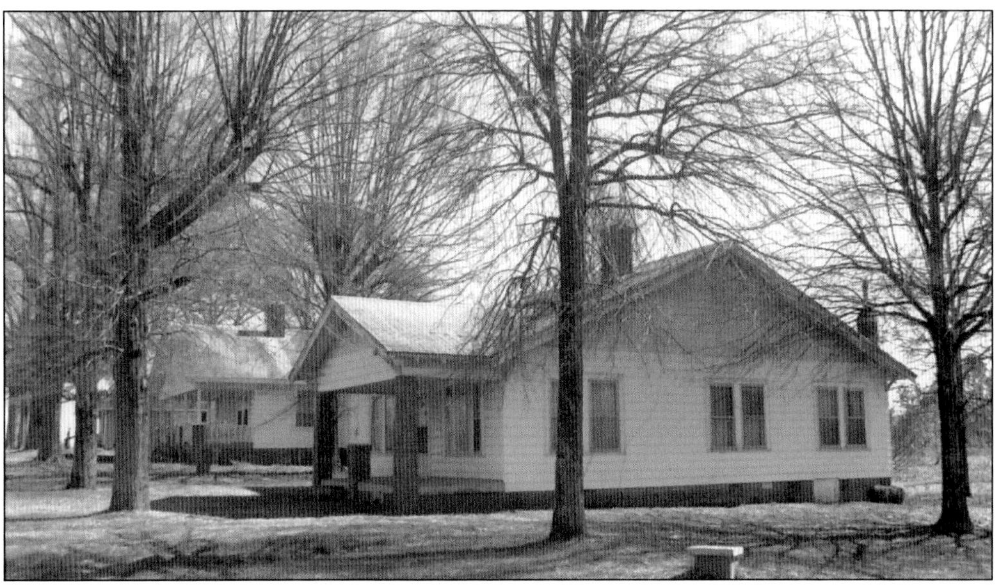

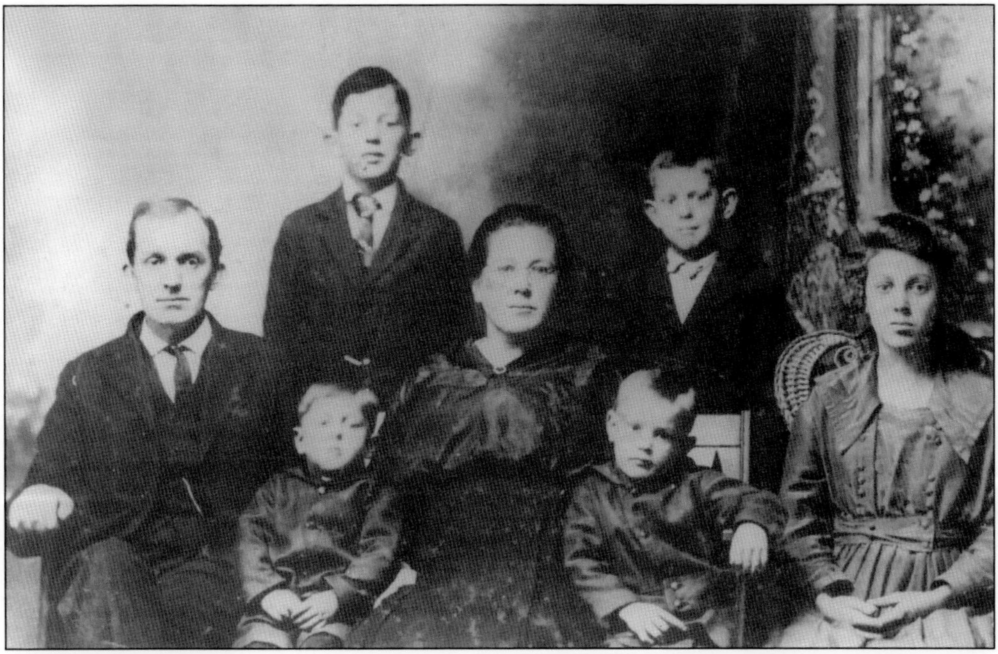

This portrait of Benjamin Rogers and his family includes, from left to right, (seated) Benjamin Rogers, son Robert, wife Emma, son Paul, and daughter Velma; (standing) sons Arthur and Ray. At the time this image was captured, son John Rogers had not yet been born.

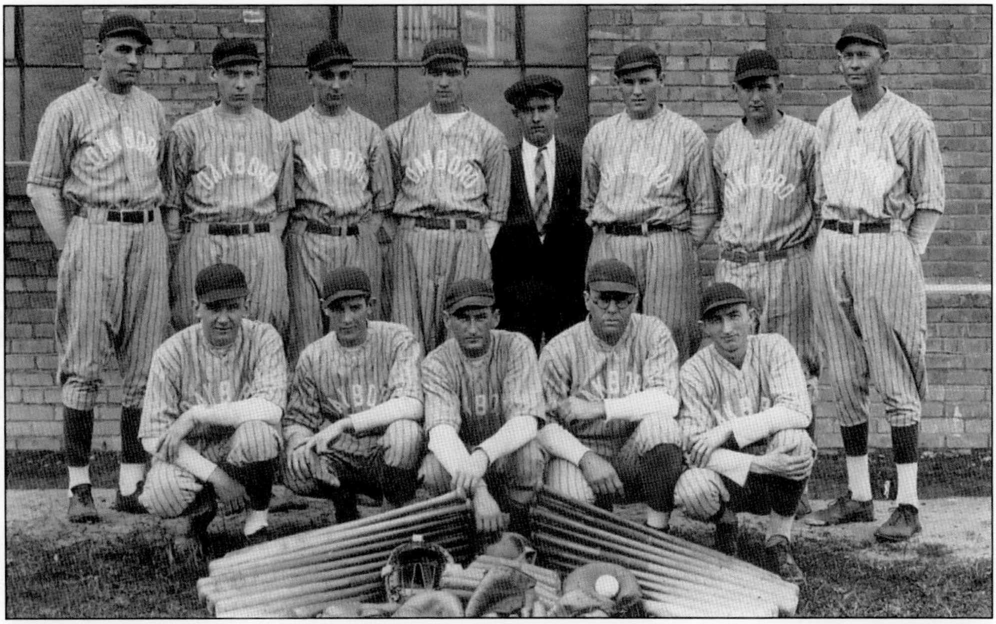

Oakboro Cotton Mill created a baseball field at the rear of their property and sponsored teams for several years. The 1932 team included, from left to right, (first row) Jake Clegg Whitley, Paul Rogers, Mose Horton, James Harward, and Horace Howard; (second row) Claude Goodman, Lane Coble, Paul Barnhardt, Horace Hartsell, Ben Eudy, Vernon Curlee, Paul Hartsell, and Milton Kennedy.

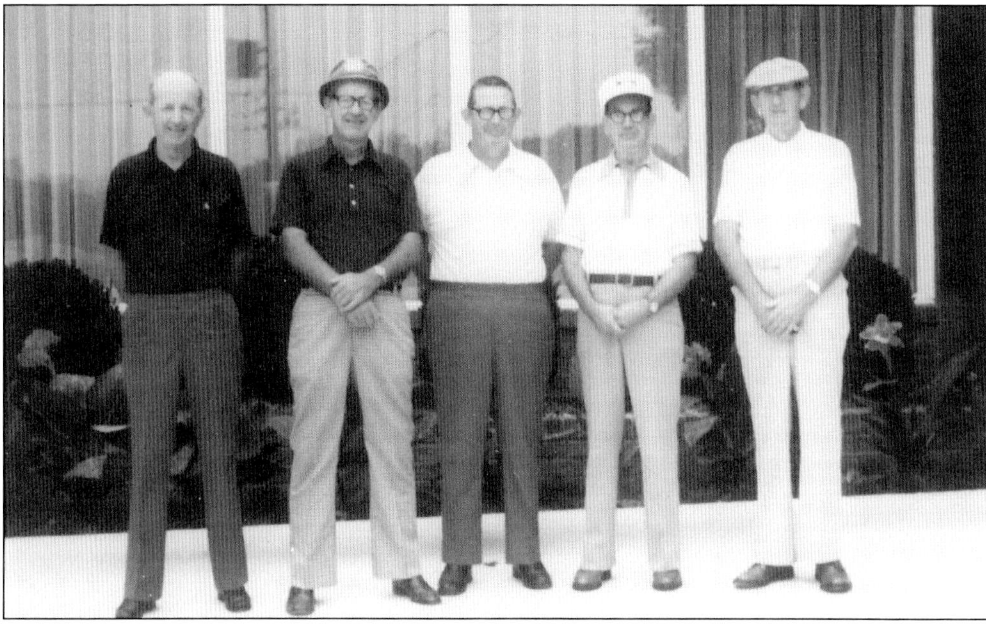

The five Rogers sons were all active in the textile industry. John Rogers started Stanly Knitting Mill in 1946 using his GI loan after serving in World War II from 1942 to 1946. Arthur Rogers worked at Glen Raven, developing contacts who would help them in the future. Paul Rogers started working at Stanly in the late 1950s, and Ray Rogers joined in the 1960s. The mill closed its doors permanently in 2001.

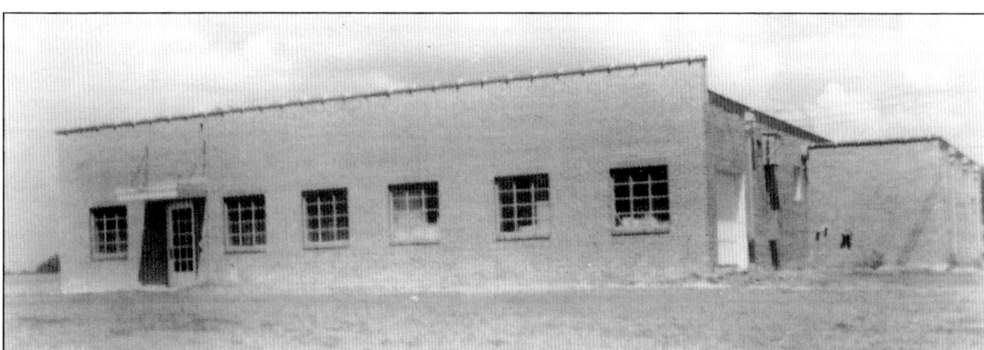

The first Stanly Knitting Mill building was on Highway 742. After the process outgrew the facility, the company added on to the structure. The original building is seen here in the late 1950s.

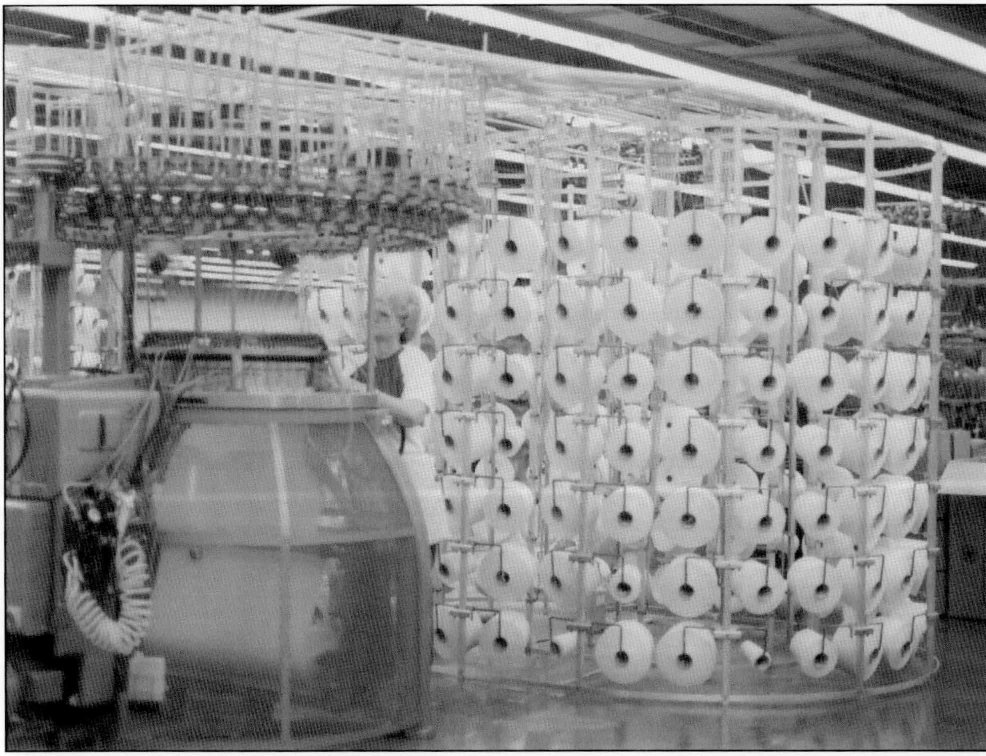

After Stanly Knitting Mills stopped hosiery production, it began making its own fabric for outerwear. It opened a sales office in New York City's Empire State Building in 1963 and also had offices in Boston and Los Angeles. The above image shows the spinning room for the fabric. Tenders kept close check on the spools of thread. Below is the dye house, which was used initially to dye hosiery and later for fabric dying. (Courtesy of Debbie Edwards.)

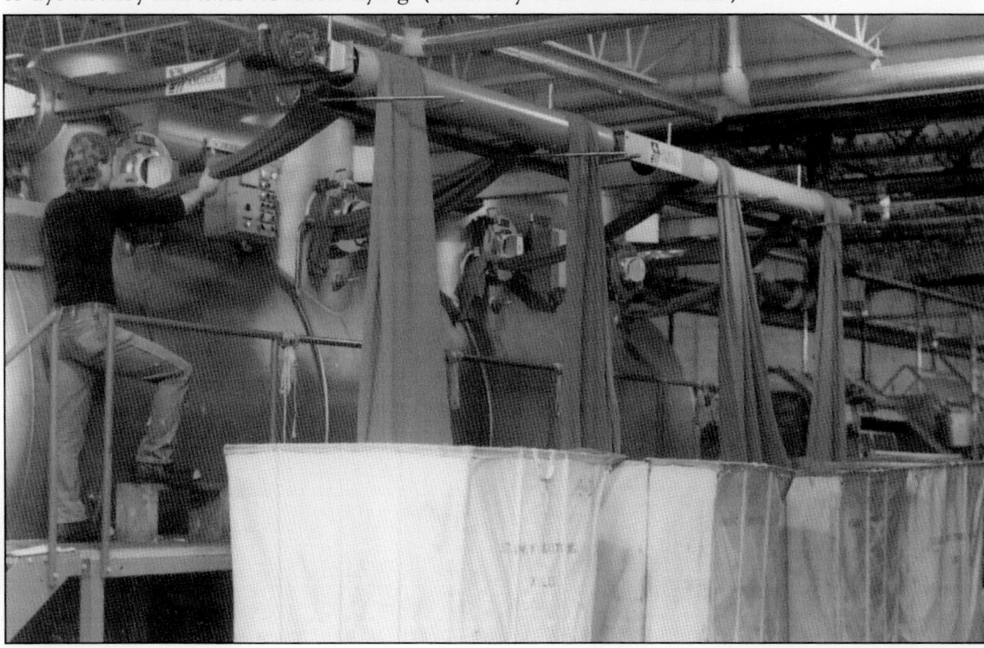

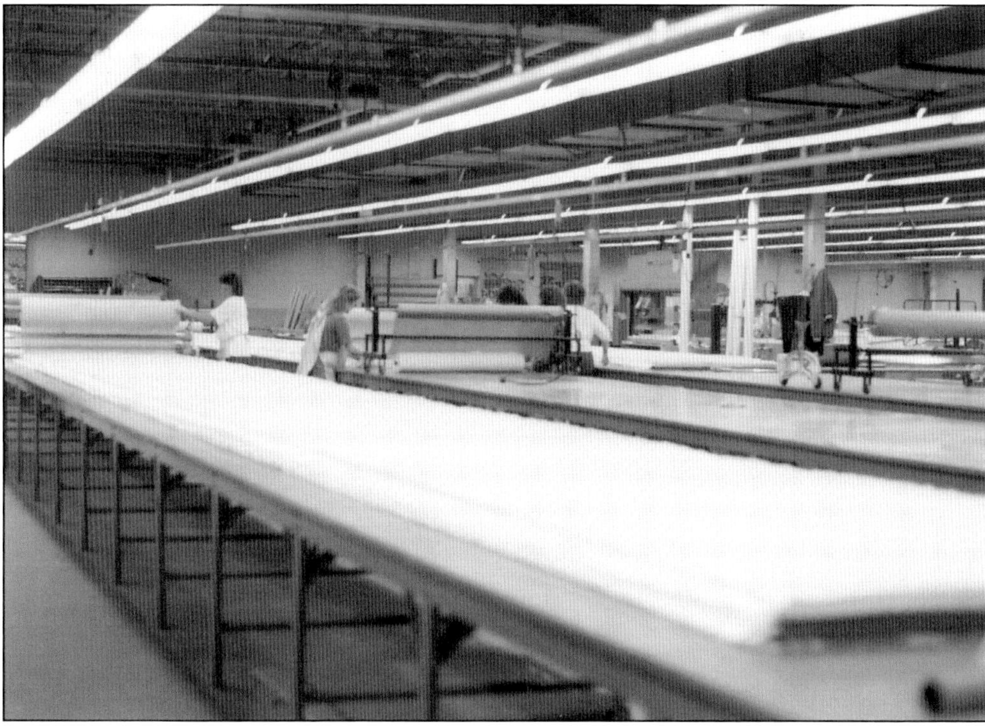

After the fabric was dyed, it was rolled out on long tables and cut according to the style of garment being assembled. The material was then sent to the sewers. Each lady had one specific part of a garment to sew, like the right or left sleeve for example. In these two images, employees complete their assigned tasks in the manufacturing process. (Courtesy of Debbie Edwards.)

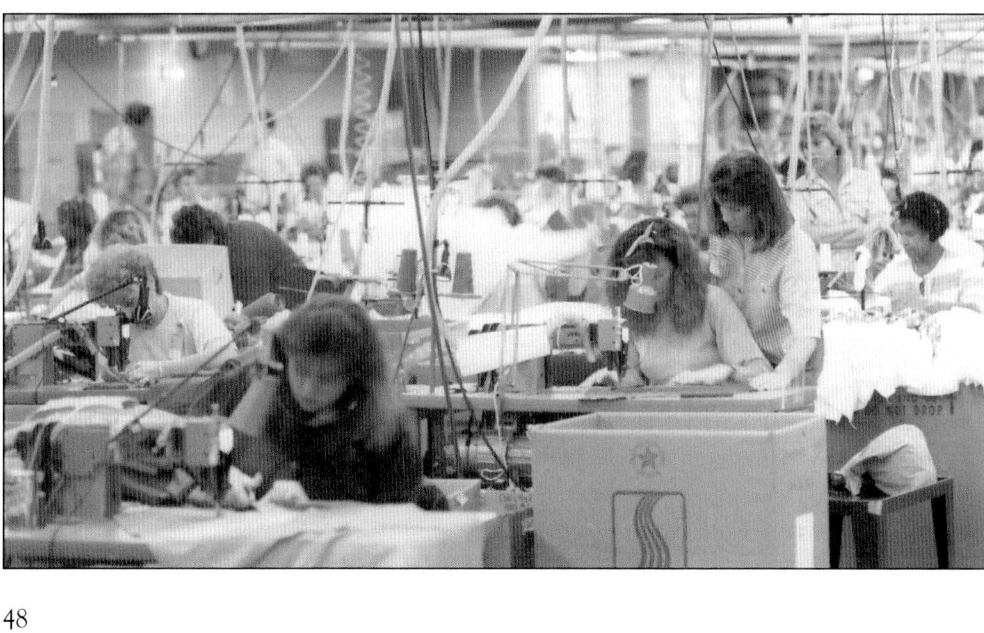

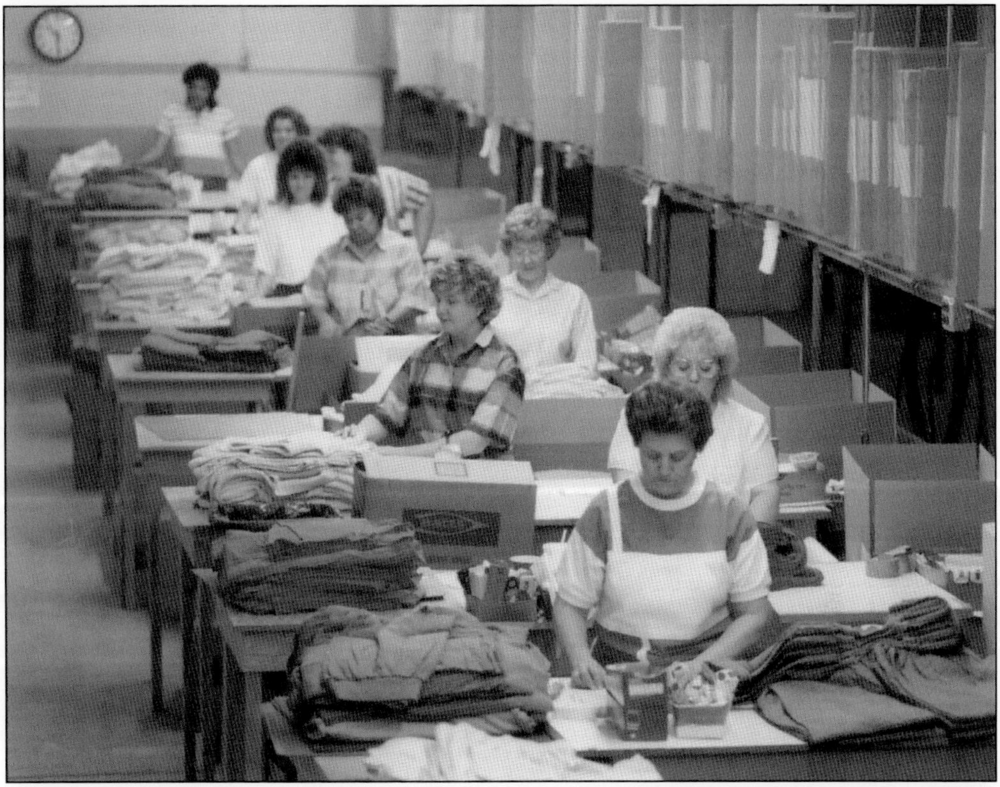

After the garments were sewn, they were inspected, pressed, and then shipped. These ladies perform the final step in the shipping department. The mill shipped to many different retail stores, including Macy's, Belk, Saks Fifth Avenue, Kmart, and Walmart. (Courtesy of Debbie Edwards.)

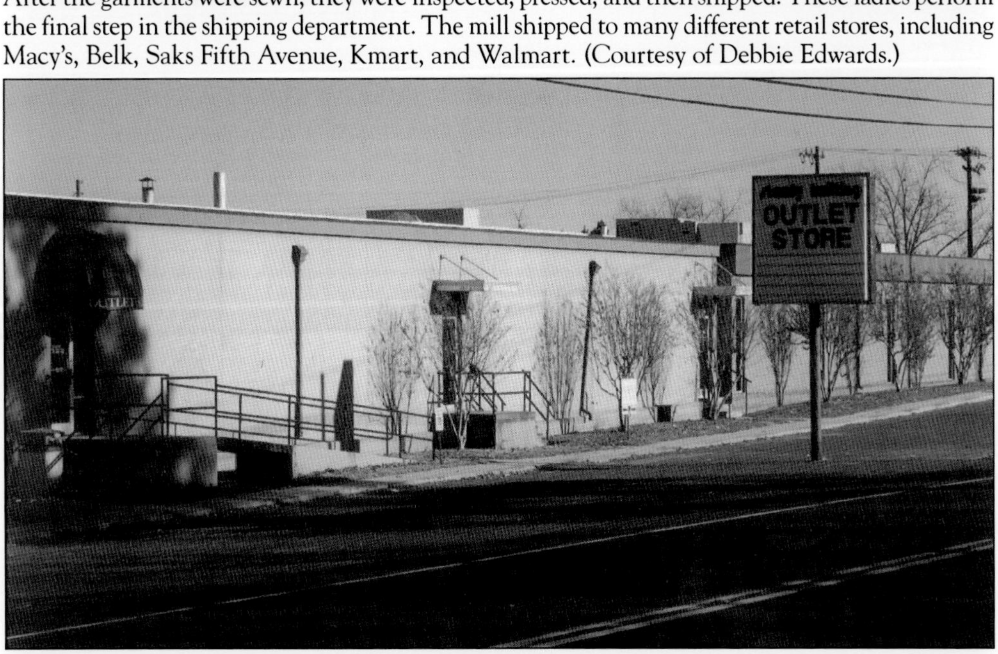

John Rogers's wife, Margaret, started the Stanly Knitting Mills Outlet Store for the employees to purchase merchandise. The outlet eventually became so popular, it was opened to the public as a retail outlet. (Courtesy Debbie Edwards.)

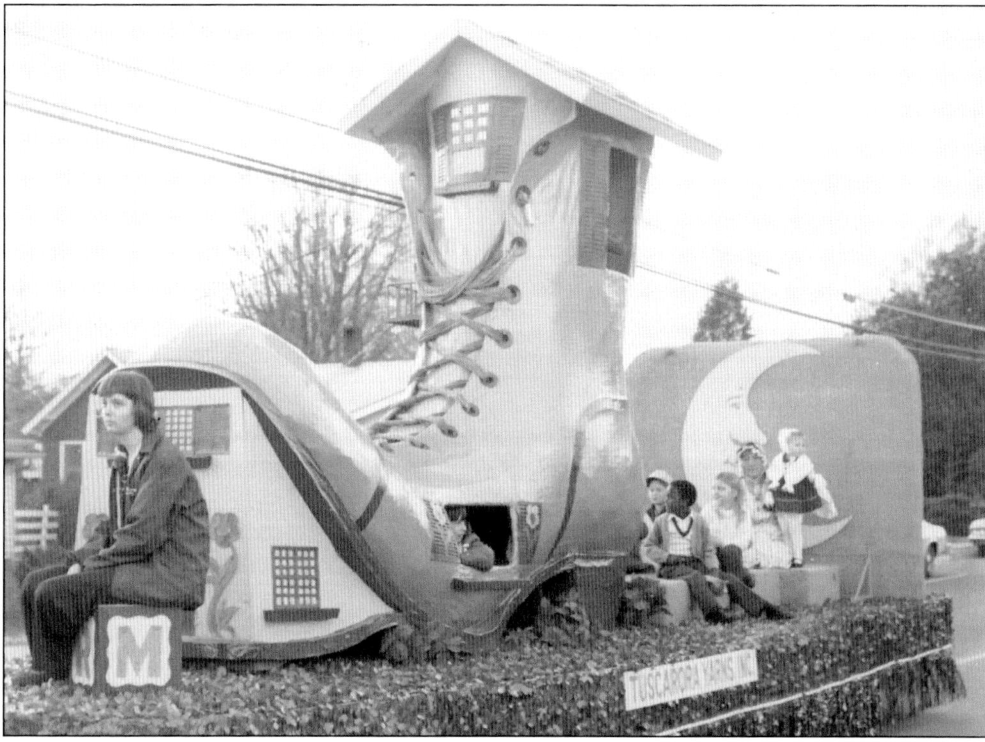

Stanly Knitting Mills and Tuscarora (the former Oakboro Cotton Mill) both celebrated the seasons with the town of Oakboro. In these shots taken at a Christmas parade, nursery rhymes were honored, and employees' children were packed onto floats. Both businesses continued to support the community with participation in town events and, on occasion, by making financial contributions to town projects.

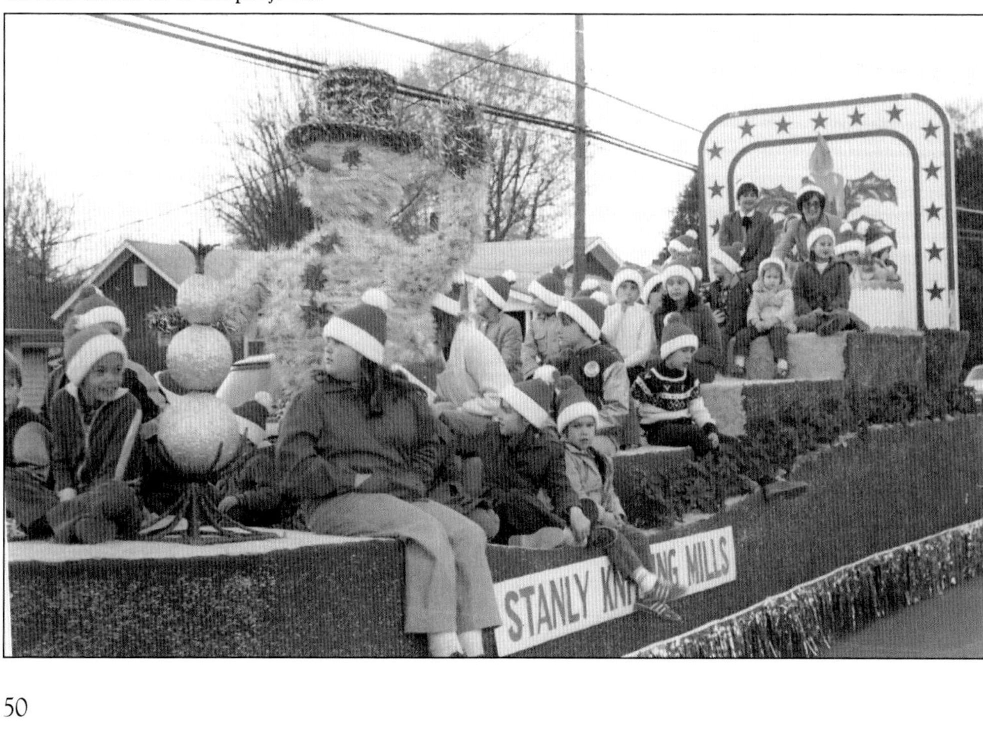

Four

Churches of the Area

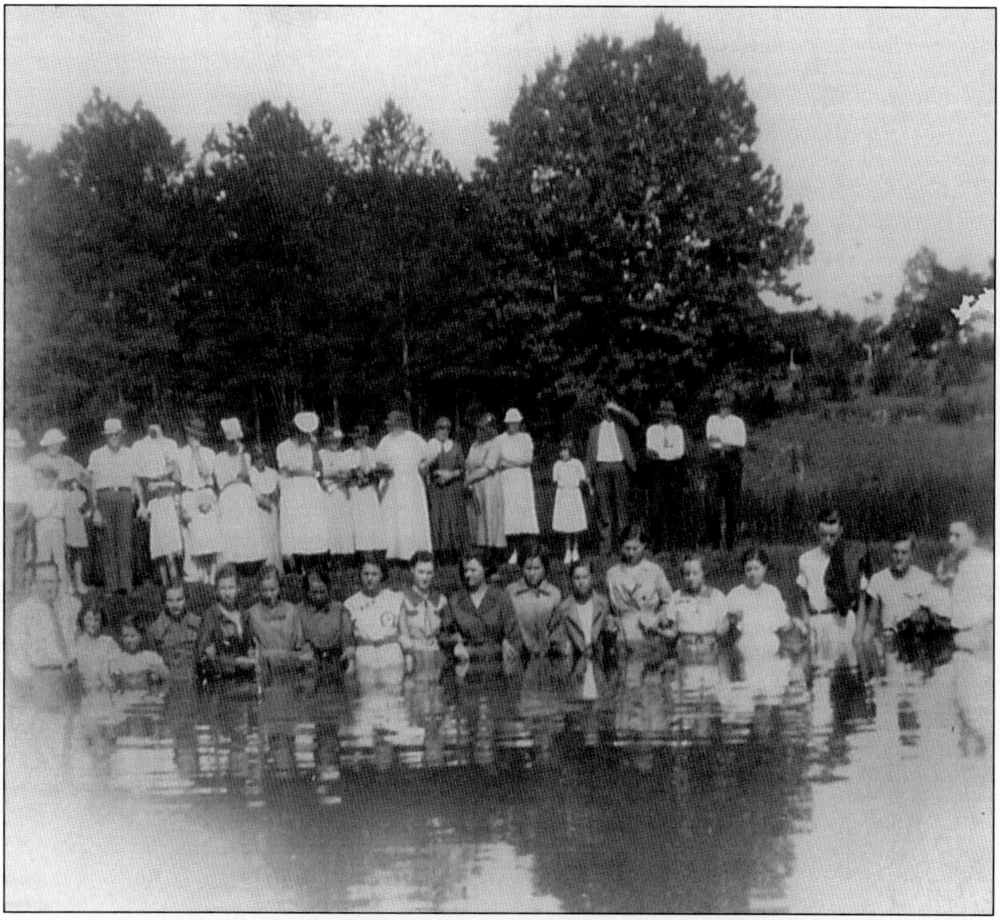

It is customary with certain churches to perform outdoor baptisms. This 1940s baptism was held at the pond on the D.A. Hinson farm in Red Cross for the Red Cross Baptist Church. Other churches used the shallows of Rocky River or some other body of water near their buildings.

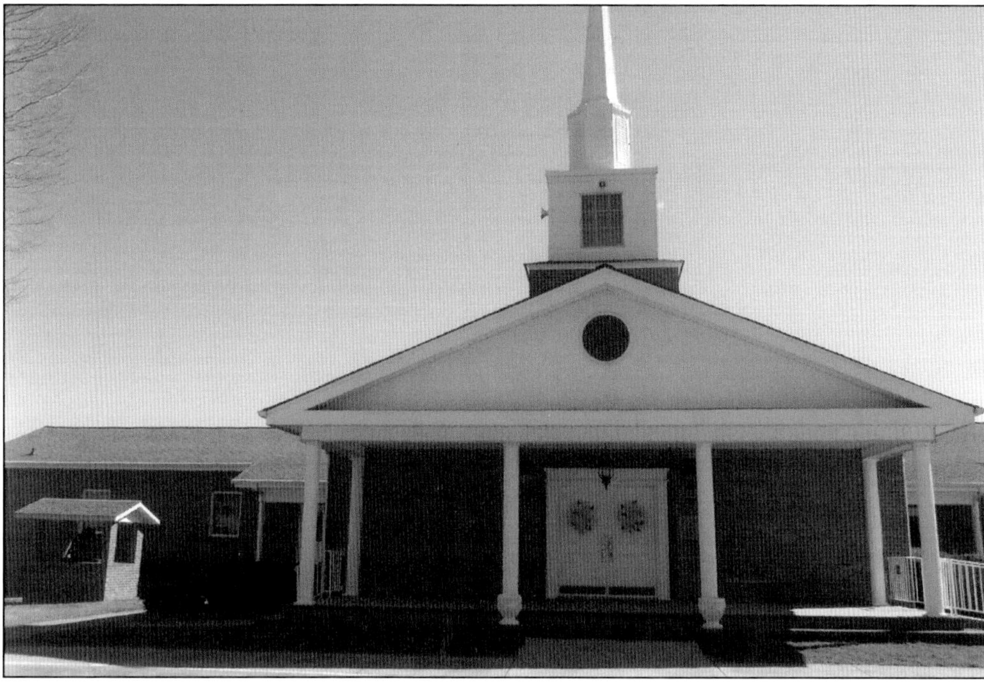

Mineral Springs Baptist Church was formed in 1845 as a member of the Pee Dee Association. The first building was a log cabin one mile east of the present location. The second structure was swept away by a windstorm, but the members persevered and built again in 1910. Services were held in a building constructed in 1928 until the present facility was erected in 1976.

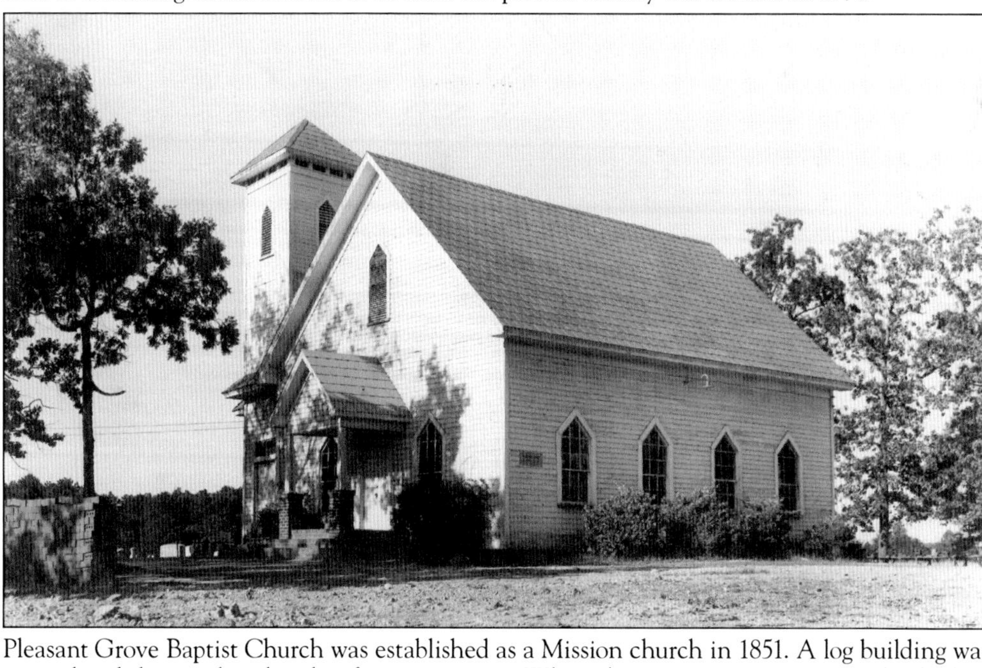

Pleasant Grove Baptist Church was established as a Mission church in 1851. A log building was erected and then replaced with a frame structure. When the congregation outgrew the facility, they built this new church with the help of pledges and loans from members. The church is in the Frog Pond community on the corner of Newsome and Frog Pond Roads.

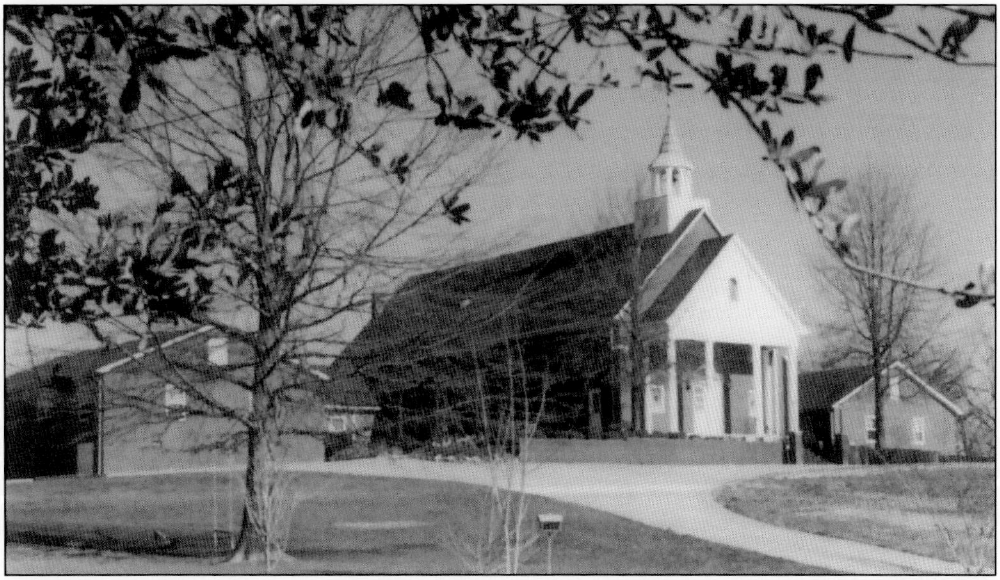

Big Lick Baptist Church was established as Mount Olive in 1860. Progressing from a brush arbor to a pine-pole structure and eventually to a frame building in 1902, the church changed its name to Big Lick after the salt licks that gave the community its name. The church is on Big Lick Road north of Oakboro.

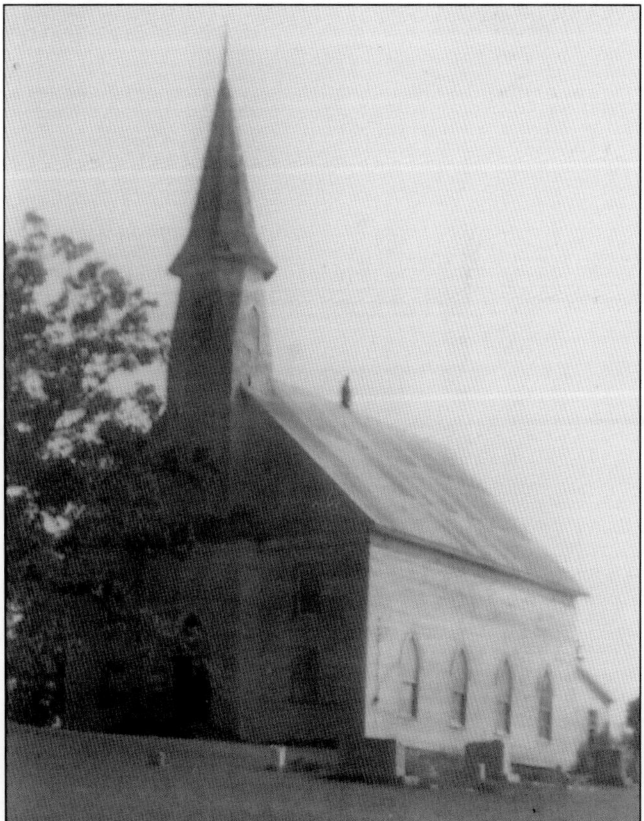

Barbee's Grove Baptist Church was started in the home of Allen Barbee, and when the Barbee family donated the land for the church building, it was named after them. Several structures were used for worship before the current building was constructed three miles east of Oakboro on Barbee's Grove Road in 1963.

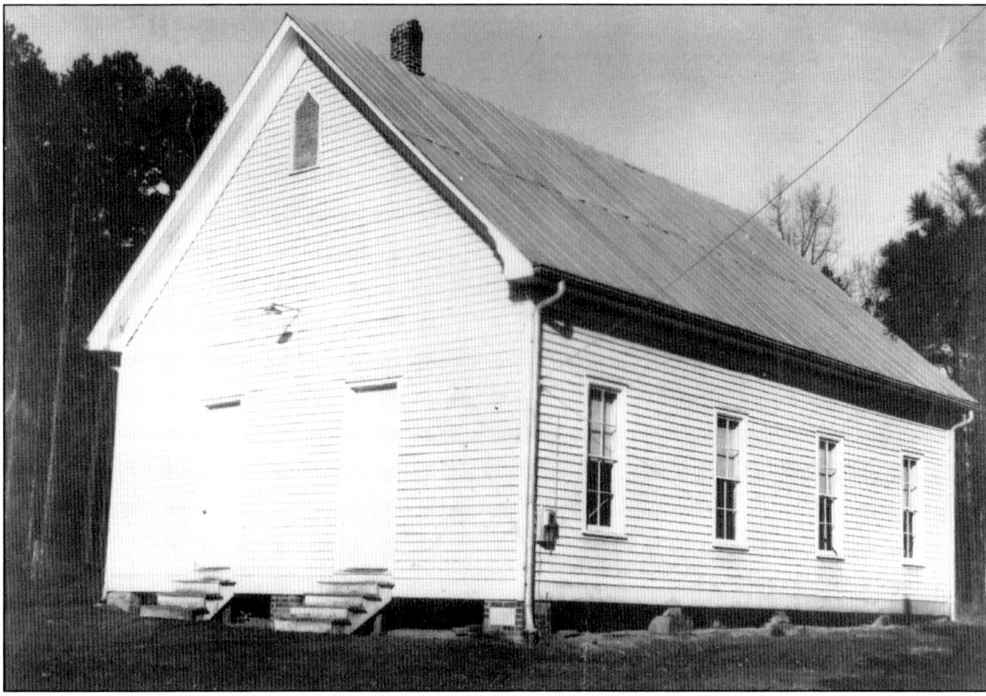

Liberty Hill Primitive Baptist Church was organized in 1846, and this white clapboard building was erected in 1903. It remained in use until 1953, when the congregation erected a new brick structure on Highway 24/27 two miles east of Red Cross.

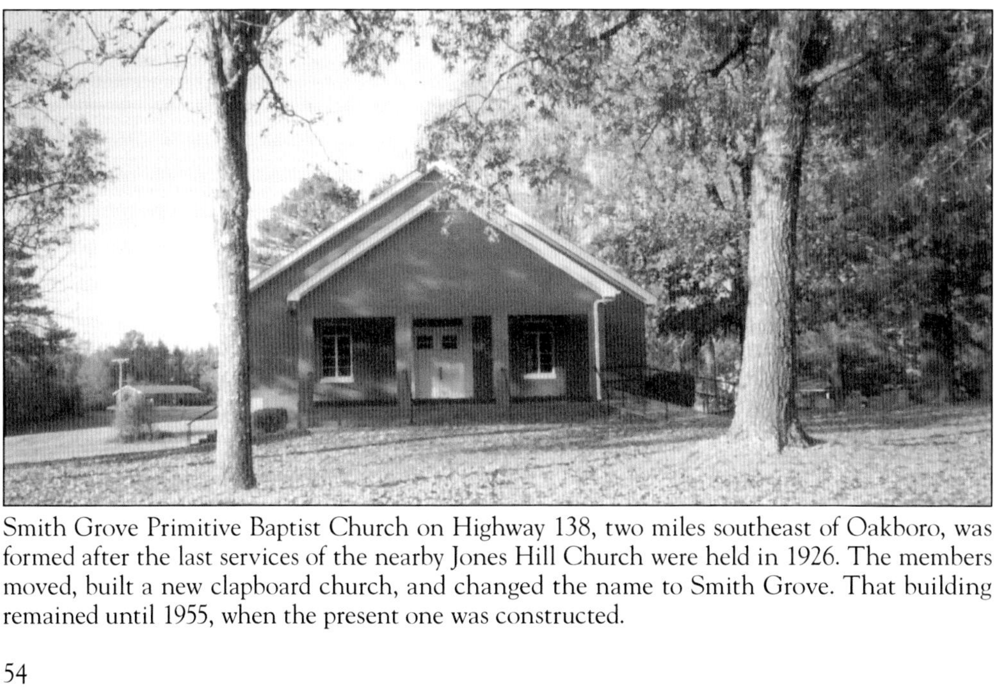

Smith Grove Primitive Baptist Church on Highway 138, two miles southeast of Oakboro, was formed after the last services of the nearby Jones Hill Church were held in 1926. The members moved, built a new clapboard church, and changed the name to Smith Grove. That building remained until 1955, when the present one was constructed.

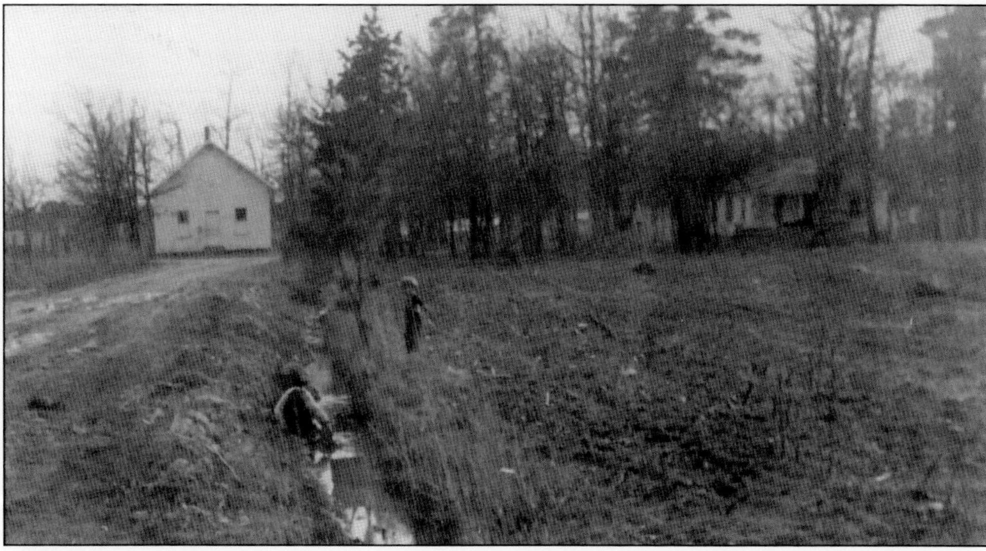

The Oakboro First Baptist Colored Church was organized and held services in a brush arbor. One acre of land was purchased from C.C. Furr, a building was constructed, and the first service was held in May 1918. The name remained for two years until Sister Caroline Billingsley moved to change the name to Galilee Baptist Church. The congregation approved, and the new name was adopted. The current church building, seen below, has undergone extensive remodeling to accommodate its growing membership.

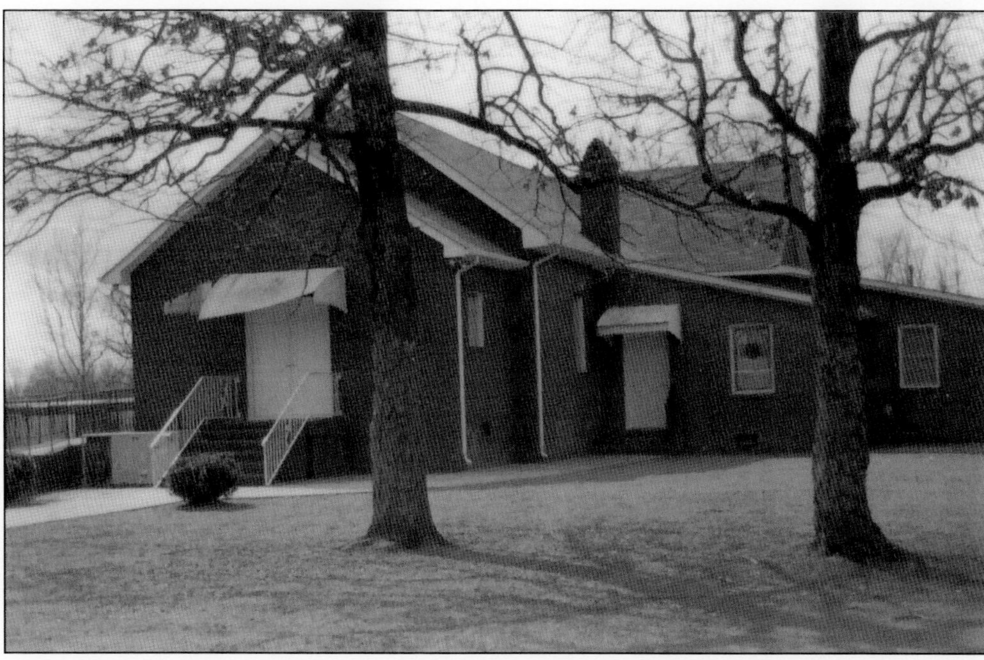

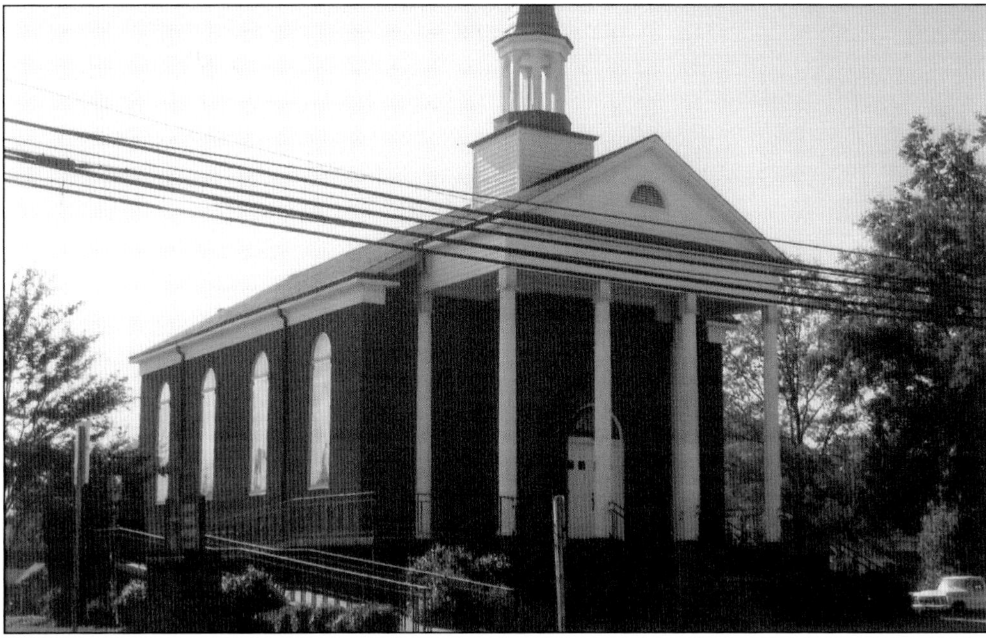

The Oakboro United Methodist Church was formed from the Big Lick Methodist Episcopal Church South. The old church was moved to Oakboro and placed on a lot donated by C.C. Furr between what is now Wayside Restaurant and the Coble Teeter house in 1914. The name was changed to Oakboro Methodist in 1921. Plans were eventually made for a new church two blocks east, which opened in 1950.

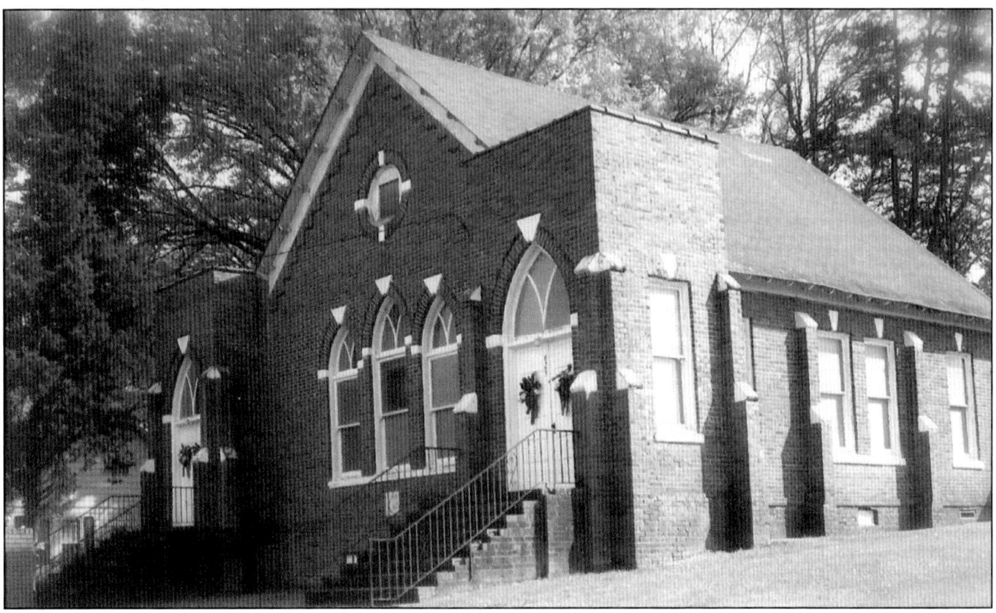

Oakboro Presbyterian Church was organized in 1914 and its members built Oakboro's first brick house of worship in 1916. The outside of the church remains unchanged, and while the interior has been modified for comfort, the original pews and furnishings remain. The church is now owned by the Oakboro Regional Historical Foundation, which plans to return it as closely as possible to its original condition.

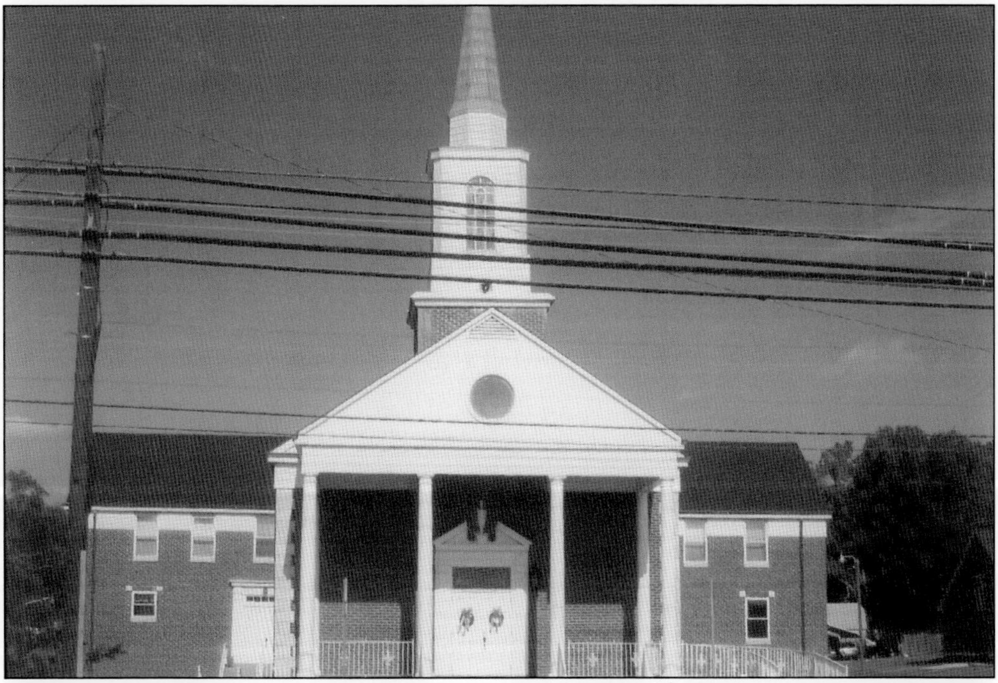

Oakboro First Baptist Church was organized on February 23, 1916. Charter members were D.C. Whitley, C.M. Smith, Rosa Smith, J. Walter Helms, and Mary Helms. In October of that year, they called their first pastor, J.A. Grubb. Members held meetings in the Methodist church before building a structure about 1920. The facility has undergone several renovations, and a family life center has been added.

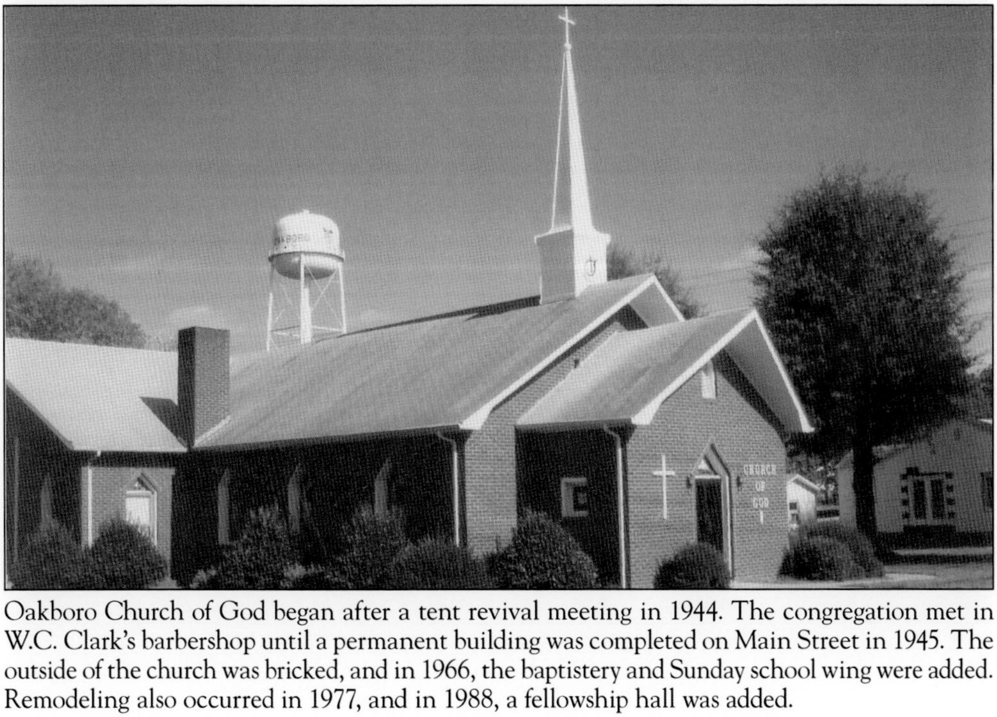

Oakboro Church of God began after a tent revival meeting in 1944. The congregation met in W.C. Clark's barbershop until a permanent building was completed on Main Street in 1945. The outside of the church was bricked, and in 1966, the baptistery and Sunday school wing were added. Remodeling also occurred in 1977, and in 1988, a fellowship hall was added.

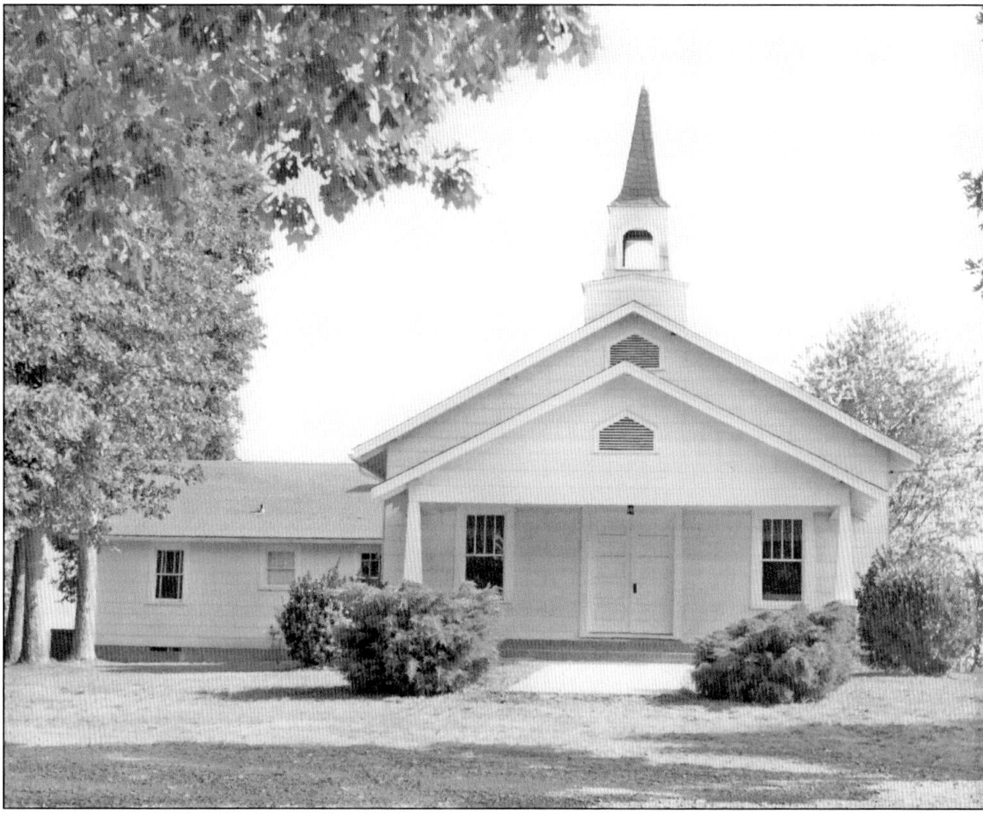

In an August 1943 tent revival in a field on the southeast corner of Highways 24/27 and 205 at Red Cross, the Red Cross Tabernacle was founded under the direction of Rev. Lee Hartsell. In November 1943, a building was erected on the opposite corner on land given by Lawson Burris. The name was changed to Red Cross Baptist Church in September 1944.

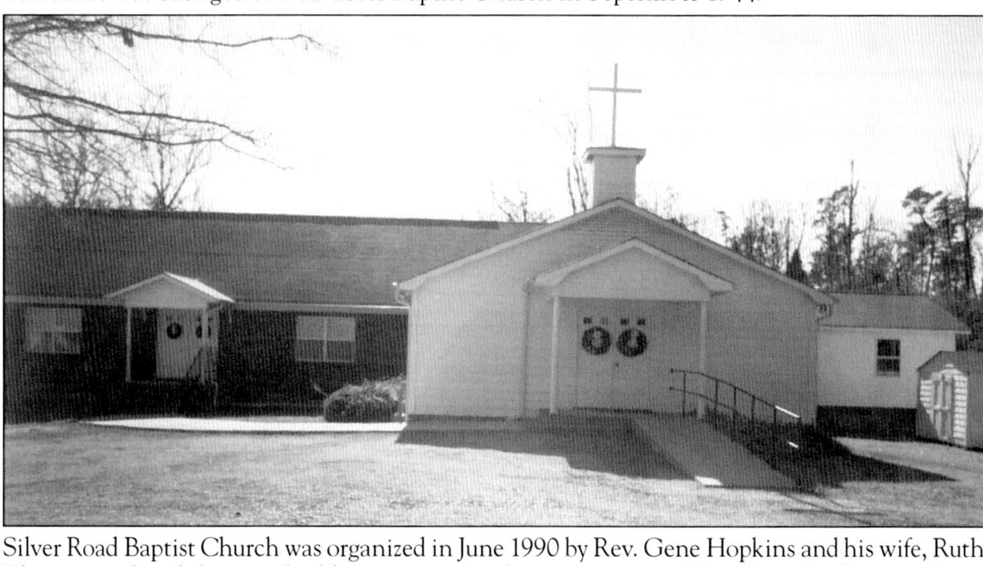

Silver Road Baptist Church was organized in June 1990 by Rev. Gene Hopkins and his wife, Ruth. The young church began a building program with a sanctuary and Sunday school rooms. Later, they added a fellowship hall and additional Sunday school rooms.

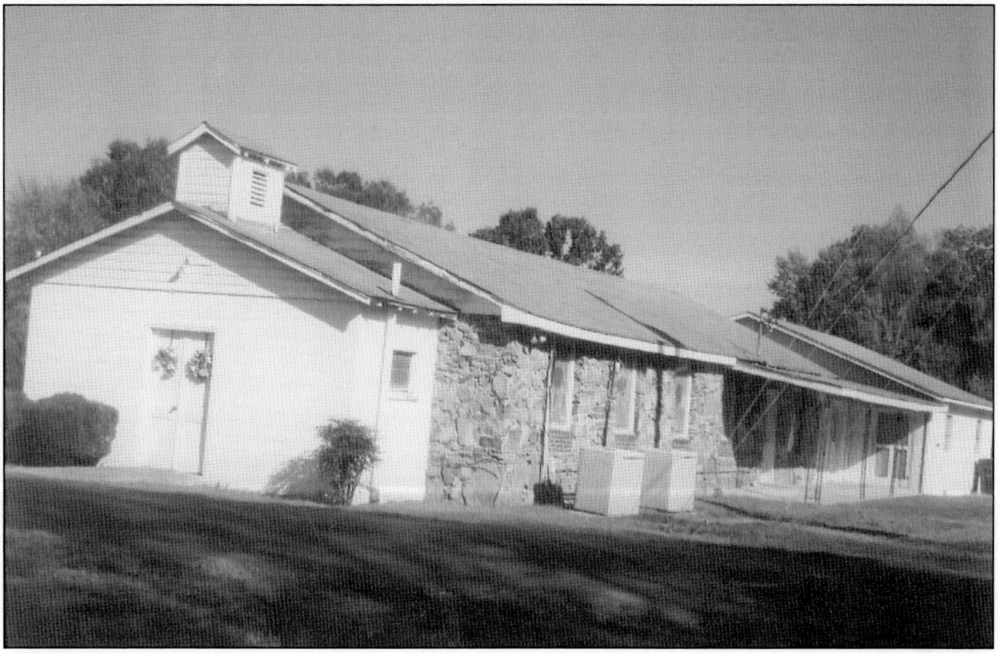

In the early 1930s, members of Saint Matthews United Church of God in South Oakboro made elder J.D. McLendon their first pastor. The pastor then built the small church himself, loading rocks from nearby fields on a wagon and pulling them to the construction site by mule. The random pattern of the rock is still evident on the exterior and in certain places of the interior. Now housed in the new modern facility below, the congregation plans to maintain the original building for use as a fellowship hall.

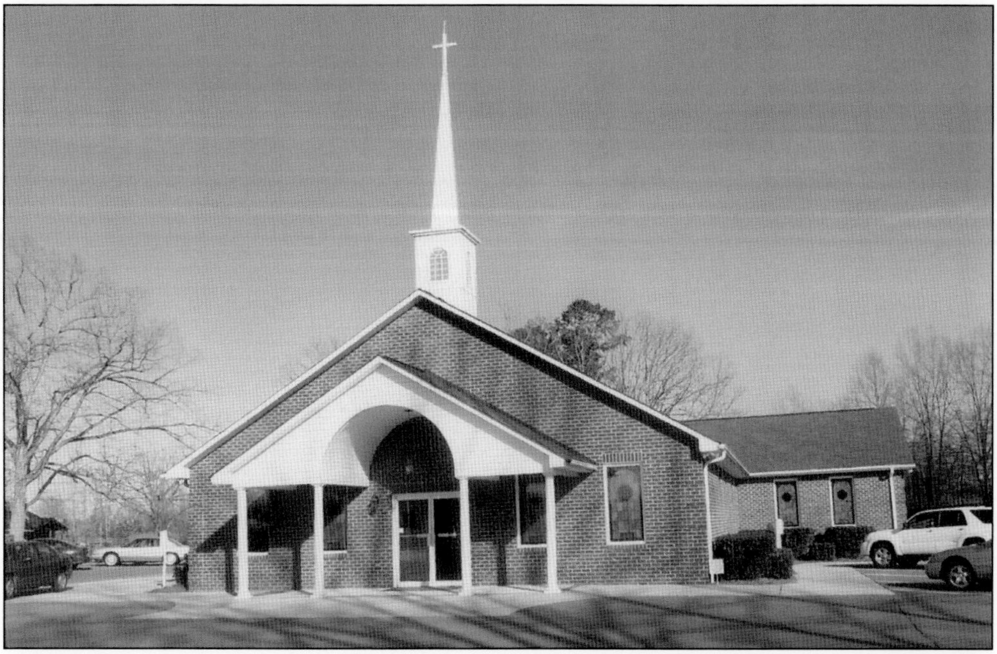

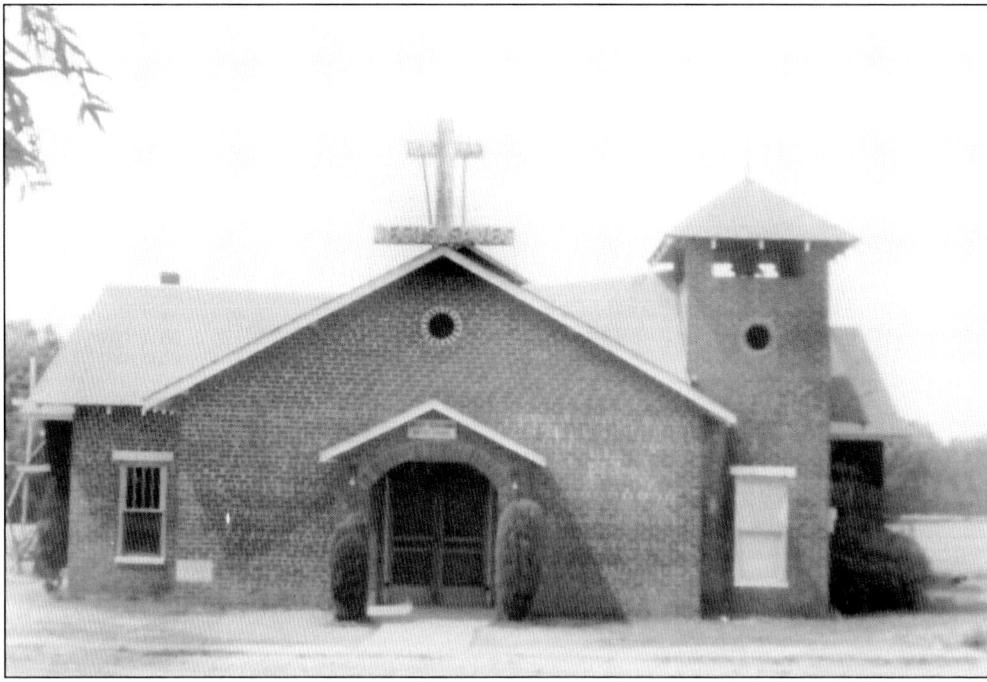

On a Sunday afternoon in May 1926, a group gathered in the grove near the mills of Oakboro. After a sermon, the group retired to a private house to organize a Baptist church at that location, which became West Oakboro Baptist Church, situated 100 yards from the present church building.

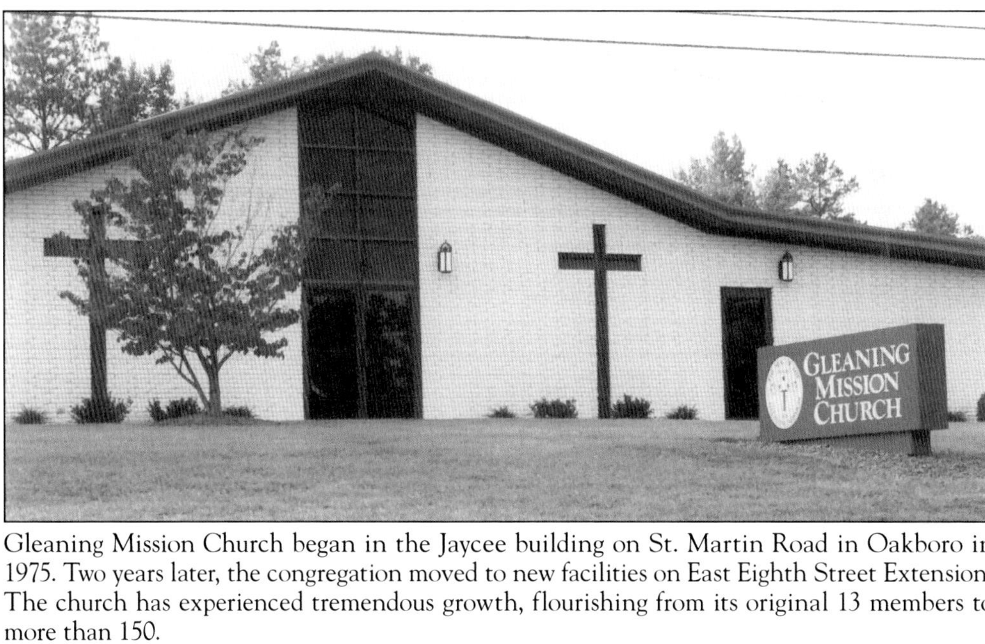

Gleaning Mission Church began in the Jaycee building on St. Martin Road in Oakboro in 1975. Two years later, the congregation moved to new facilities on East Eighth Street Extension. The church has experienced tremendous growth, flourishing from its original 13 members to more than 150.

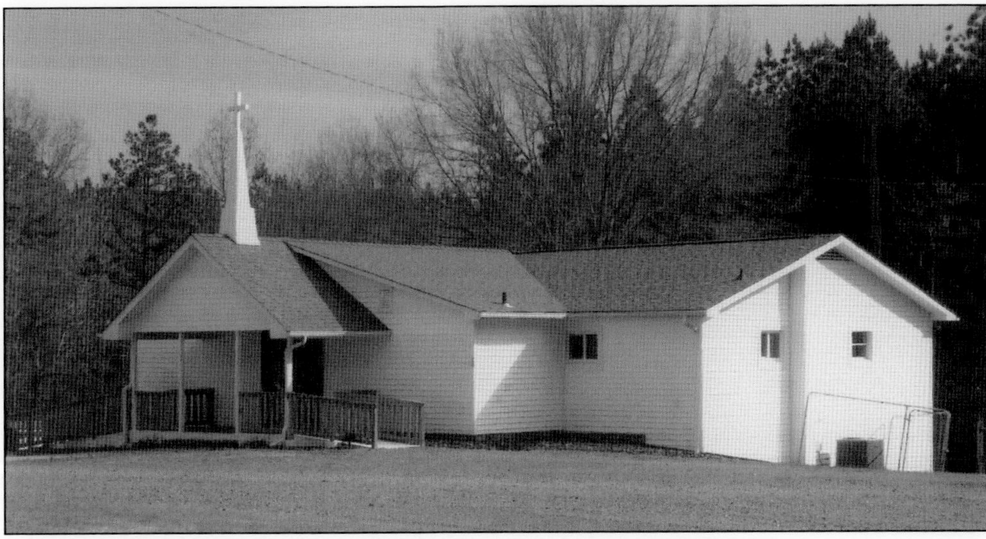

Tabernacle Baptist Church was established in 1994 on St. Martin Road in the former home of Gleaning Mission Church. The congregation has remodeled a portion of the structure and has grown in recent years.

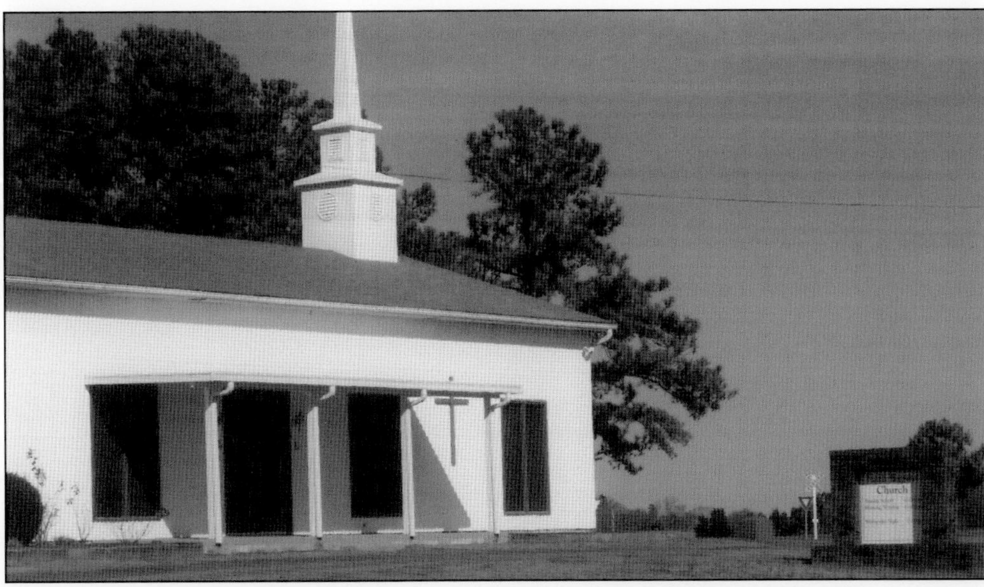

Faith Baptist Church is on Highway 138 in the Barbee's Grove community. Church members are now making use of the Internet for Bible studies and other communications.

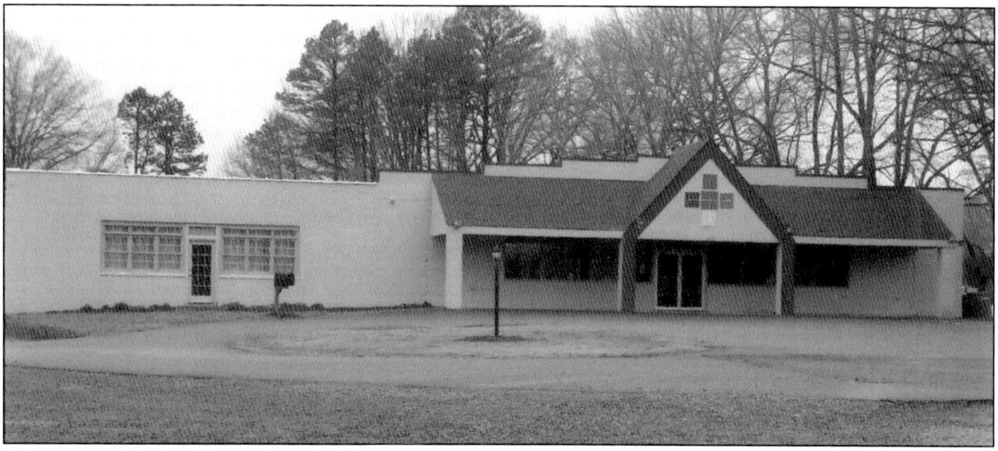

Centerpoint Church was started by Rev. Reece Linelle and his wife, Roxanne (Efird) Linelle. It holds worship celebrations in the former Oakboro skating rink and has attracted many new members. The skating rink was owned and operated by Jonah Huneycutt, and the building has also been home to a hardware store.

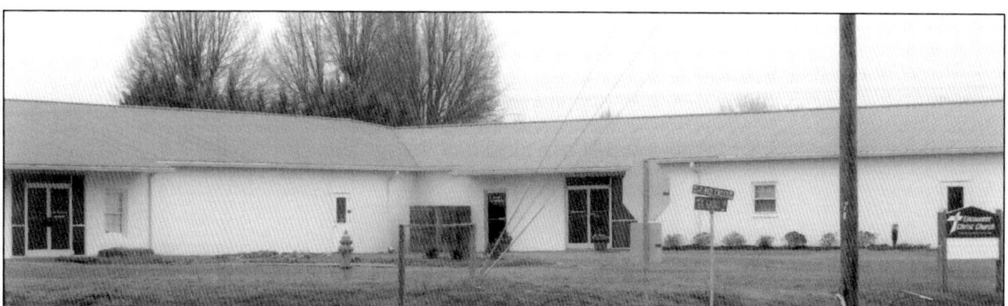

Encounters Christ Church was started in 2011 by Rev. Alan DiDio in the Red Cross community across from West Stanly High School. This group is also experiencing growth.

Five

Schools Through the Years

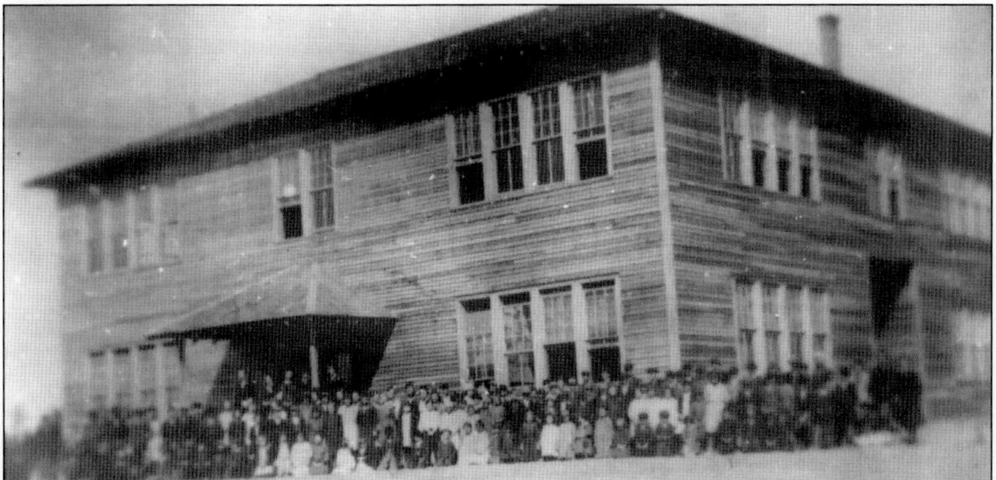

For many years, children were taught in one- or two-room schoolhouses, which were eventually consolidated into this two-story wooden building on Highway 205 north of the city limits. The structure was designed to house grades 1st through 11th.

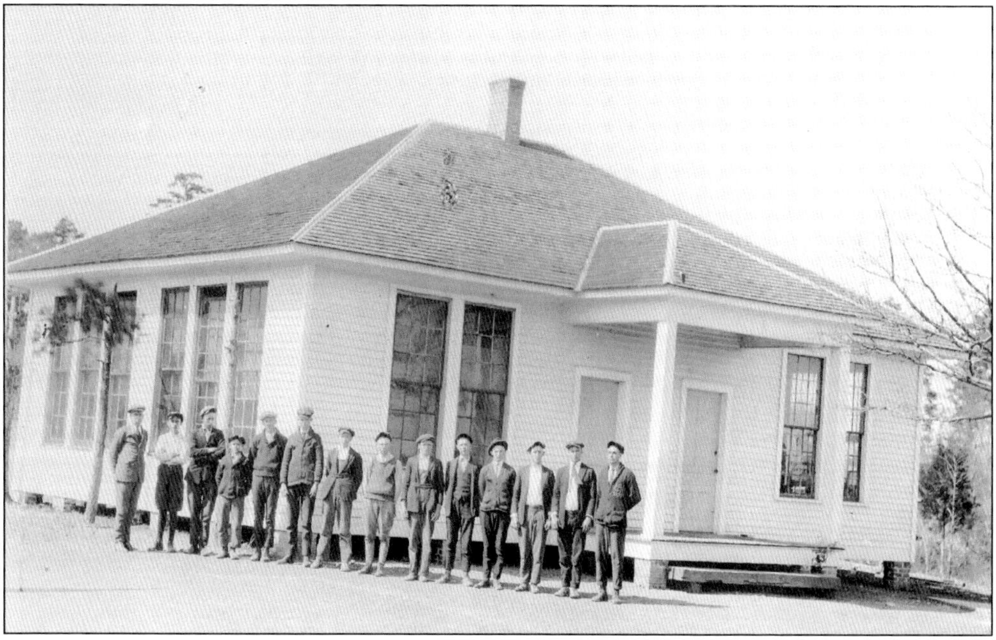

The 1920–1921 agriculture class at Oakboro School stands proudly in front of the agriculture building. The class included, from left to right, ? Colvard, Lewis Barnhardt, two unidentified boys, Vesta "Gus" Parker, Raymon Hatley, unidentified, ? Barnhardt, Roy Hatley, Furman James, Horace Howard, Harry Mills, Otha Curlee, and Claude Goodman.

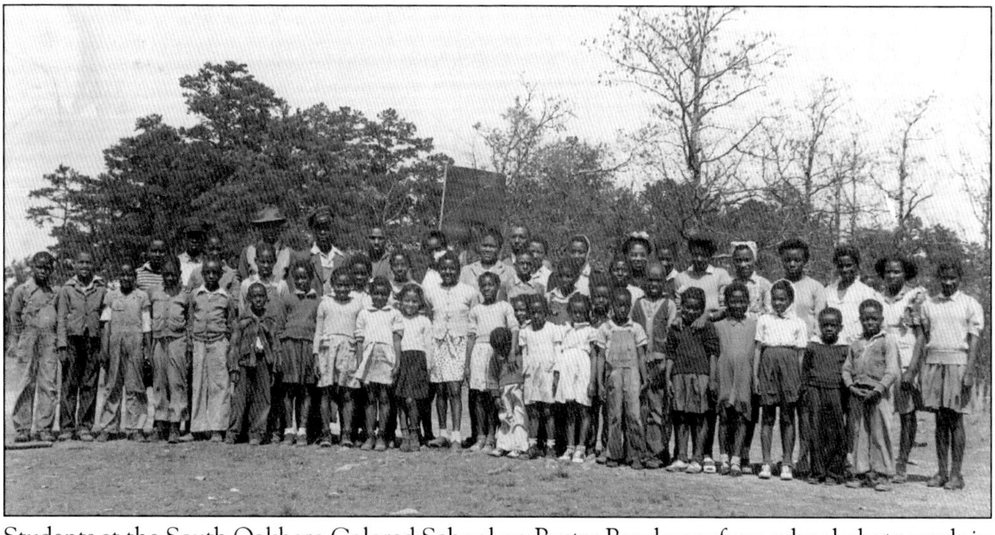

Students at the South Oakboro Colored School on Buster Road pose for a school photograph in the 1945–1946 school year. Teachers at the school included a Mr. Campbell, Lettie Davis, and John Ray Davis.

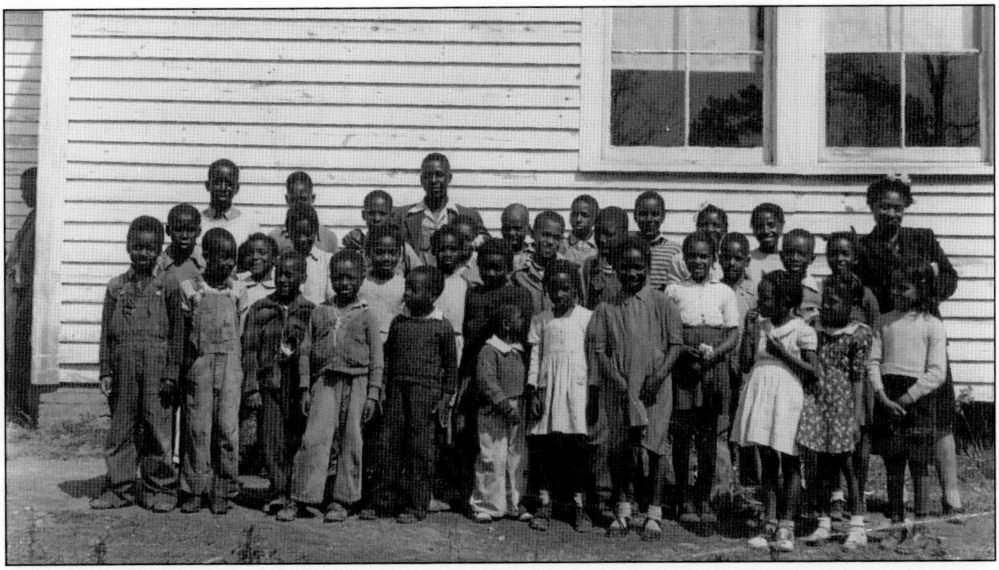

This old school building on Buster Road once housed the South Oakboro Colored School, serving grades 1st through 7th. High school students attended Kingville School in Albemarle. When schools were integrated in the late 1960s, the building became the home of the June Hamilton family. It was later converted into a church.

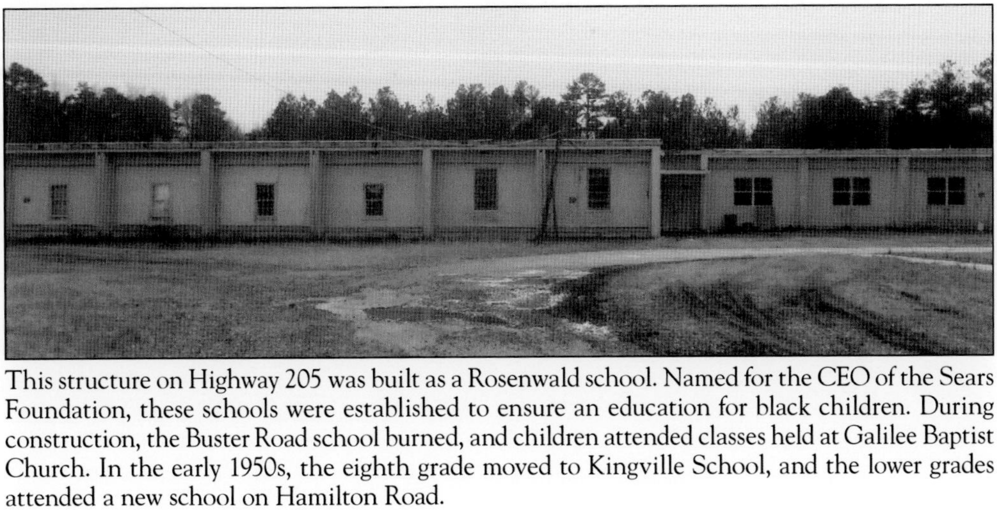

This structure on Highway 205 was built as a Rosenwald school. Named for the CEO of the Sears Foundation, these schools were established to ensure an education for black children. During construction, the Buster Road school burned, and children attended classes held at Galilee Baptist Church. In the early 1950s, the eighth grade moved to Kingville School, and the lower grades attended a new school on Hamilton Road.

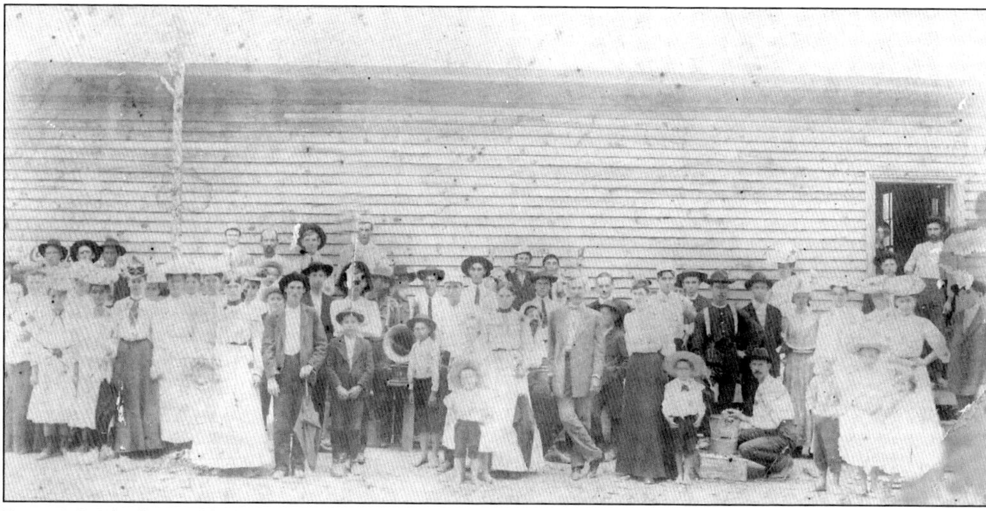

Rev. C.J. Black established Big Lick Academy during his tenure at the Big Lick Baptist Church. It soon earned an excellent reputation as an educational institution, and students came from miles around. After the decline of the town of Big Lick, the school was closed.

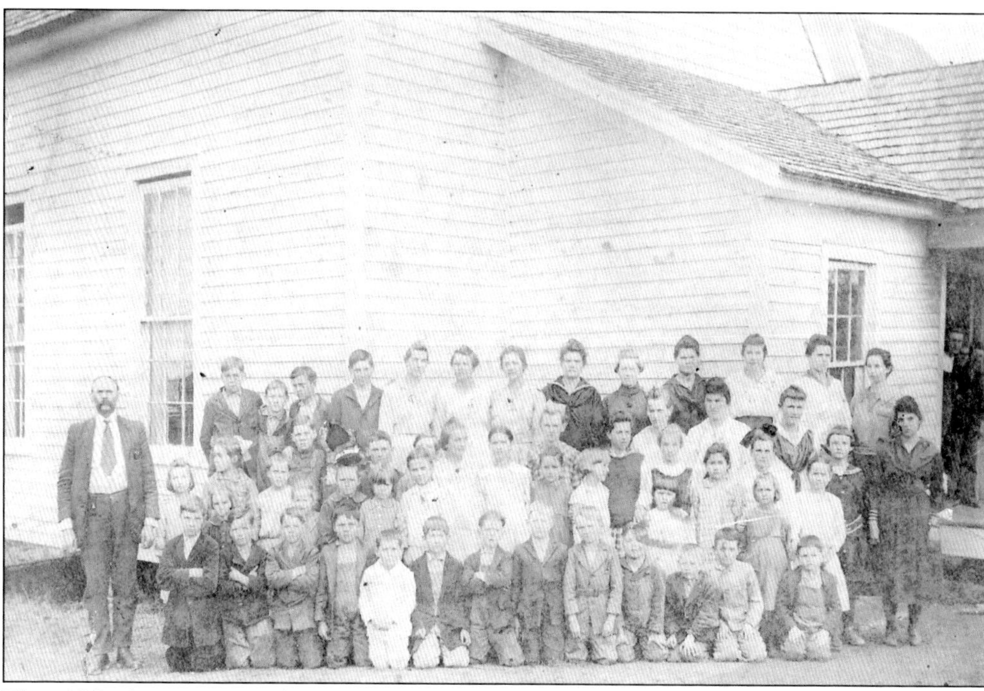

The old Barbee's Grove School was built on the Fred Smith property on Old School Road. In this 1920s photograph, teacher Masurah Whitley stands on the far left. This school was one of the largest in the community.

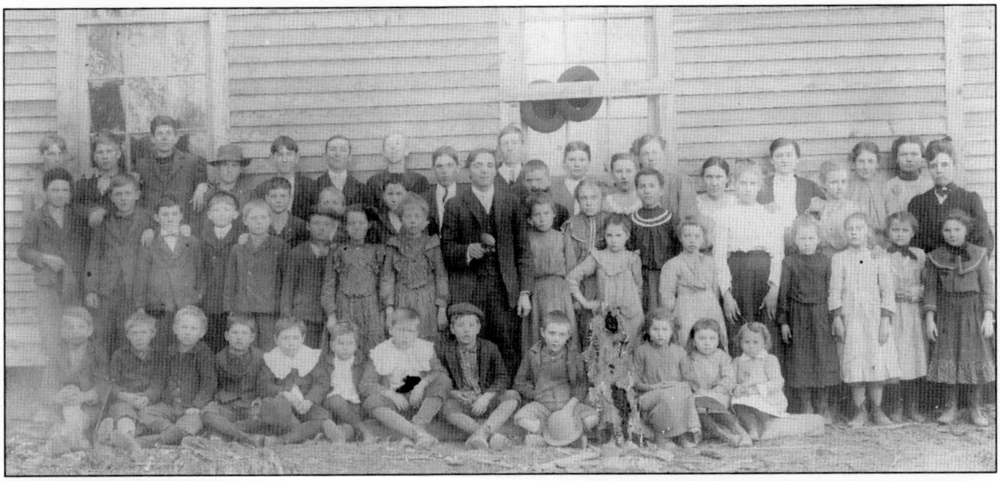

Students dressed up for this 1908 class photograph in front of the Drye School on Stanfield Road in Big Lick. Notice the hats in the window.

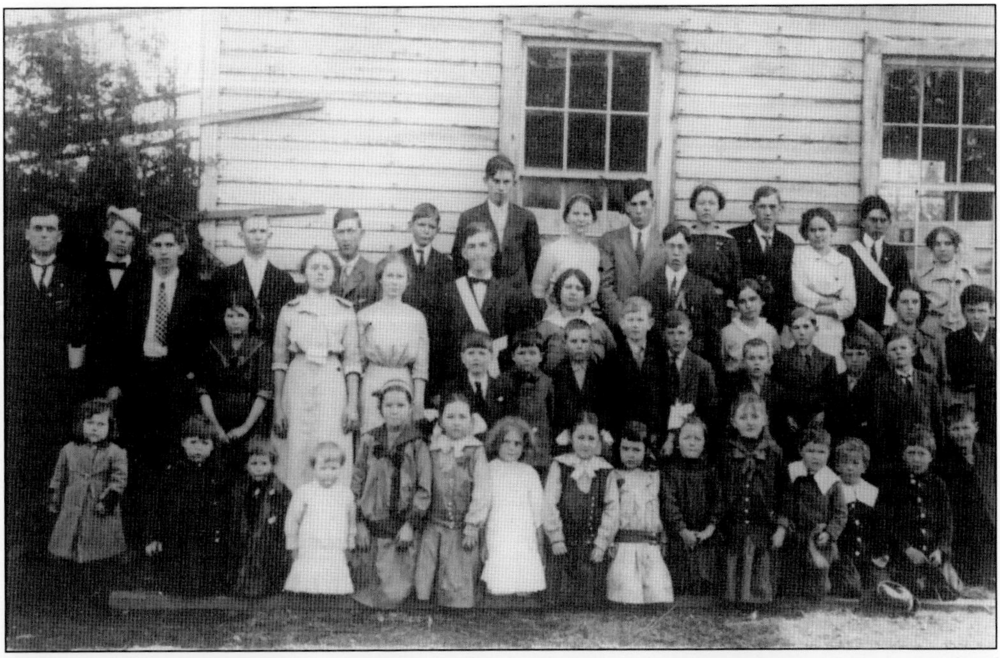

Pondsville School (sometimes called Pond School) was in the Mineral Springs area south of Oakboro. Adam Alexander Hathcock (first man on the far left) was the headmaster. He taught the Sacred Harp Shaped Note method of singing from a collection of old Baptist tunes dating from 1844. This collection was the forerunner of the church hymnal of today.

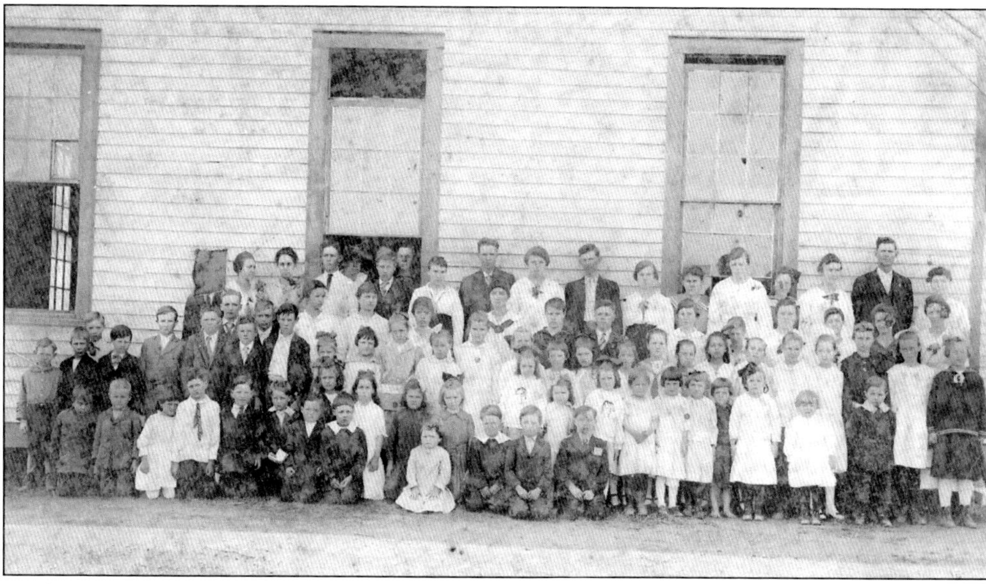

Students are lined up in front of the Brattain School on Pless Mill Road just south of Highway 24/27 on April 4, 1918. Nola Reap of Albemarle was the principal, and she was assisted by Bessie Smith of Stanfield.

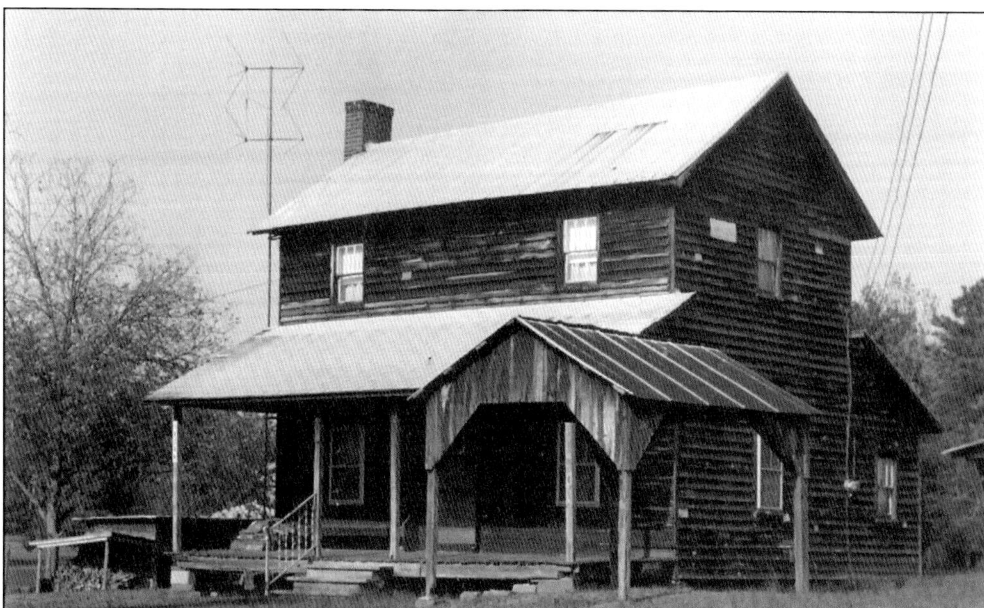

The old Brattain house, still standing after more than 100 years, is on the same property as the Brattain School, which was behind the woodshed on the left.

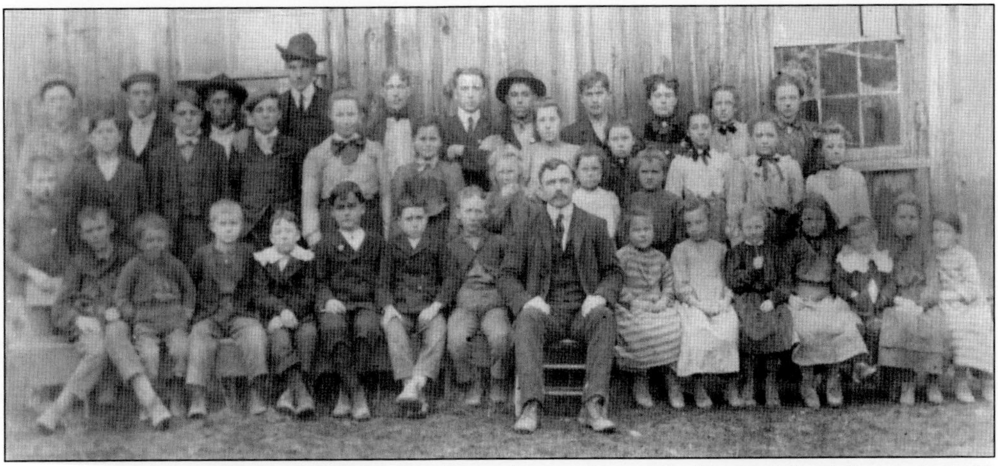

In 1904, W. Henry Whitley (seated, center) was the teacher at the Burris School, located a half-mile from Pleasant Grove Church.

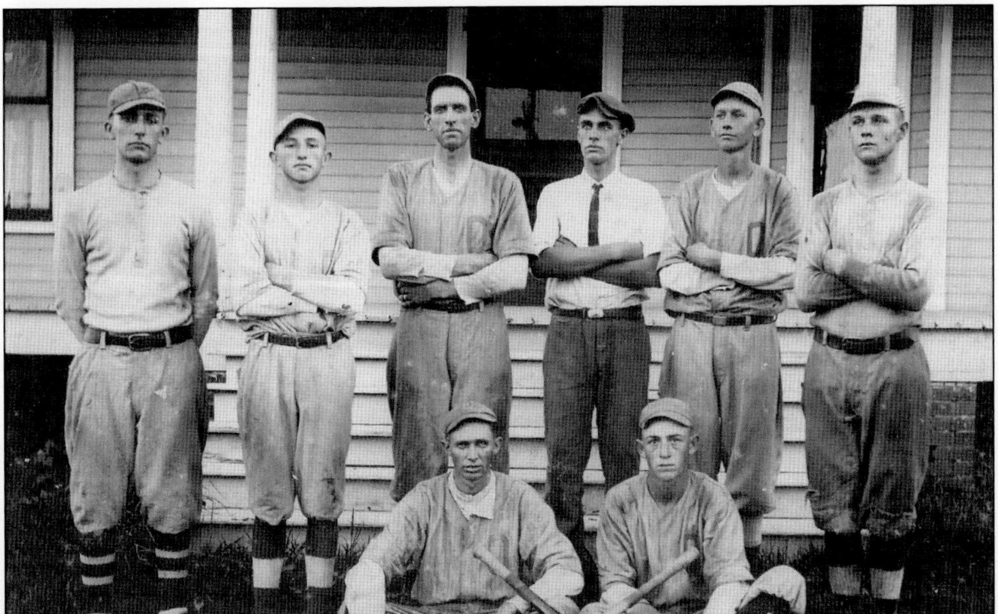

The Oakboro School baseball team of 1922 included, standing from left to right, Crayton Efird, Horace Howard, Claude Goodman, Milton Kennedy, Jack Hartsell, and Harry Mills. The two seated players are unidentified.

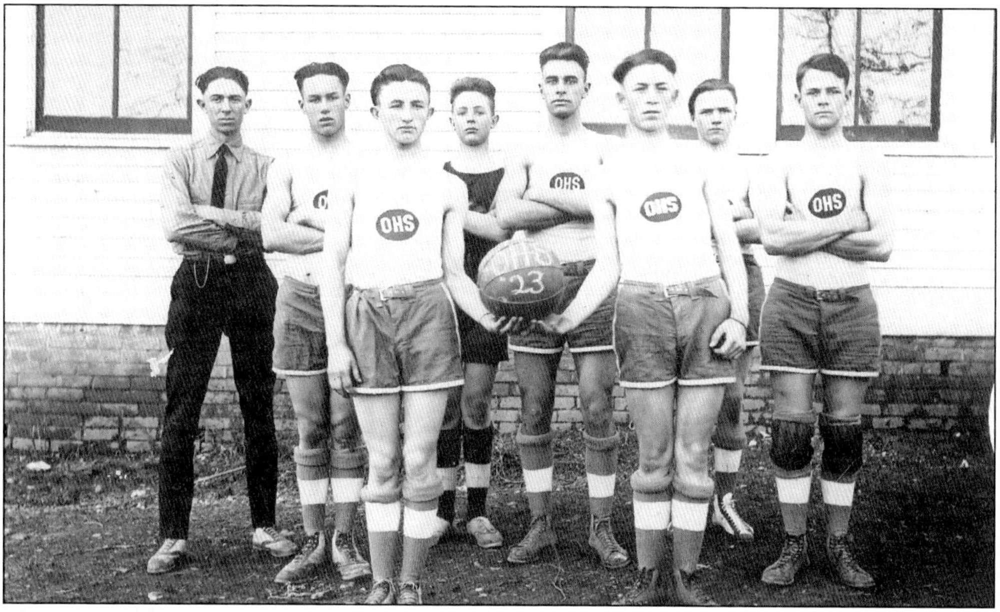

The 1923 Oakboro basketball team included, from left to right, coach L.S. Summers, Otha Curlee, Horace Howard, Furman James, Claude Goodman, Harry Mills, Roy Hatley, and Jack Hartsell.

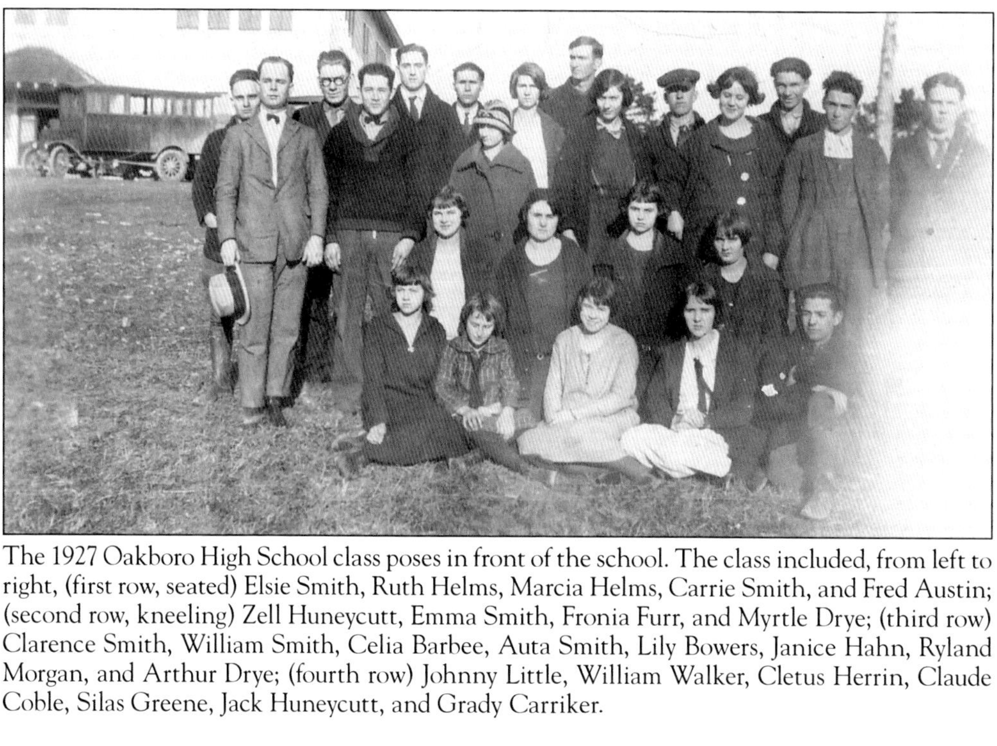

The 1927 Oakboro High School class poses in front of the school. The class included, from left to right, (first row, seated) Elsie Smith, Ruth Helms, Marcia Helms, Carrie Smith, and Fred Austin; (second row, kneeling) Zell Huneycutt, Emma Smith, Fronia Furr, and Myrtle Drye; (third row) Clarence Smith, William Smith, Celia Barbee, Auta Smith, Lily Bowers, Janice Hahn, Ryland Morgan, and Arthur Drye; (fourth row) Johnny Little, William Walker, Cletus Herrin, Claude Coble, Silas Greene, Jack Huneycutt, and Grady Carriker.

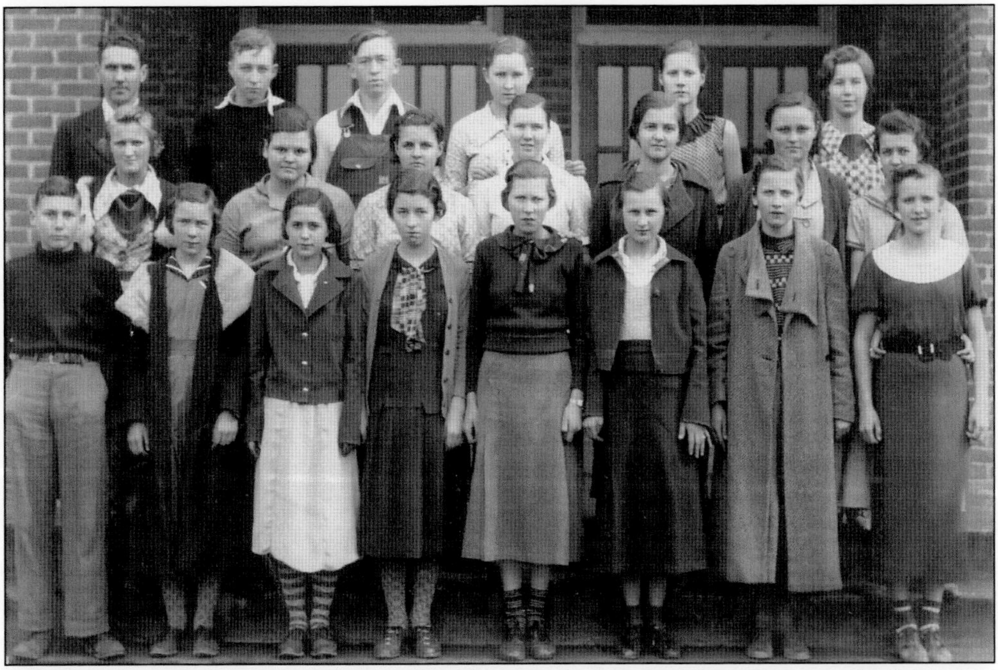

Only three students are identified in this photograph: Leonard Furr (first row, far left), Faye Huneycutt (first row, far right), and Braudis Whitley (second row, second from left).

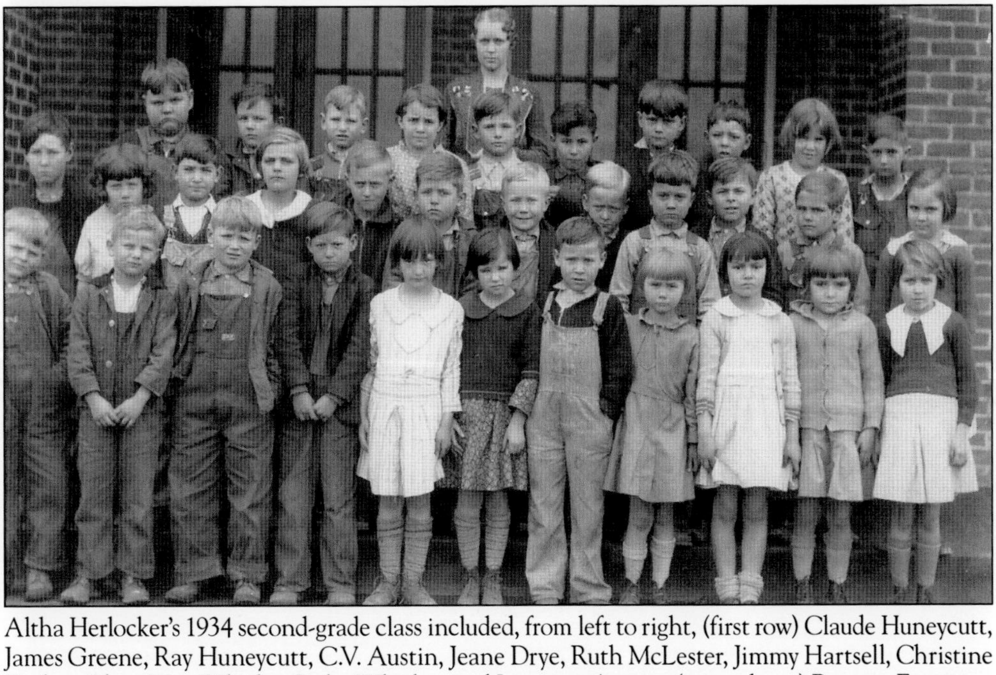

Altha Herlocker's 1934 second-grade class included, from left to right, (first row) Claude Huneycutt, James Greene, Ray Huneycutt, C.V. Austin, Jeane Drye, Ruth McLester, Jimmy Hartsell, Christine Tucker, Clara Mae Whitley, Ruby Whitley, and Imogene Austin; (second row) Rayvon Foreman, Geneva Lambert, Eugene Osborne, Minerva Hathcock, Farrington Hathcock, Junior Furr, Lemoan Turner, Billy Huneycutt, Junior Burris, Bruton Smith, Cebron Smith, and Mildred Whitley; (third row) John Hill, Carl Barbee, Calvin Huneycutt, Lucille Huneycutt, Lloyd Whitley, James Helms, R.L. Russell, Connis Huneycutt, Annie Lee Smith, and W.T. Whitley.

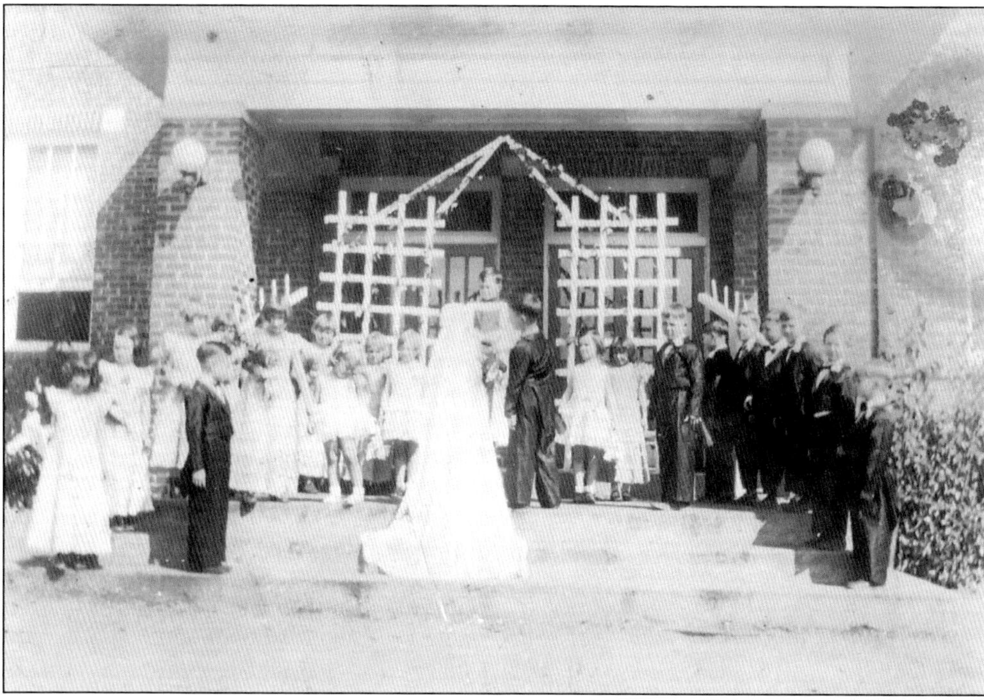

Tom Thumb weddings were in vogue in the 1930s and 1940s and these schoolchildren dressed as members of a wedding party and performed for parents in front of the school. The photograph was taken in 1932, and this class would graduate 10 years later. J.C. Furr was the minister, Maxine Turner was the bride, and Joyce (Hinson) Hill was a flower girl.

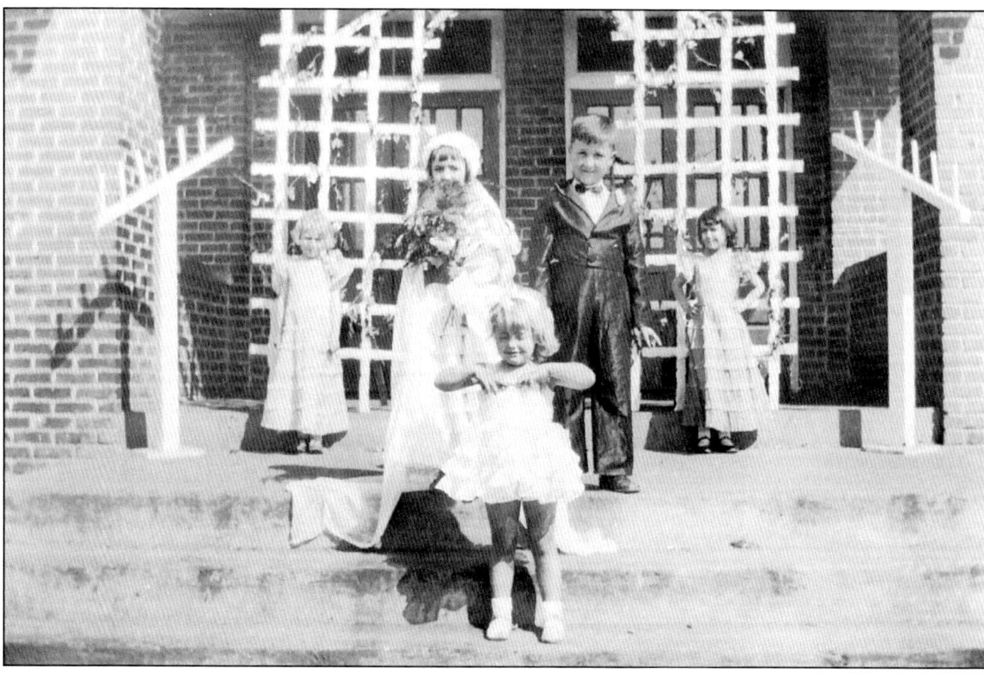

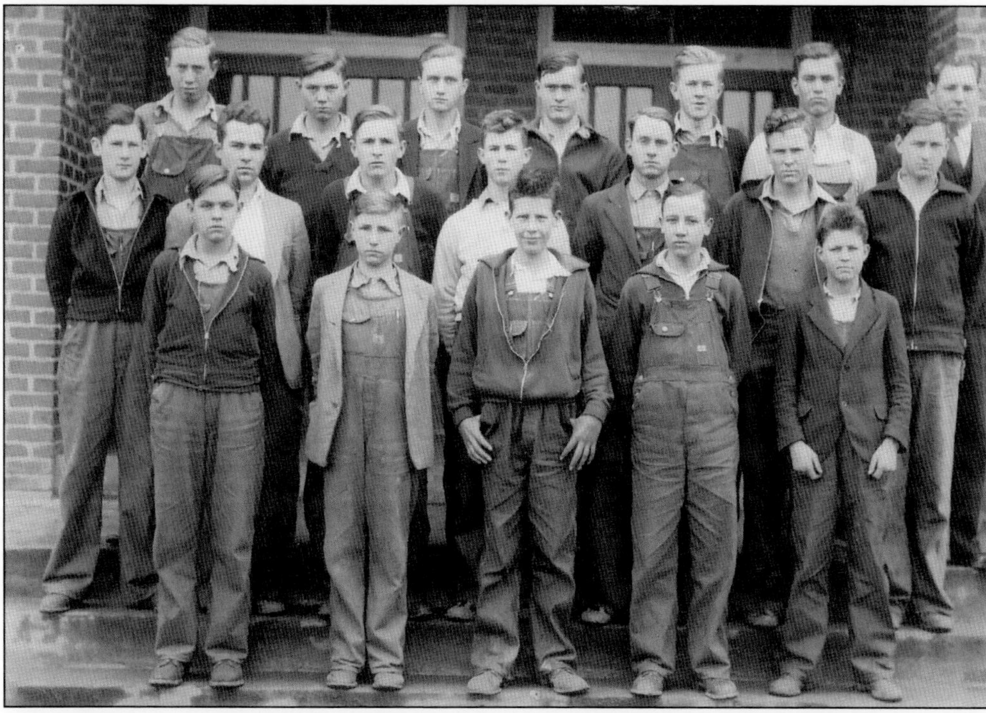

This 1935 ninth-grade agriculture-education class stands at the front of the high school building. The students from left to right are (first row) Marshall Whitley, Louis Brooks, Grover Hinson, J.D. Tucker, and Frelon Thomas; (second row) Loys Austin, Locke Turner, Paul Ed Page, Ethan Smith, Clonnie Smith, Bennie Hathcock Jr., and William Hatley; (third row) Clayton Hatley, Lloyd Green, Afton Lambert, W.C. Blalock, Crowell Smith, Clinton Burris, and teacher Paul Strickland.

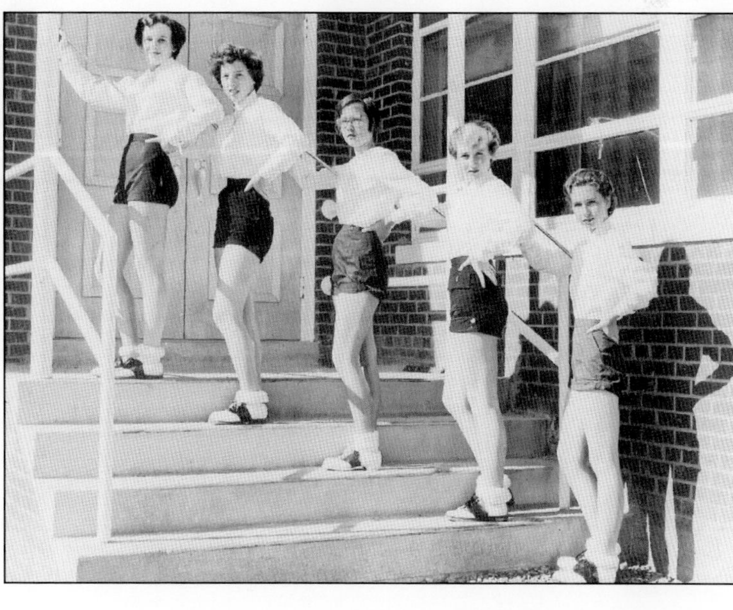

Oakboro High School majorettes from the marching band pose on the cafeteria steps. The girls, all seniors in the class of 1957, from left to right are Sue Barbee, Doris Huneycutt, Peggy Smith, Carolyn Morton, and Louise Tucker.

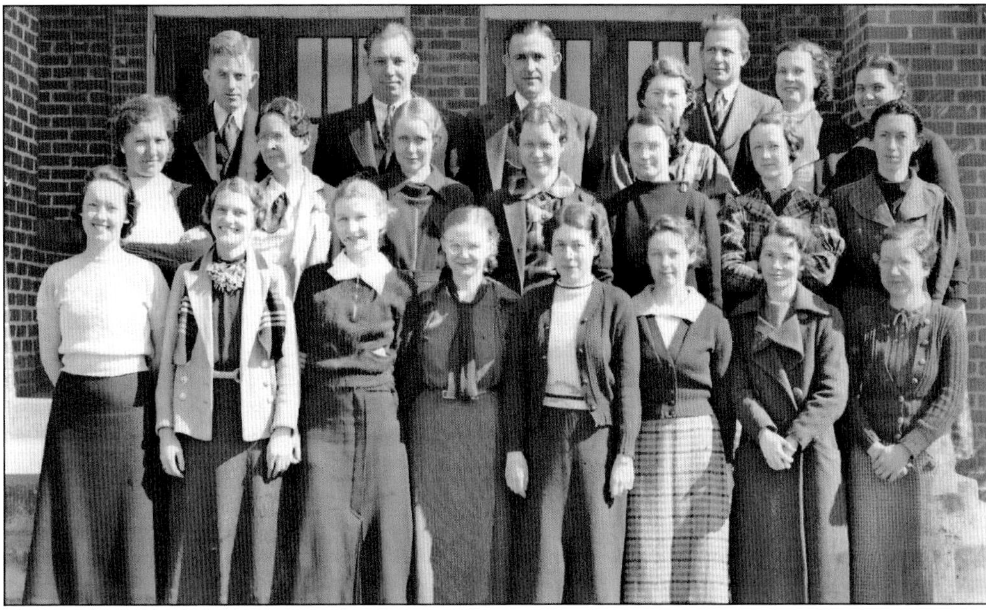

The 1936 Oakboro School faculty included, from left to right, (first row) Mildred Little, Ruby Griffin, Hazel Little, Margaret Coble, Lois Watson, Mary Weaver, Mary Simpson, and Linda Bost; (second row) Elizabeth Rummage, Esther K. Williams, Altha Herlocker, Mary Frances Helms, Fannie Winfree, Kathleen Newsome, and Janie Morrison; (third row) Thomas Sinclair, Paul Strickland, Glenn Taylor, Lillian Morgan, principal George Henry Hill, Bess Thompson, and Inez Pitts.

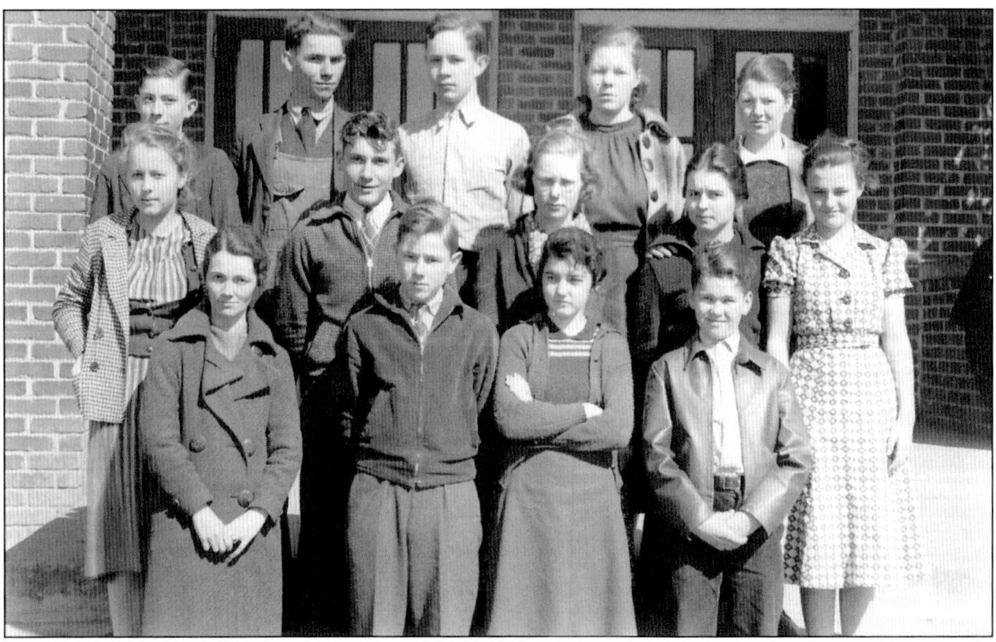

This 1936–1937 Oakboro School class included, from left to right, (first row) teacher Mary Simpson, Melvin Furr, Ruth Burris, and Warren Coble; (second row) Margaret Crowell, Kenneth Herman, Beatrice Coble, Evelyn Newsome, and Mary Virginia Harward; (third row) Bruce Osborne, Winfred Morgan, Keith James, Kathleen Eudy, and Rachel Austin.

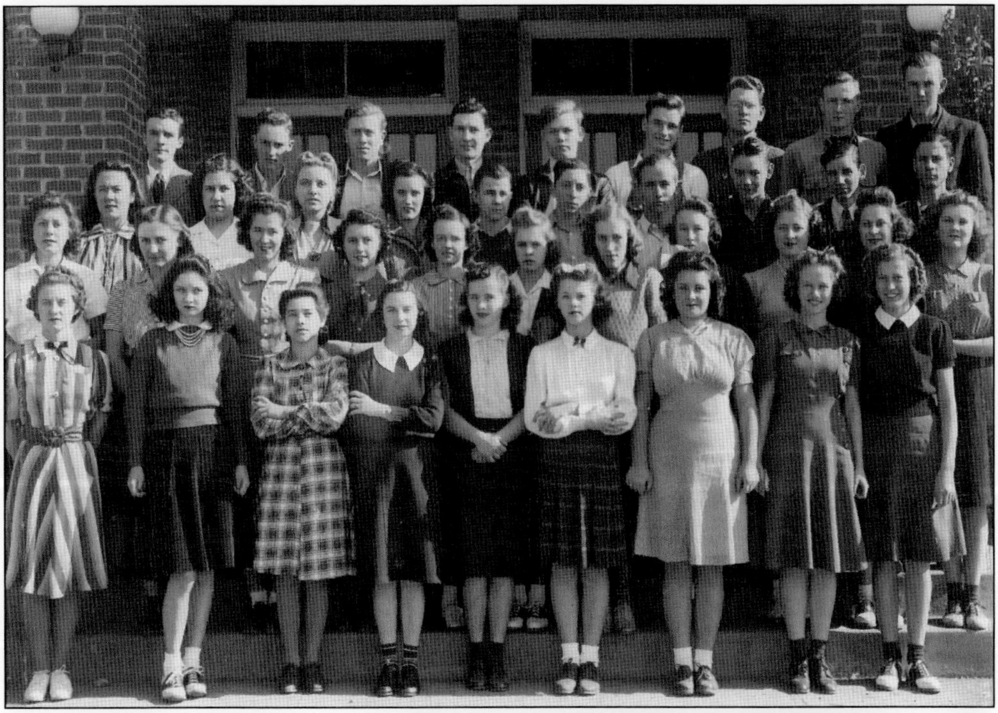

This photograph shows the eleventh grade class of 1941. The population of the town was growing, as evidenced by the increasing numbers of students in every grade level.

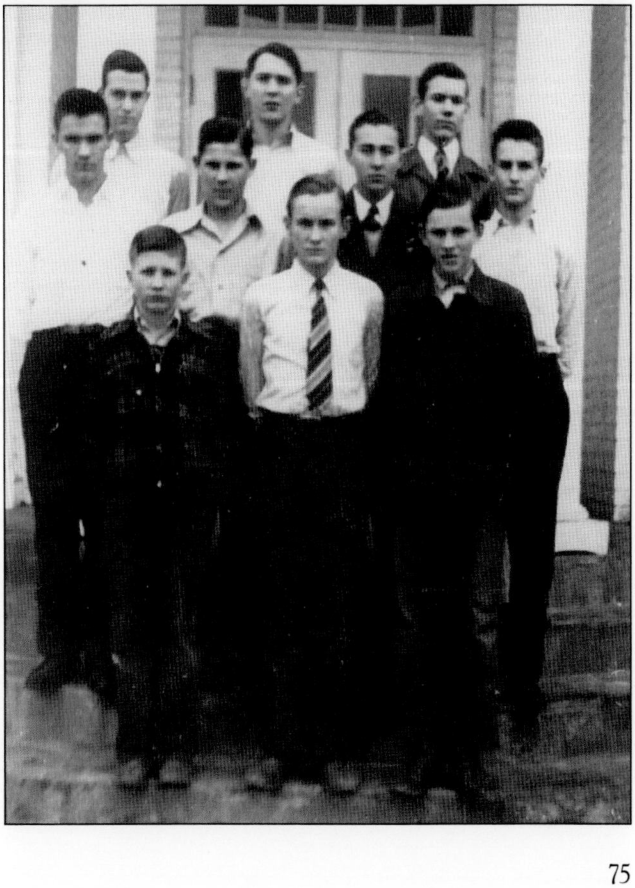

In 1944, a number of boys who lived in the city could not get into the agriculture program, so the school created a special class, allowing them to take advantage of the agriculture curriculum. The class included, from left to right, (first row) Curtis Smith, Marvin Little, and Frank McCellan; (second row) Ken Eudy, Boyd Lee Hinson, Fred Poplin, and Melvin Curlee; (third row) Wallace Howell, Roy Crisco, and Carl Drye.

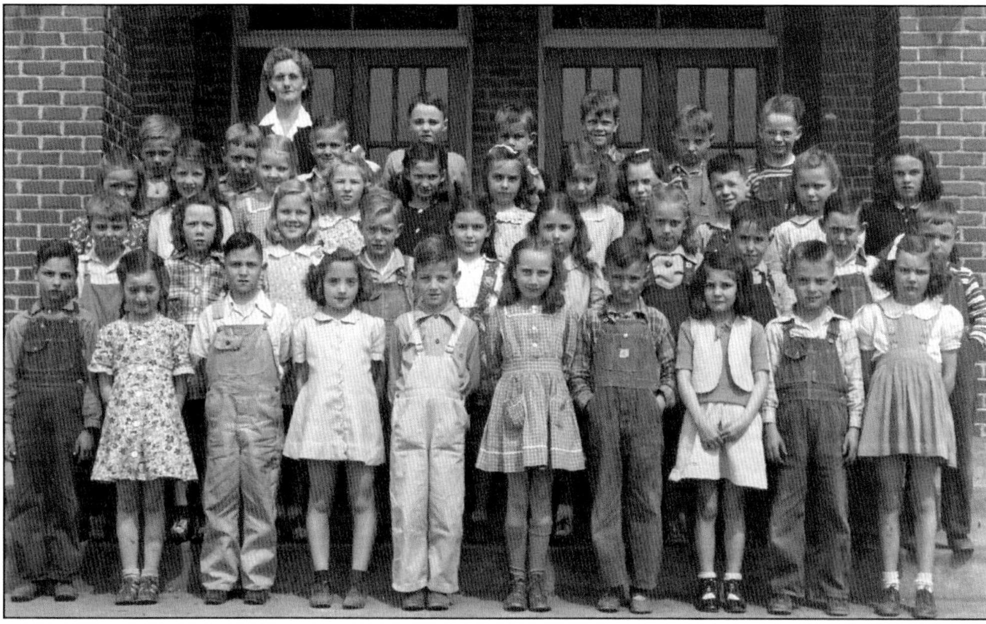

Odessa Hatley taught the second grade at Oakboro School in 1945–1946. She was also a poet, and some of her work was published by the Oakboro Regional Historical Foundation.

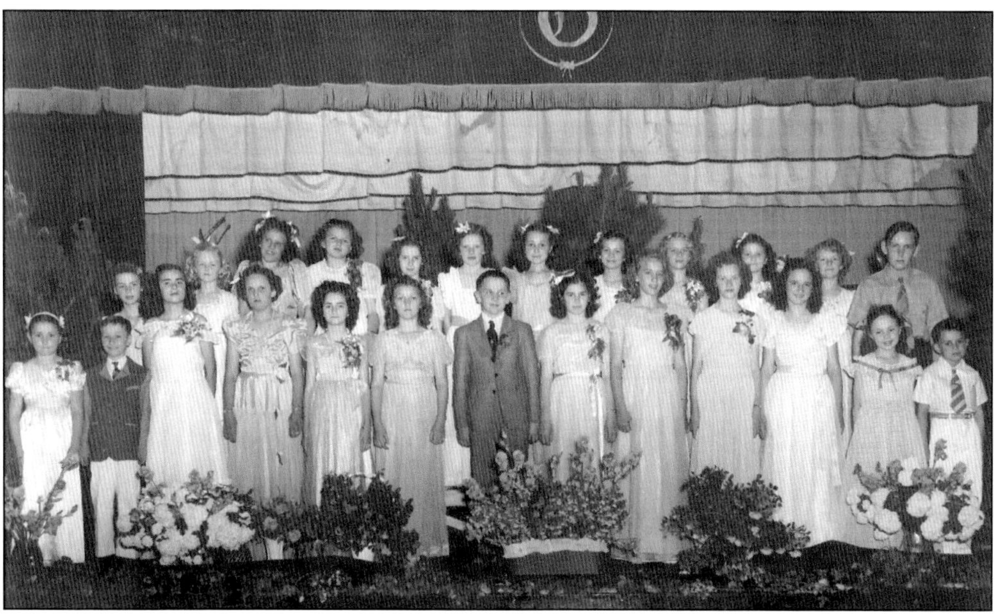

These students perform at a recital in the Oakboro School auditorium in the late 1940s. Ruby P. McIntyre taught piano lessons at Oakboro School at the time.

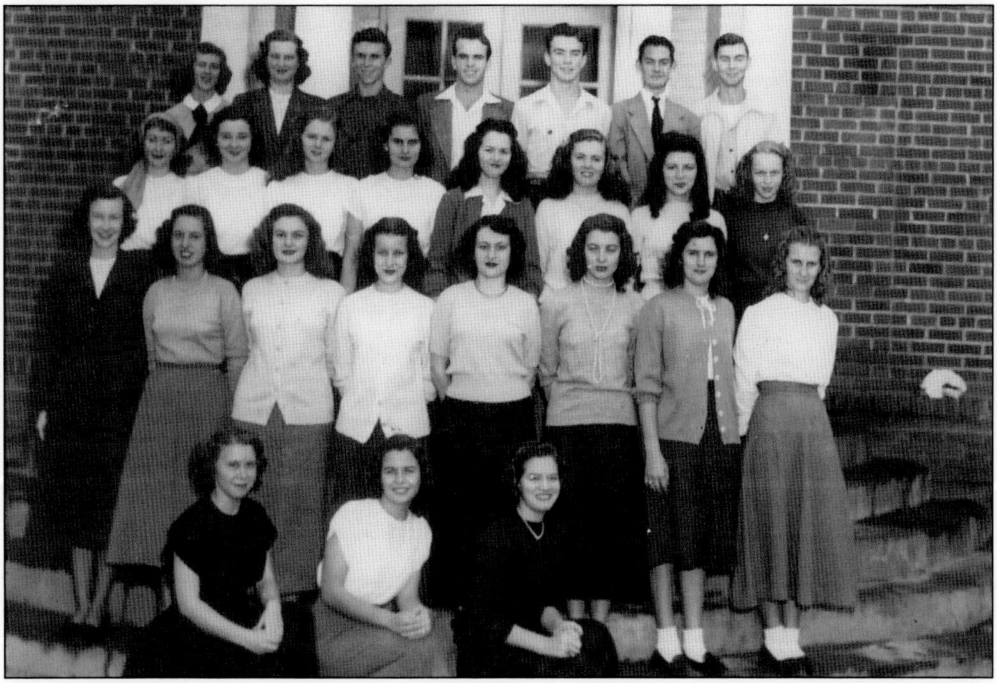

The 1949 Beta Club poses in front of the school. Sponsored by Jean Grantham, some of the members included Imogene Poplin, Cora Lee Whitley, Joy Mae Stoker, Alta Barger, Peggy Goodman, Rosa Little, Doris Crayton, Pearl Morgan, Lib Hartsell, Wanda Beechum, Blevyn Hathcock, Ted Furr, Dwight Carpenter, C.J. Hartsell, and Ted Parker.

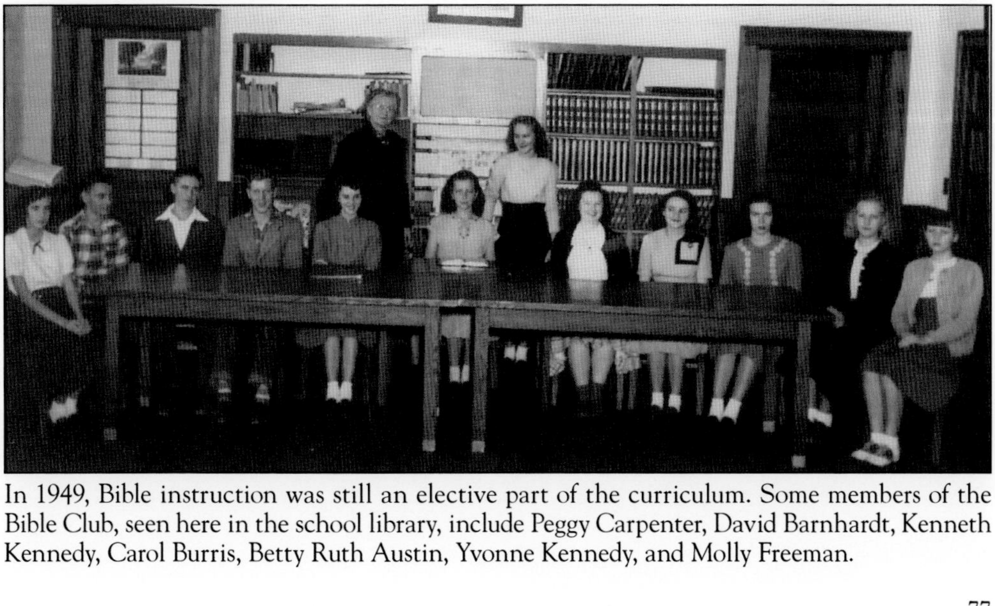

In 1949, Bible instruction was still an elective part of the curriculum. Some members of the Bible Club, seen here in the school library, include Peggy Carpenter, David Barnhardt, Kenneth Kennedy, Carol Burris, Betty Ruth Austin, Yvonne Kennedy, and Molly Freeman.

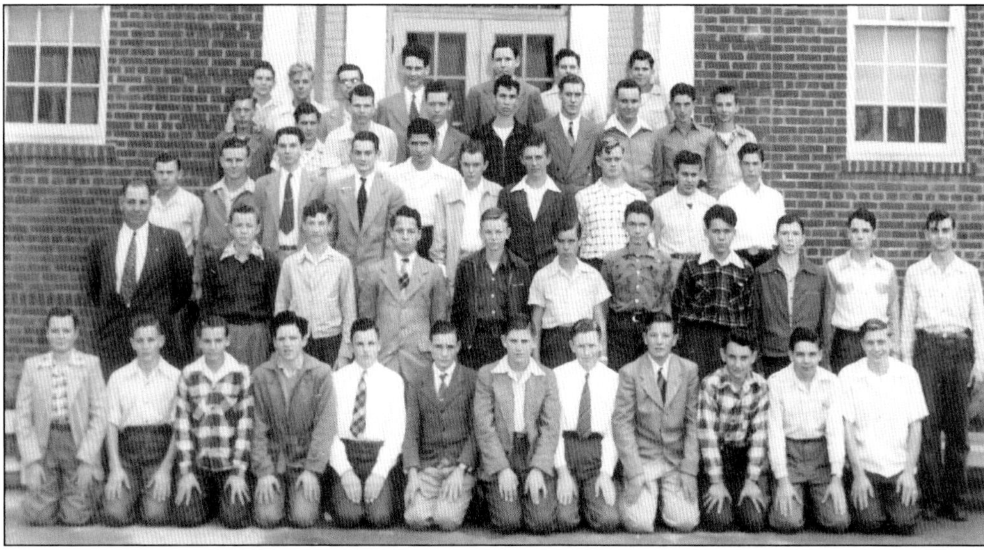

Because of Oakboro's location in the midst of a rural area, the agriculture program at Oakboro School was an extremely valuable and popular one. In this photograph of the 1949 Future Farmers of America, teacher Paul Strickland is in the second row at the far left. Many of these students became well known in local and regional agriculture.

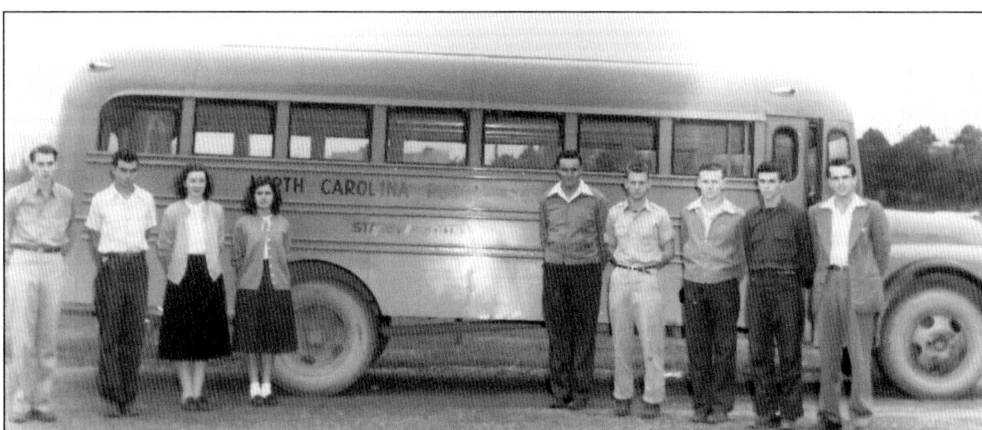

School buses served the important purpose of bringing students from the countryside into town for school. Some of the drivers pictured here in 1949 include Olin Huneycutt, Doris Crayton, Melvin Crisco, Bud Kluttz, Lowell Hill, Ted Furr, Dwight Carpenter, and Annie Jean Brattain.

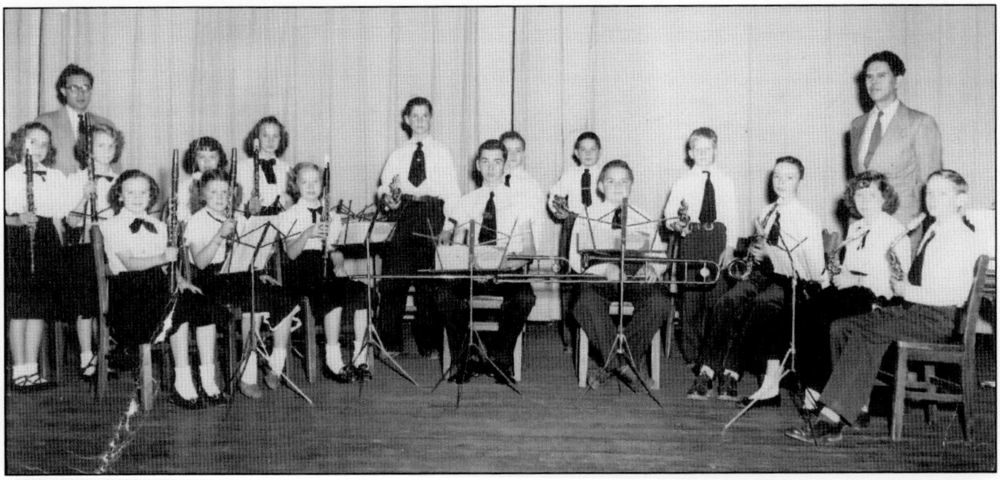

Students in 1950 prepare to perform in the school auditorium. The elementary band students were tutored by Mr. Miller (standing behind students on the left) and Mr. Alexander (standing behind students on the right).

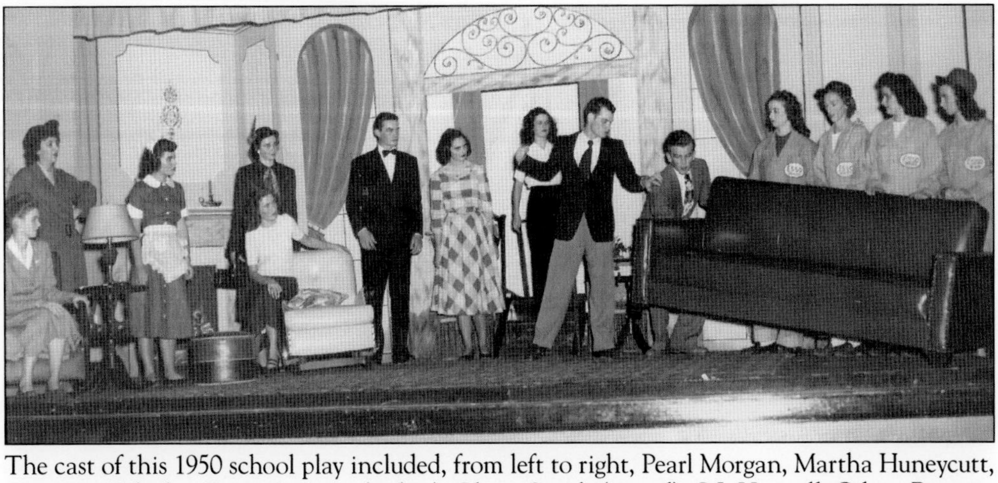

The cast of this 1950 school play included, from left to right, Pearl Morgan, Martha Huneycutt, Cora Lee Whitley, Doris Crayton (in hat), Gloria Smith (seated), C.J. Hartsell, Odene Burgess, Mary Frances Tucker, David McCellan, Edward Efird, Eunice Kennedy, Doris Dry, Beatrice Crisco, and Aileen Snyder.

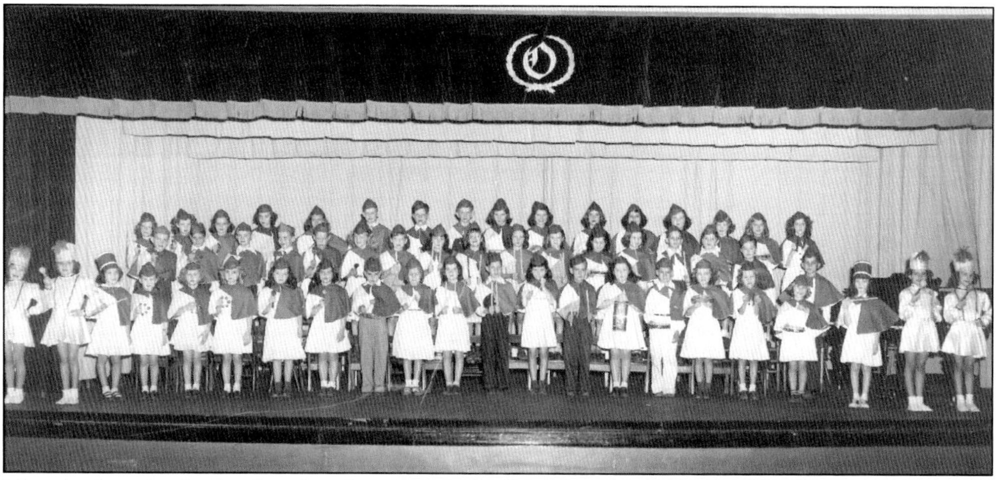

The third-grade rhythm band and majorettes held performances in the school auditorium every year. This third-grade class graduated in 1959.

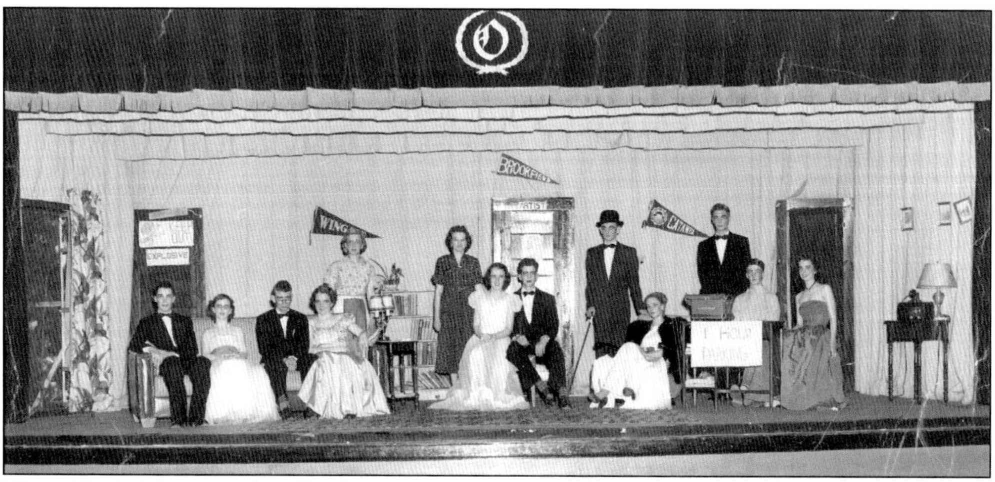

The 1951 Oakboro High School senior class play, *Spring Fever*, was performed in the school auditorium, which was torn down in 1975 and replaced by a modern facility. Seen here from left to right are Reece Allen, Lucille Furr, Wayne Burris, Gwendolyn Williams, Jeanette Huneycutt, teacher Juanita Harward, Aninell Narnee, Grady Whitley, David Barnhardt, Dema Huneycutt, W.L. Smith, Leonard Howell, and Roubenia Burgess.

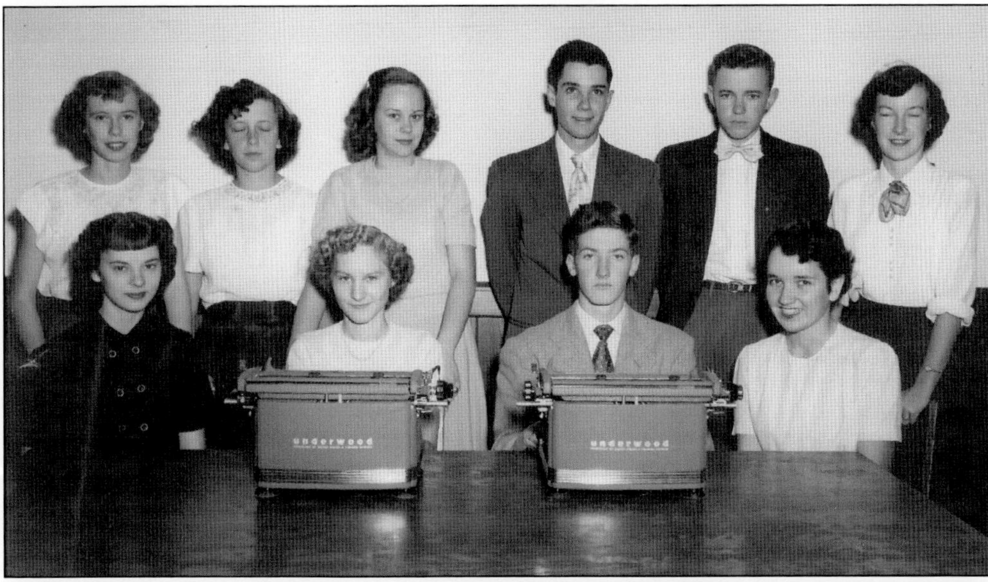

Staff members of the 1951 the Oakboro School yearbook, *Oak Winds*, are seated behind their typewriters. They are, from left to right, (first row) Carole Burris, Betty Ruth Austin, Leonard Howell, and Gwendola Williams; (second row) Christine Burgess, Janette Huneycutt, Dema Huneycutt, Reece Allen, Maurice Drye, and sponsor Jean Grantham.

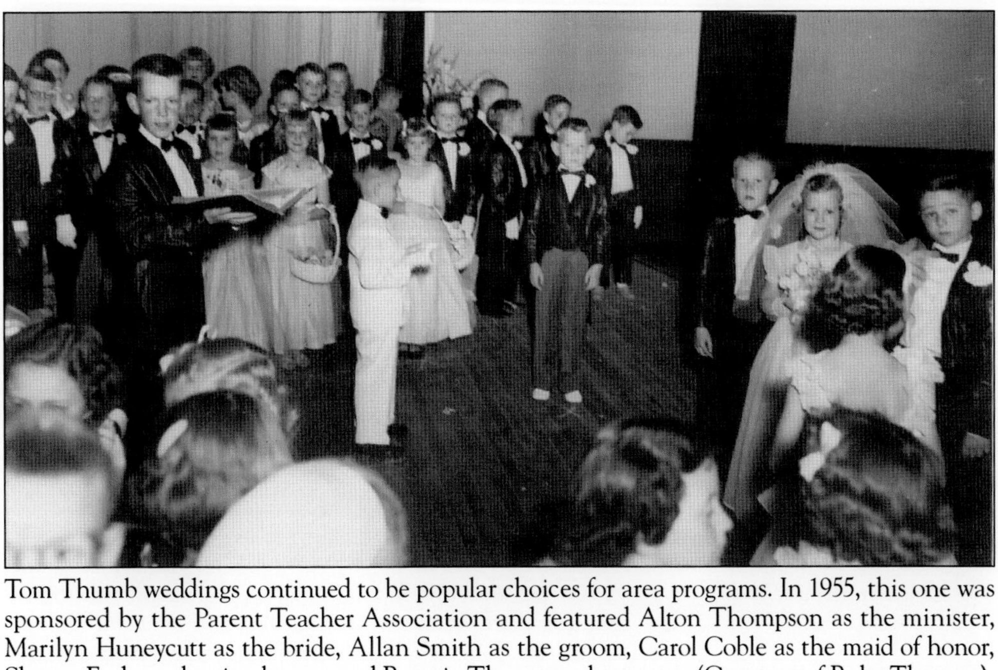

Tom Thumb weddings continued to be popular choices for area programs. In 1955, this one was sponsored by the Parent Teacher Association and featured Alton Thompson as the minister, Marilyn Huneycutt as the bride, Allan Smith as the groom, Carol Coble as the maid of honor, Sheron Eudy as the ring bearer, and Ronnie Thomas as best man. (Courtesy of Ruby Thomas.)

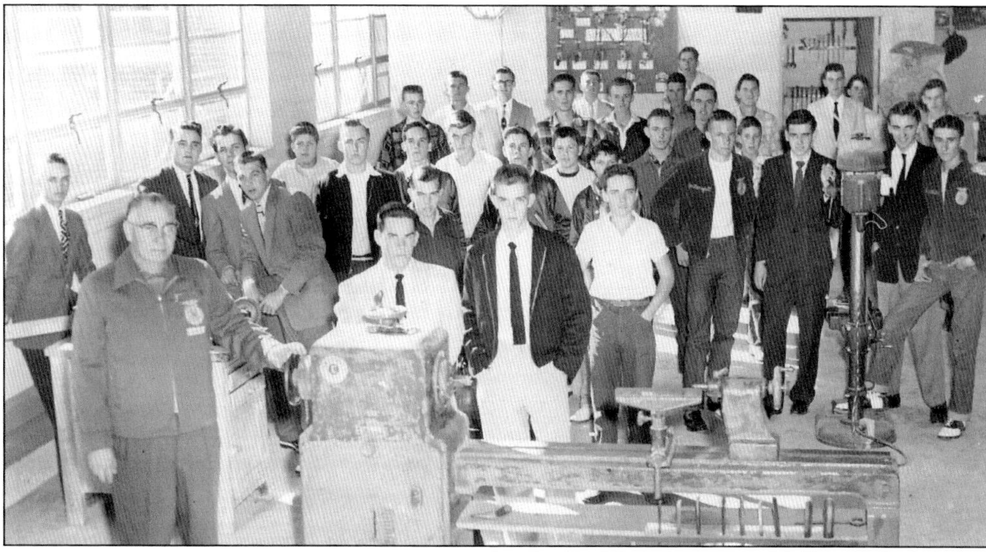

Shop teacher Paul Strickland pauses while showing students how to use a piece of machinery. He taught agriculture and shop to numerous children, both from the rural areas and from Oakboro proper. Strickland also sponsored the Future Farmers of America, an important student club focused on leadership activities in agriculture.

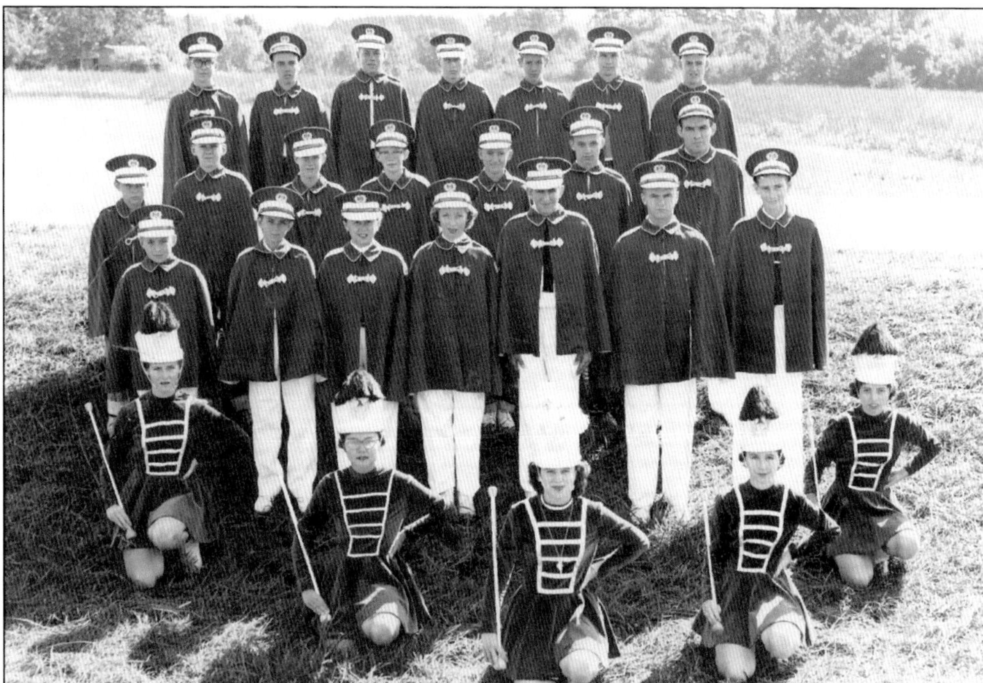

The 1956 Oakboro School band included, from left to right, (first row) majorettes Carolyn Morton, Peggy Smith, Sue Barbee, Louise Floyd, and Doris Huneycutt; (second row) Marshall Coble, Charles Coble, Joann Poplin, Polly Lee, Roger Little, Jimmy Davis, and Malcolm Huneycutt; (third row) Butch Presler, Gerald Huneycutt, Dean Carelock, Frenchie Cowan, Judge Morgan Jr., Graham Barnhardt, and Wayne Beachum; (fourth row) John Mack Coble, Bobby Hatley, Wayne Hatley, Clyde Hatley, Gerald Hinson, Mackie McLendon, and Larry Williams.

Junior marshals from 1957 wait in line for their appearance on stage. They are, from left to right, chief marshal Darrell Huneycutt, Joann Poplin, Sue Barbee, Louise Tucker, Judy Furr, and Nancy Herrin.

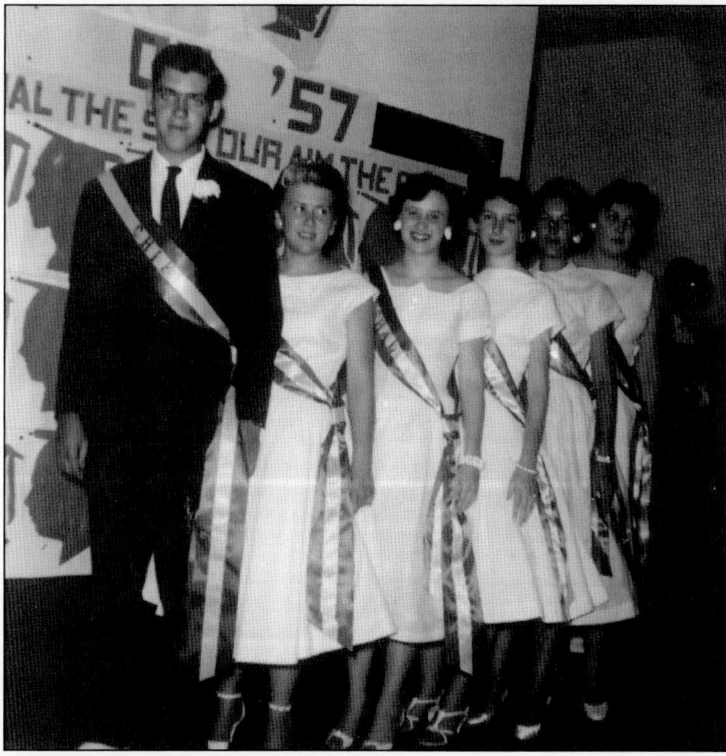

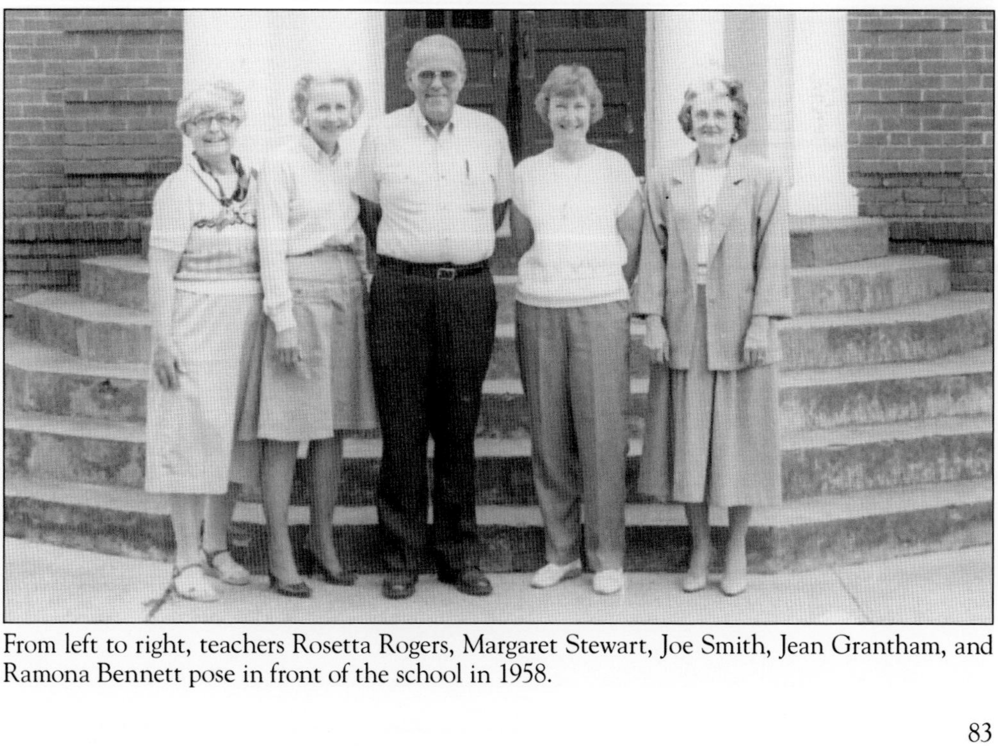

From left to right, teachers Rosetta Rogers, Margaret Stewart, Joe Smith, Jean Grantham, and Ramona Bennett pose in front of the school in 1958.

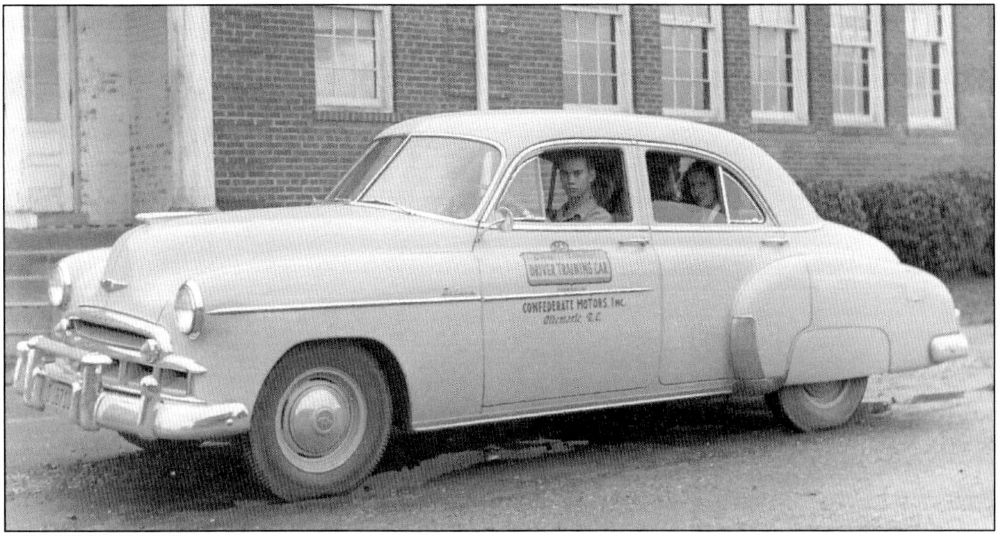

Frank Harward, who taught drivers education at Oakboro, is seen at the wheel in the 1952 Chevrolet used in the course. Below, he shows students the inner workings of the automobile. Confederate Motors of Albemarle supplied the cars for the driver-training program.

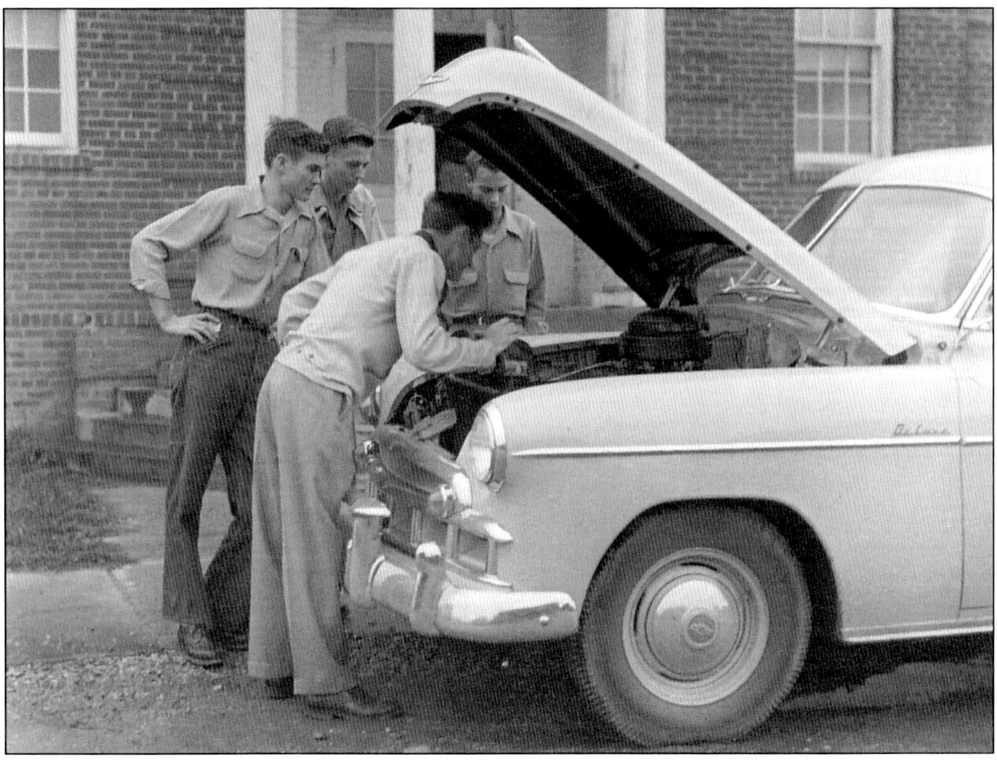

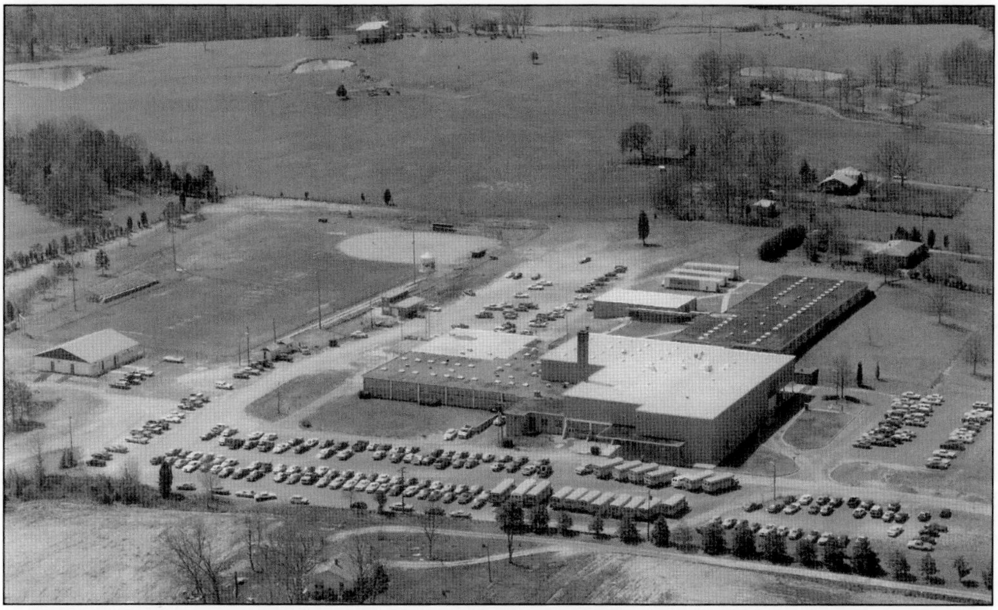

In 1962, Oakboro High School was consolidated into West Stanly High School, along with students from Endy, Locust, Ridgecrest, and Stanfield. This aerial view from the late 1990s shows the school and its setting in the rural countryside in Red Cross. (Courtesy of Wesley Tucker.)

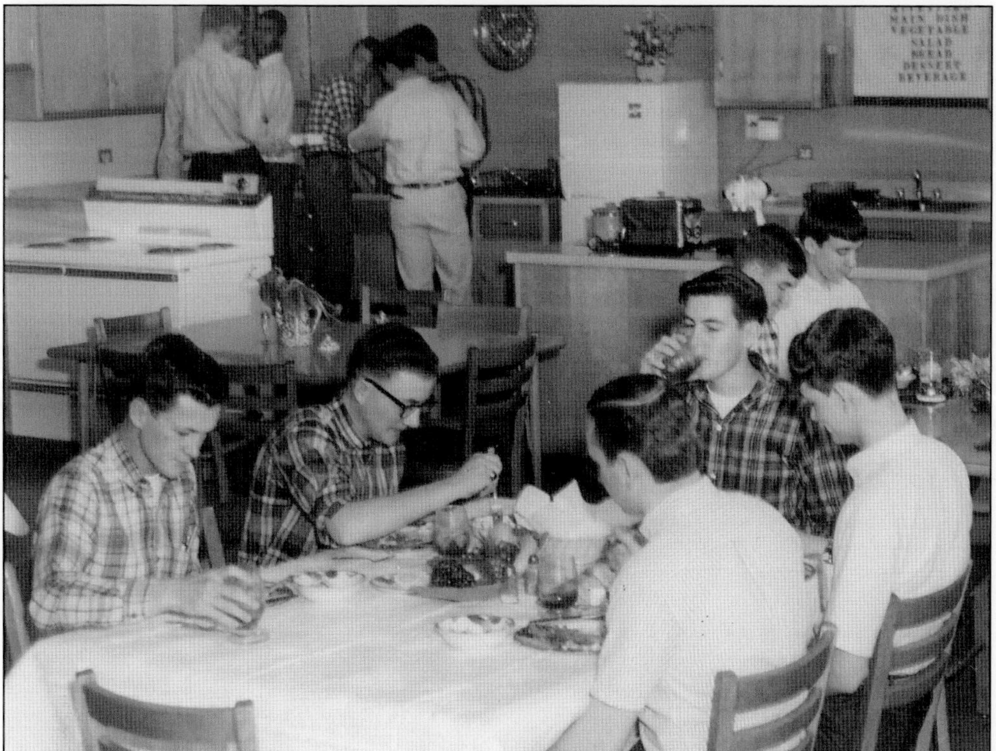

Among the offerings at the new consolidated school was a food and nutrition class for boys. This group practices good table manners while eating the meals they have prepared.

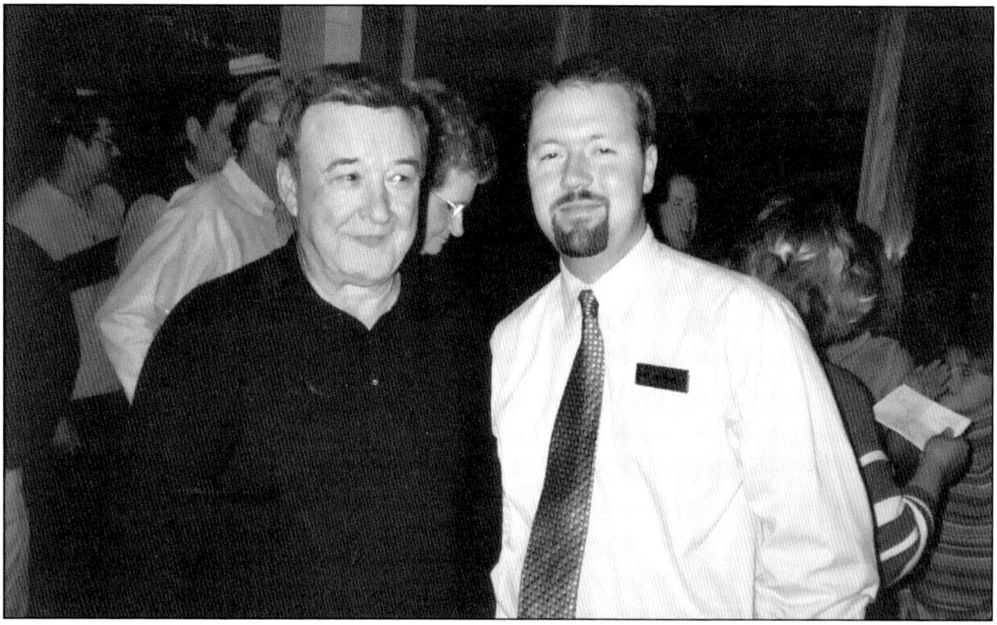

Jim Kennedy (left) began staging drama presentations at West Stanly High School in 1971 and served as the drama teacher and director of the West Stanly Players for 26 years. Upon his retirement in 1997, Wesley Tucker (right), a former student of his, inherited the position and has kept the tradition of the Players strong. (Courtesy of Wesley Tucker.)

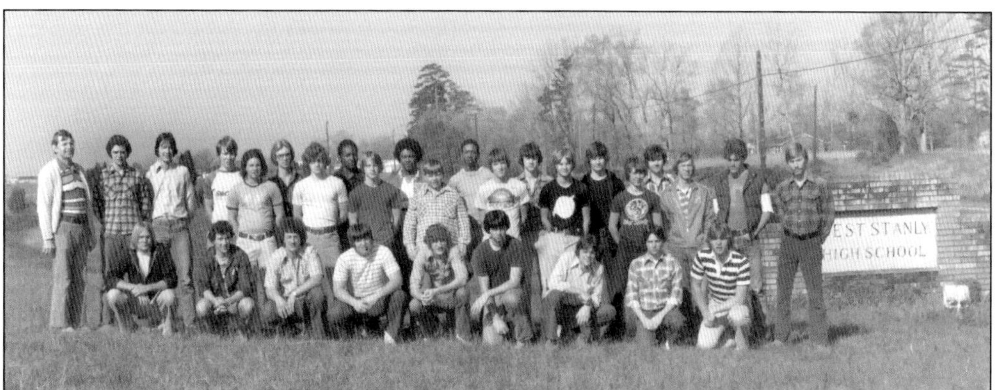

The construction program is also strong at West Stanly. In 1979, under the direction of teacher Harold Burris, the construction class built the Oakboro Library on South Main Street. The student participants posed for this group photograph with Burris (far left).

Six

Celebrations, People, and Places

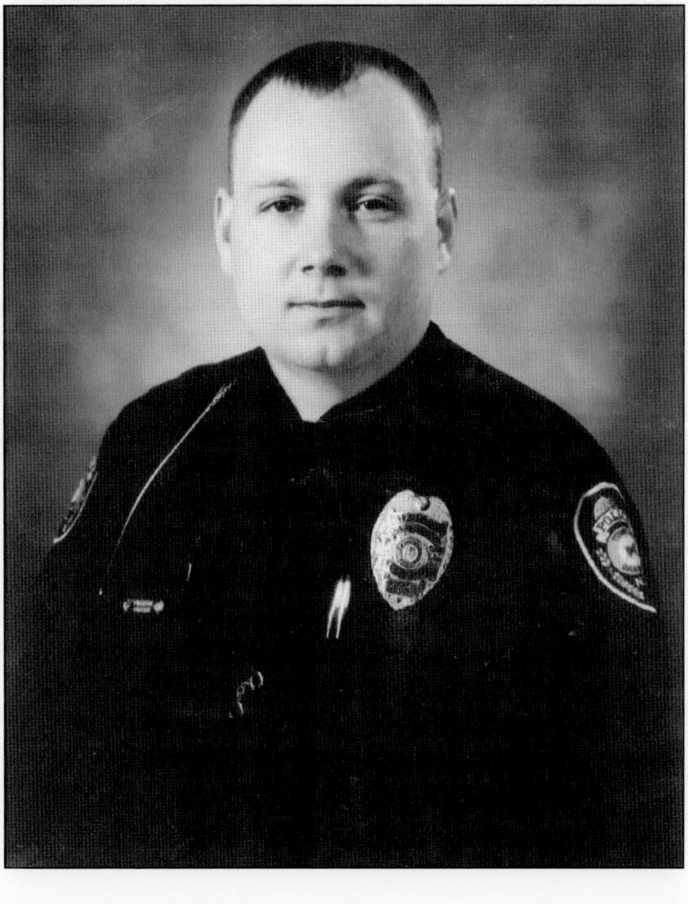

This chapter is dedicated to the memory of Damon Franklin Smith, an Oakboro police officer who was killed in the line of duty on April 15, 1996. (Courtesy of Pam Medlin and the Oakboro Police Department.)

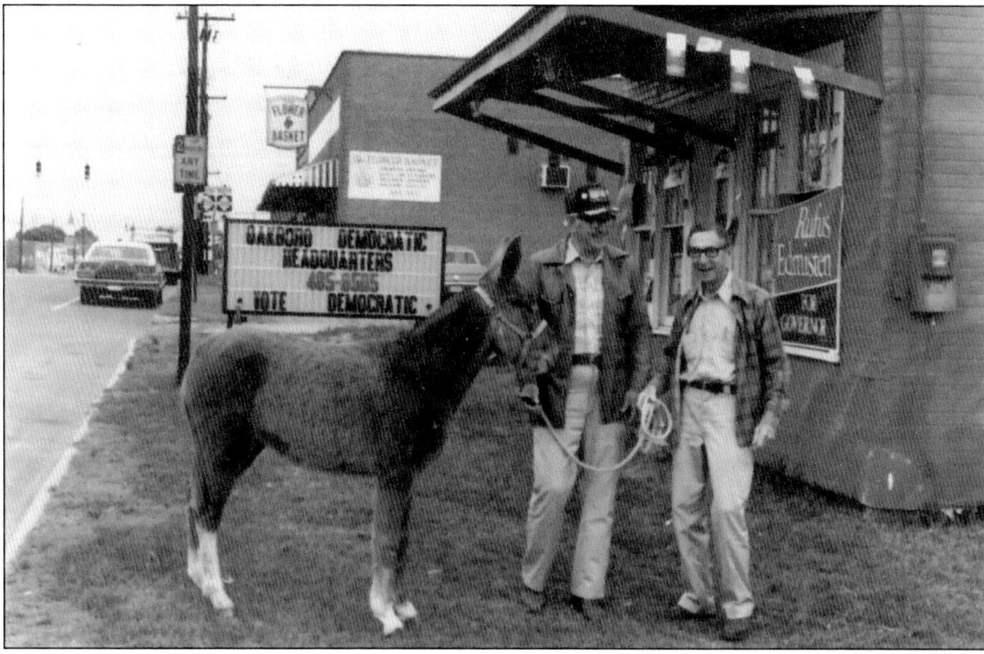

Former police chief Crowell Smith introduces a donkey to mayor Claud Teeter. Smith, who served as chief from 1955 to 1960, was a decorated World War II veteran who served with General Patton in the European Theater. This little red building housed several businesses over the years, including a barbershop, an appliance repair shop, a hot dog stand, and a fruit and vegetable stand.

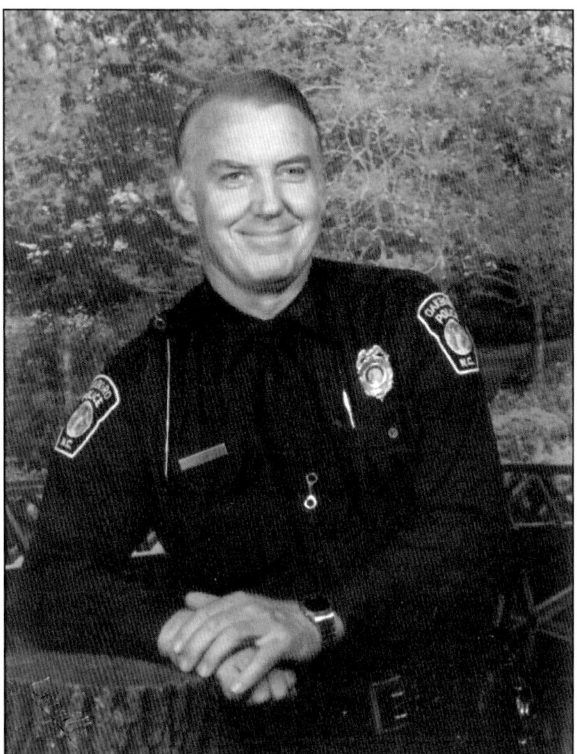

Jack Thomas took over as Oakboro police chief in November 1960 and served until 1990. He presided over the many changes in law enforcement through the years, always maintaining that one must grow in the job through education. Oakboro remained a one-man police department until 1967, and the town provided the first automobile in 1968. (Courtesy of Jack Thomas.)

The story goes that the owner of the diner on Main Street told Hubert Hahn that if he bought this dog a hot dog, he would take his picture beside the monument. And so he did. The monument once resided in the middle of the intersection, but its current whereabouts are unknown. (Courtesy of Jackie Hahn.)

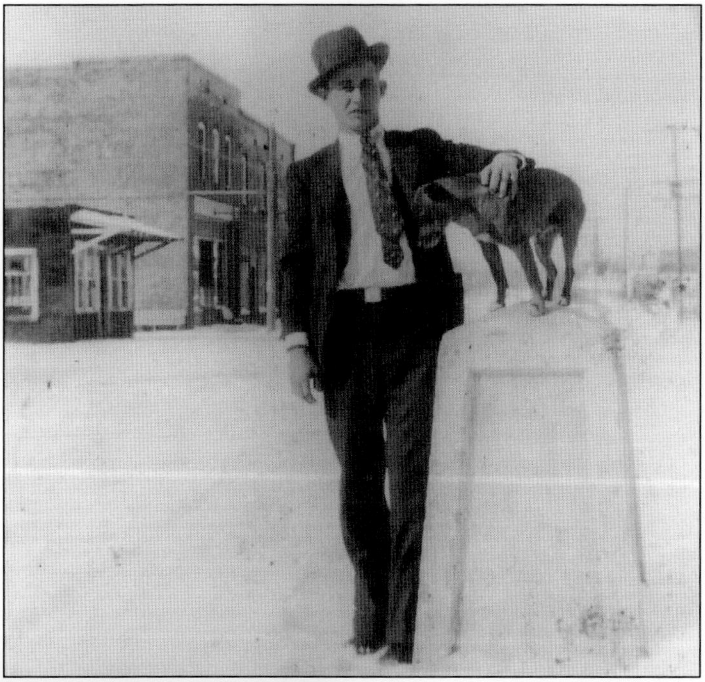

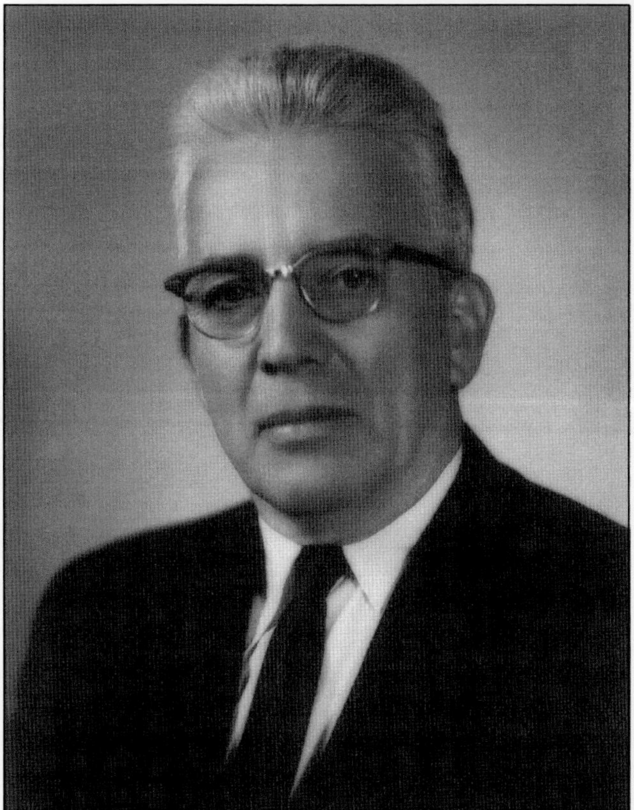

C.N. Barger was a druggist in Oakboro for many years who compounded his own medicines. People often asked him for advice rather than going to the doctor. The drugstore had a snack bar, and high school boys worked at the soda fountain, serving cherry cokes and ice cream floats.

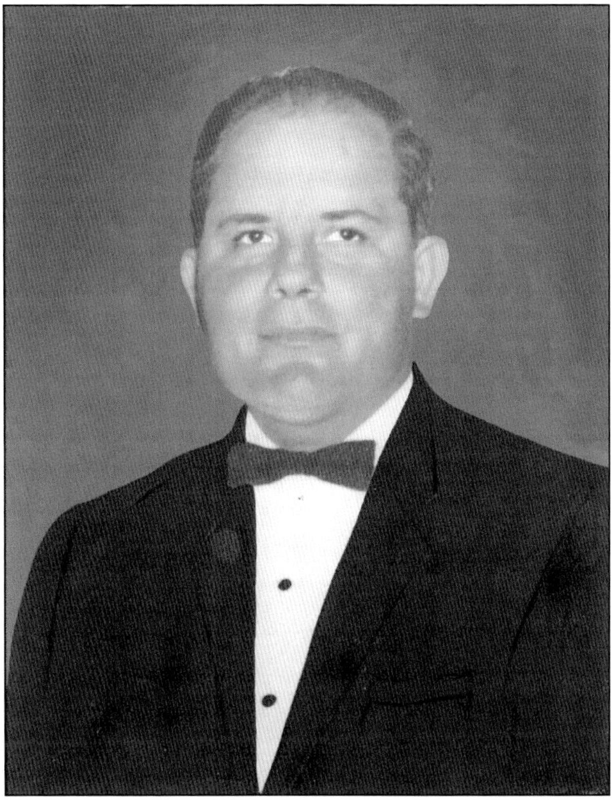

Cliff Caddell came to Oakboro in 1966 and partnered with Jesse Pike at Pike's Drug Store. In 1972, he became full owner and renamed it Caddell's Drug Store. He maintained the business until his death. (Courtesy of Mitzi Caddell.)

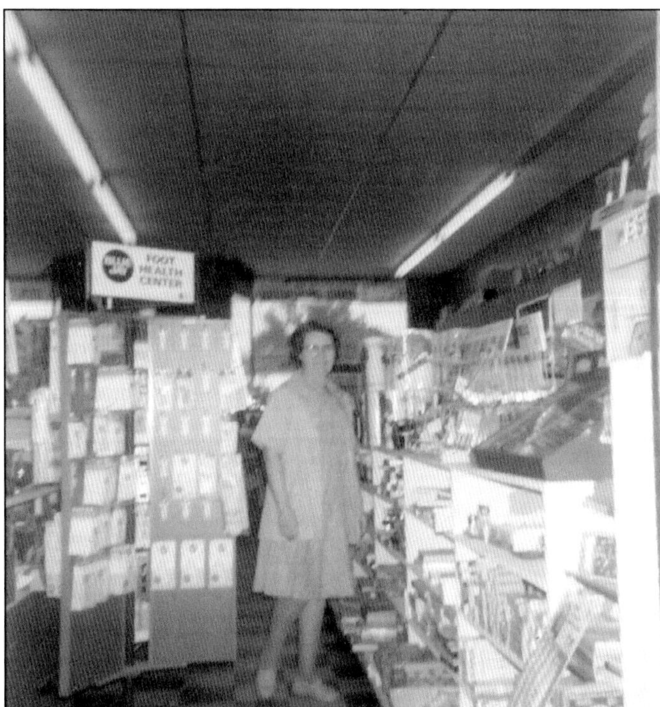

Eunice Little, seen here inventorying stock on the shelves, began working at Pike's Drug Store in 1962 and continued to work in the same place through several different owners, including its iterations as Caddell's Drug Store and Tollison Pharmacy.

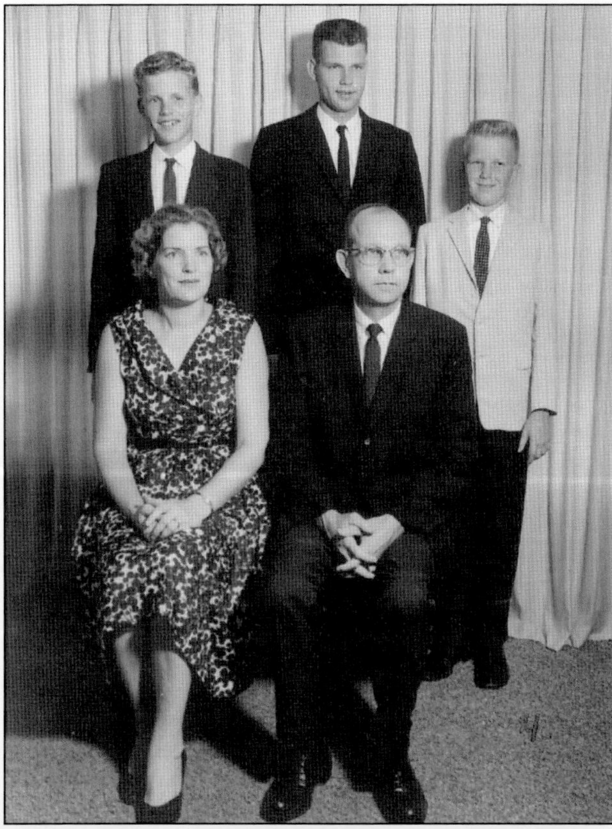

Dr. Walter L. McLendon was a physician in Oakboro for many years in the mid-1900s. He is seen right with his wife, Edith, who worked with him at the practice, and their sons, from left to right, Lennox, Mack, and Wallace. Dr. McLendon gave physicals for the high school athletes, some of whom had never been to a doctor before, and Edith was the Oakboro correspondent for the *Stanly News and Press* and the organist for the Oakboro Presbyterian Church. Dr. McLendon's office, pictured below, is now an accountant's office.

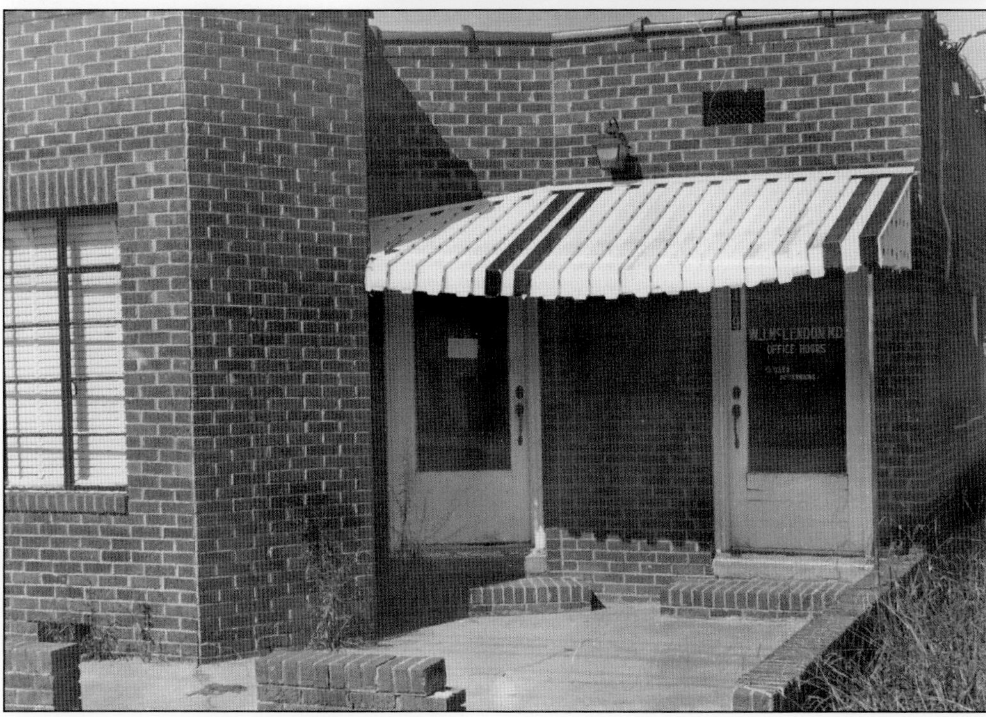

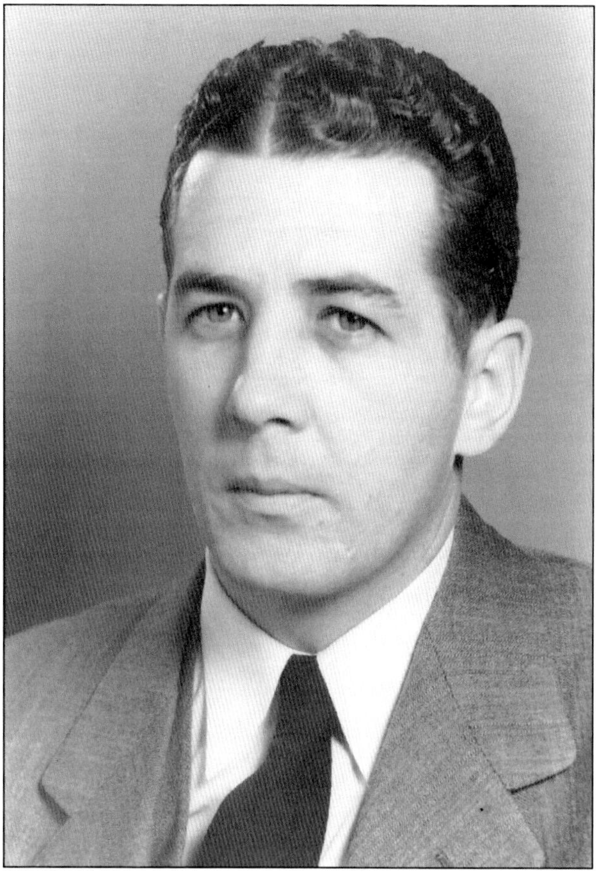

Dr. W.L. McLeod, an Oakboro physician from 1966 to 1988, was greatly respected as the last of the country doctors, even making house calls as needed. His office was on Third Street.

Postmaster Artus Howell poses at the counter of the Oakboro post office, and ? Owens stands at the boxes. This interior section of the post office personally belonged to Howell and was moved to his home after his retirement. Howell had served as postmaster and rural mail carrier a total of 31 years.

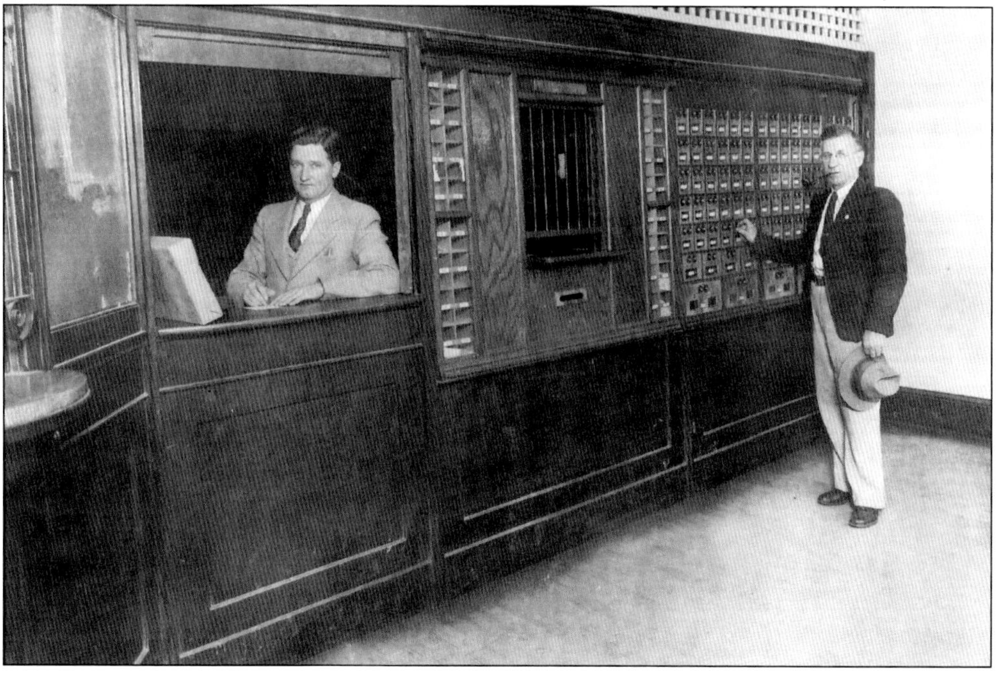

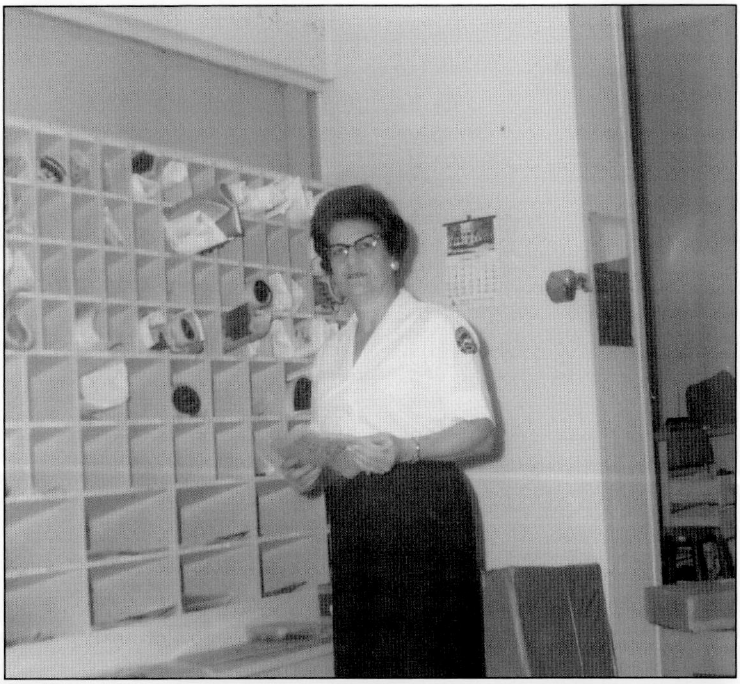

Nellie "Bill" Church served as Oakboro's postmaster from 1944 until 1974. She was the daughter of Dr. Flavius E. and Mary (Seago) Hartsell and was married to Rev. Forrest Church. When she retired, Dillon Whitley, pictured below, replaced her as postmaster.

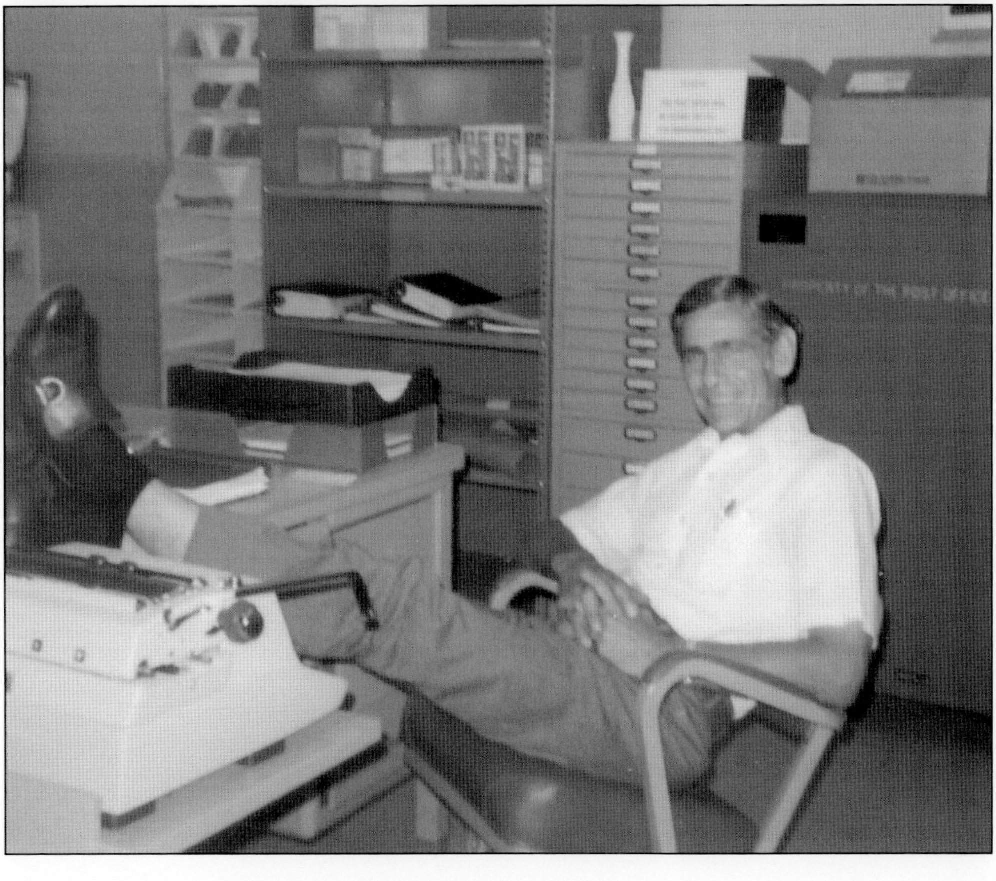

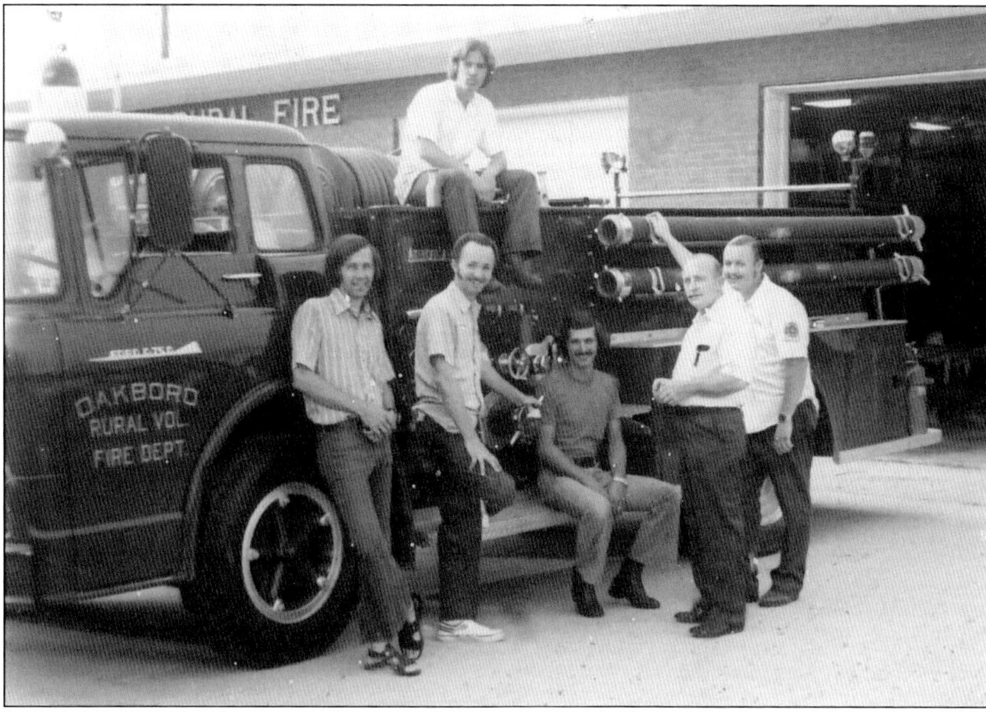

The Oakboro Rural Volunteer Fire Department received their first fire truck in 1959. Seen here admiring the truck from left to right are Larry Tucker, Wayne Huneycutt, Terrell Whitley, C.J. Barbee, and Gary Hinson. Seated on top of the truck is Randy Huneycutt. (Courtesy of Larry Tucker.)

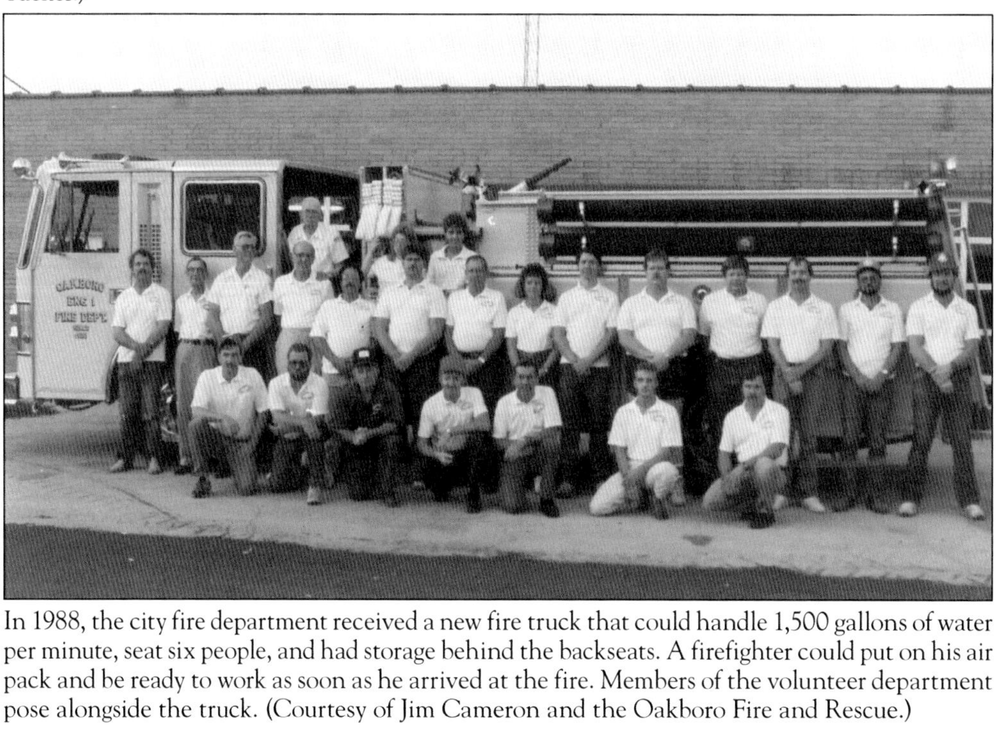

In 1988, the city fire department received a new fire truck that could handle 1,500 gallons of water per minute, seat six people, and had storage behind the backseats. A firefighter could put on his air pack and be ready to work as soon as he arrived at the fire. Members of the volunteer department pose alongside the truck. (Courtesy of Jim Cameron and the Oakboro Fire and Rescue.)

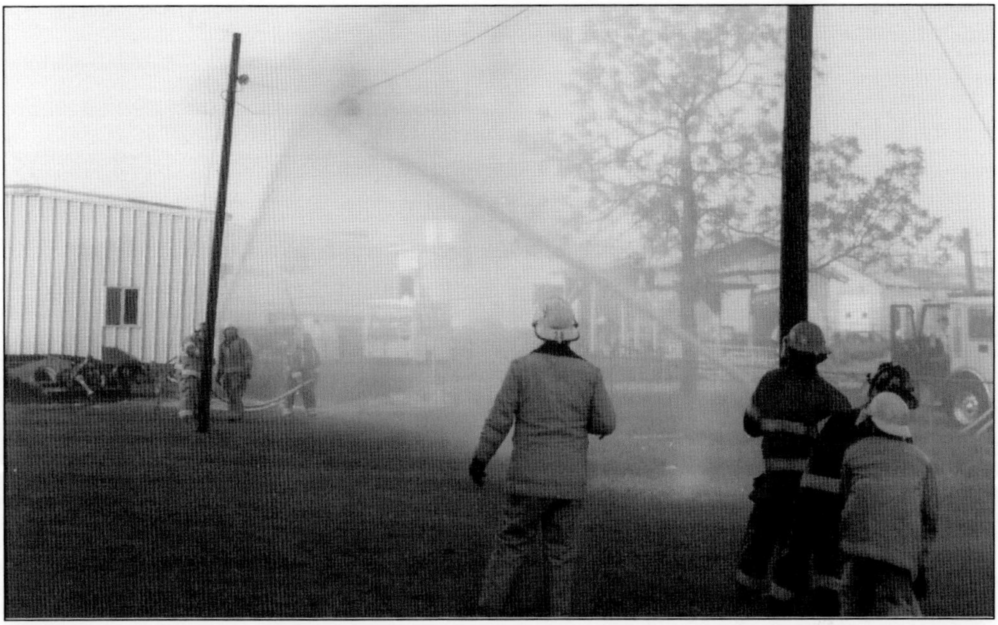

Each year at the Fourth of July celebration, fire departments from around the county compete in various events. Pictured here, in the firemen's duel, members try to keep the bucket in the middle during a timed event.

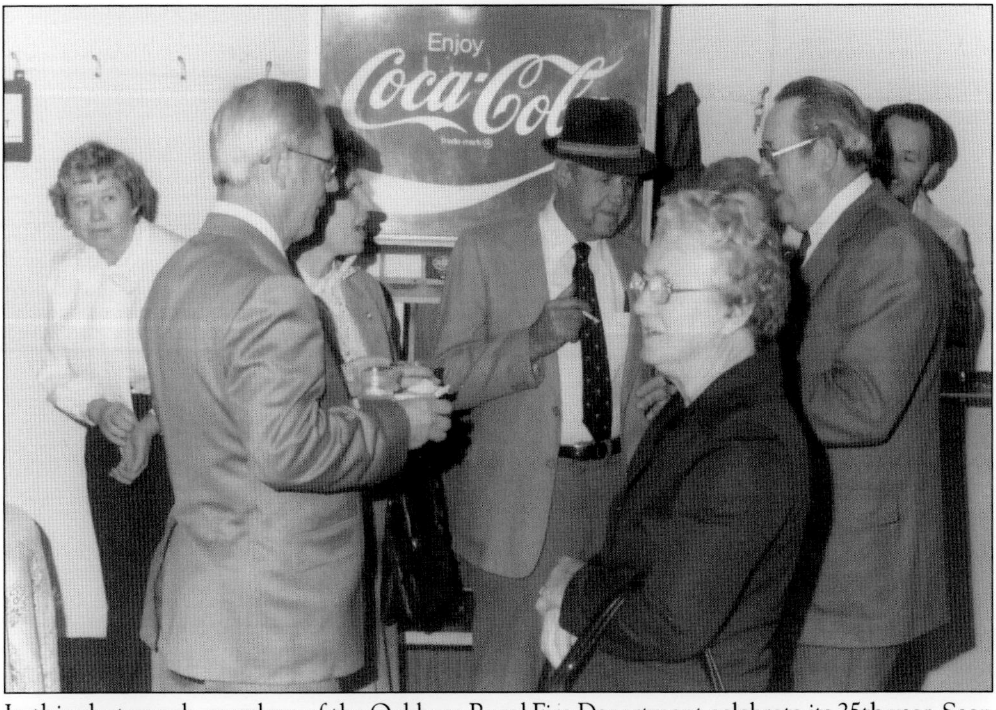

In this photograph, members of the Oakboro Rural Fire Department celebrate its 25th year. Seen at the celebration from left to right are Teen Crisco, Oakboro mayor Fetzer Hartsell and his wife Betty, T.W. Coble, Emma Tucker, Johnnie Drye, and Wayne Huneycutt.

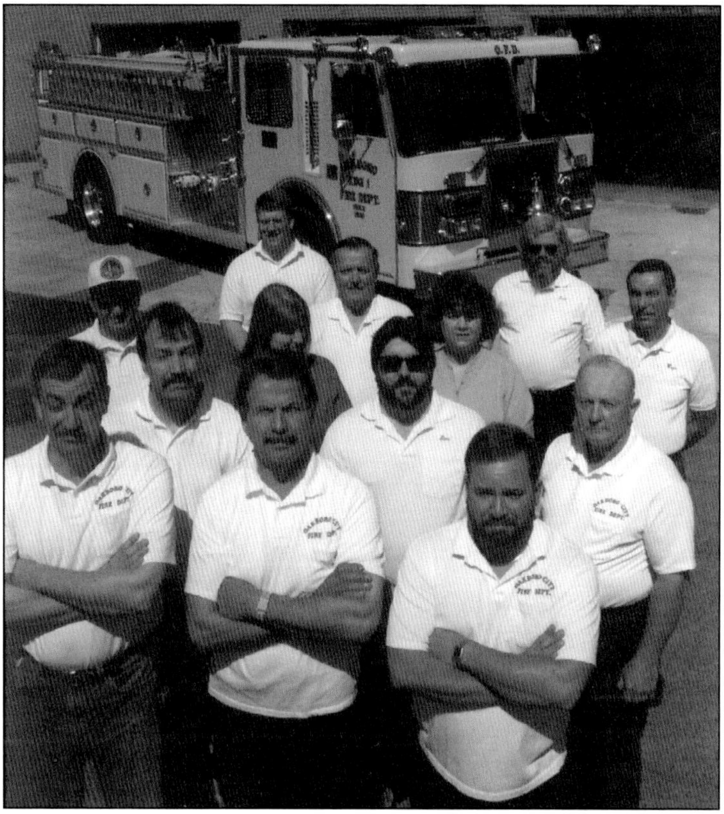

The Oakboro City Fire Department, left, and the Oakboro Rural Fire Department, below, are pictured here before the two departments merged as one in 1997.

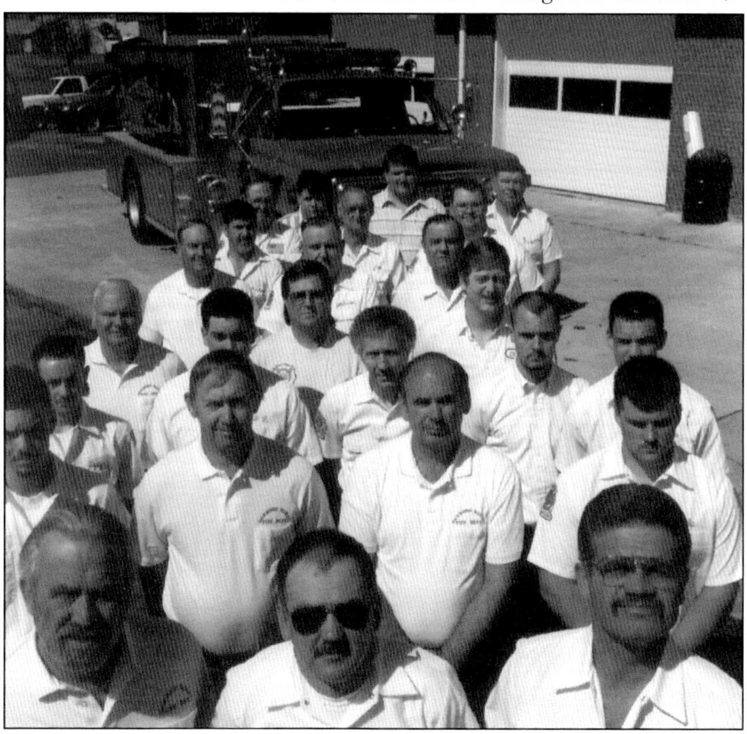

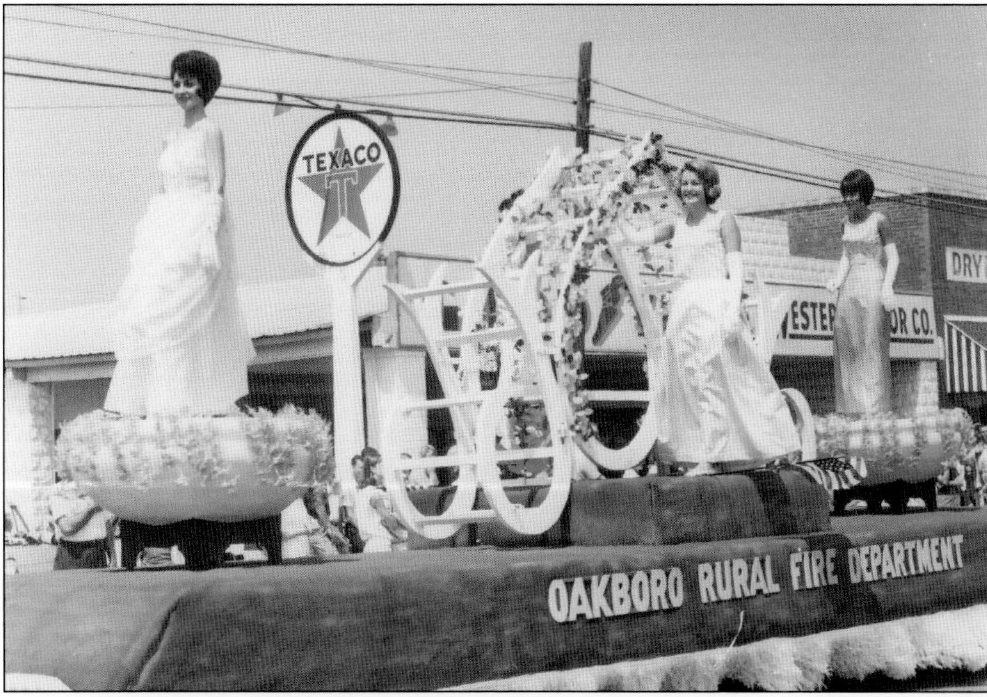

Both fire departments were active in sponsoring the annual Fourth of July celebration in Oakboro, and each group presented a float in this 1966 parade.

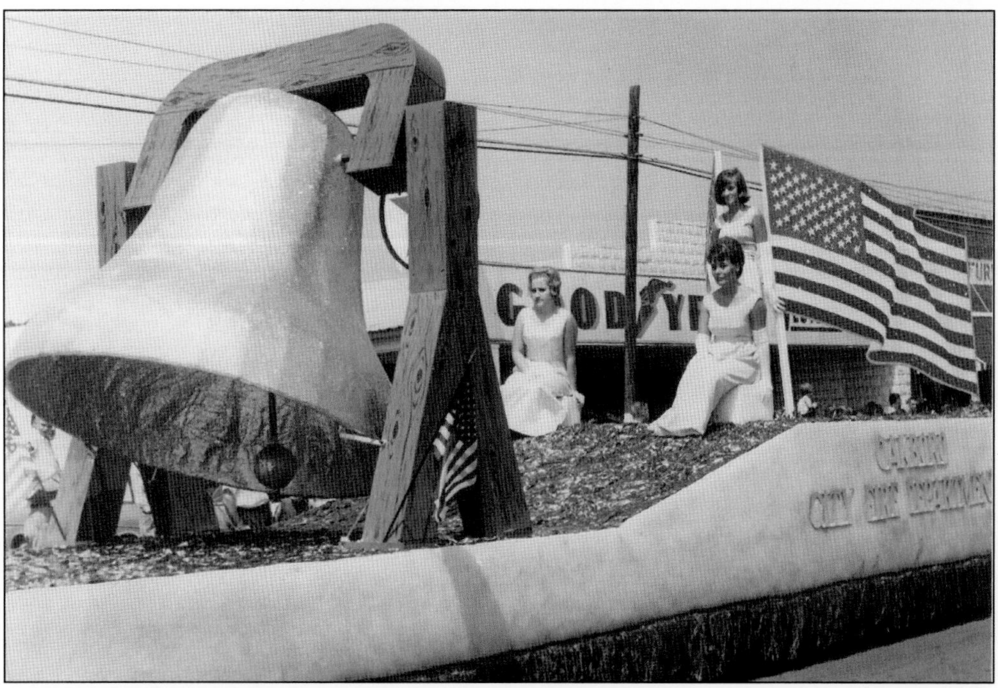

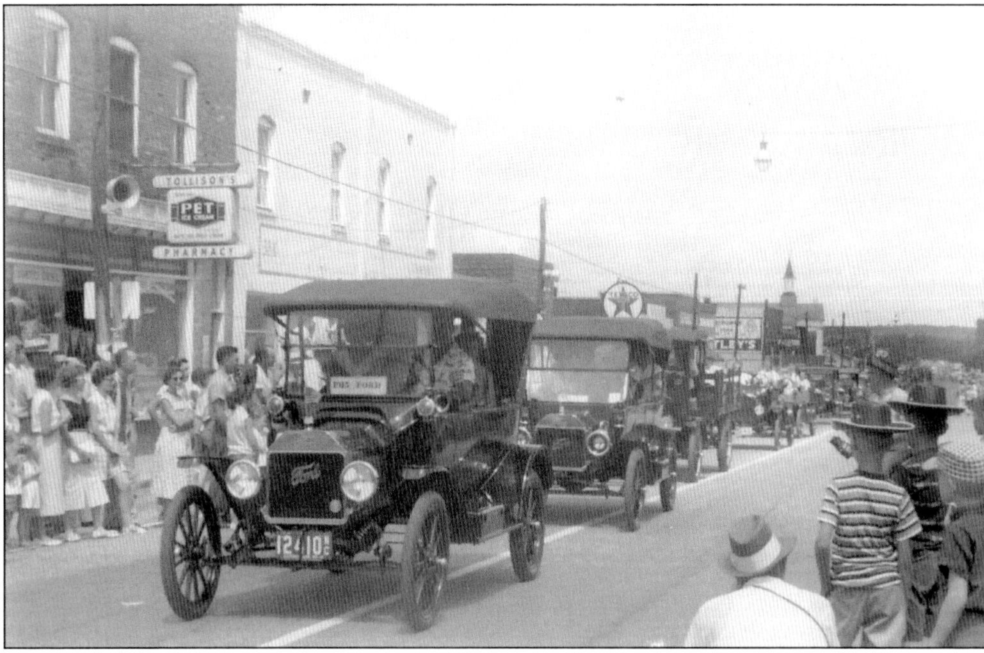

The Fourth of July parade has been a mainstay for the town of Oakboro since 1958. Started as a way to make money for a much-needed truck, the first celebration was an immediate success. The lengthy annual parade down Main Street features floats, automobiles, beauty queens, horses, and clowns, and rides in the park and fireworks give the celebration a fine finish. These two pictures from the 1958 parade offers an idea of the number of spectators who came to experience the day.

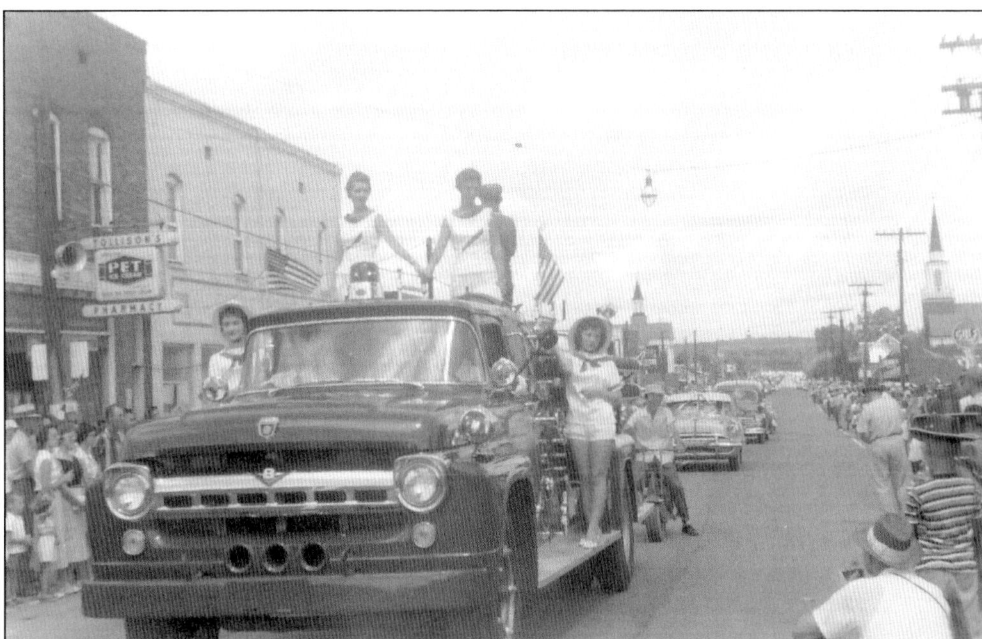

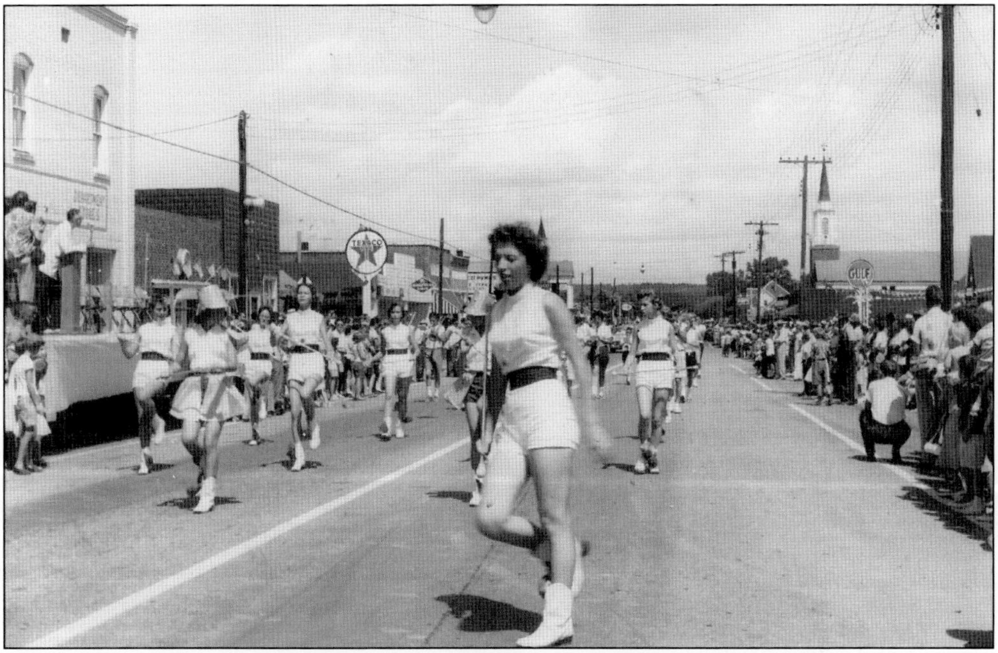

The Oakboro High School band was out in full force to participate in this parade. Doris Huneycutt leads the majorettes as the band marches down the street.

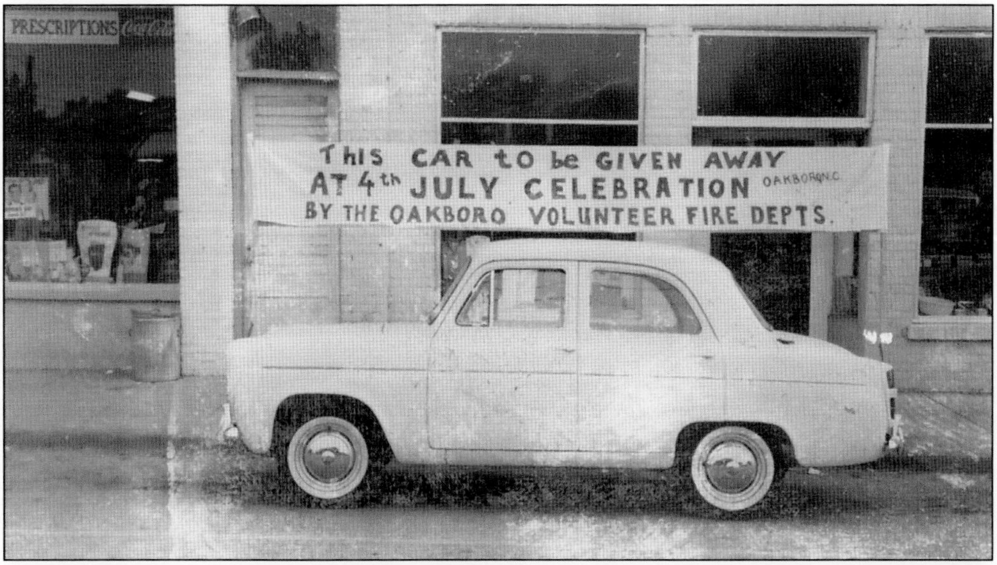

As a fundraiser and enticement to participate in the activities of the celebration, an automobile was raffled off each year for a three-year period. While the project was a success, the decision was made not to continue it. After the winner of the raffle was announced at 11:00 p.m., it was time for fireworks, which was often the children's favorite part of the celebration.

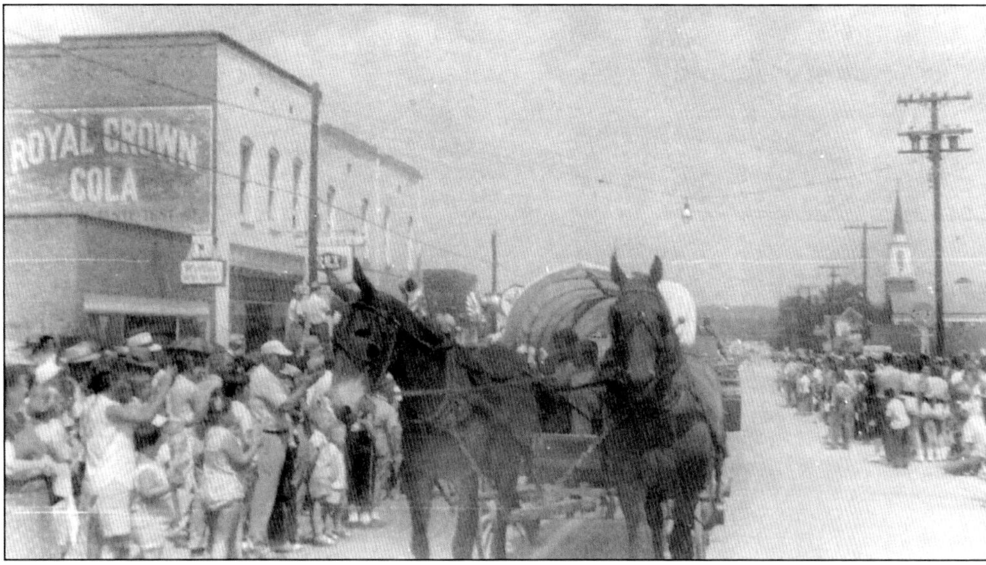

In 1959, these beautiful animals paraded down Main Street pulling a covered wagon. From the size of the crowd, the celebration appears to be a success.

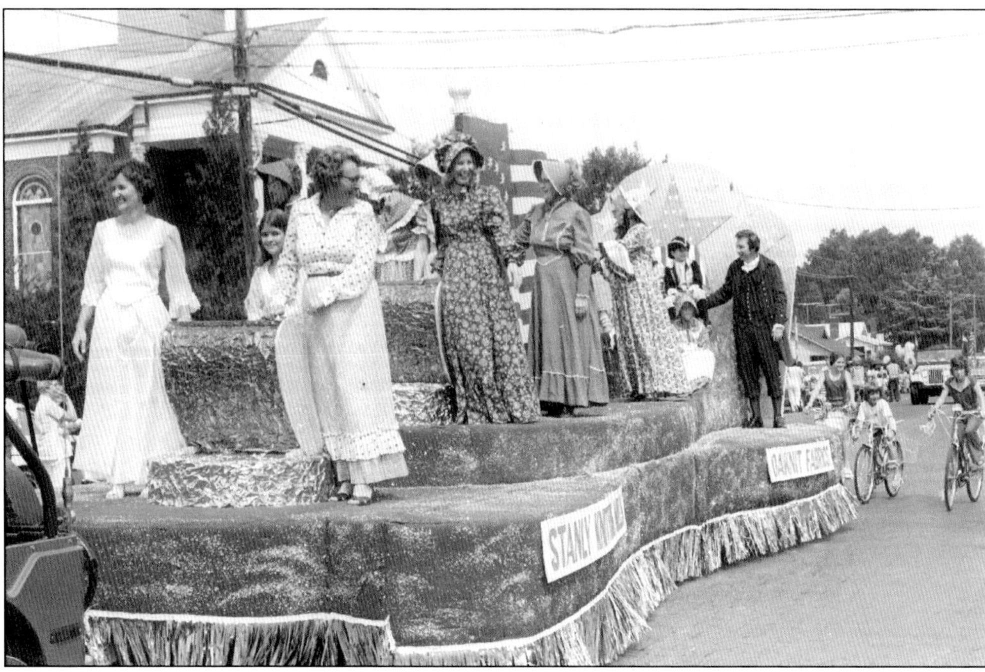

In 1976, the celebration took on an even more festive note as participants recognized the bicentennial of the United States. Riders on this float were dressed as the early settlers of the country. Stanly Knit and Oak Knit, two active mills in the community, sponsored the float, which children followed on bicycles.

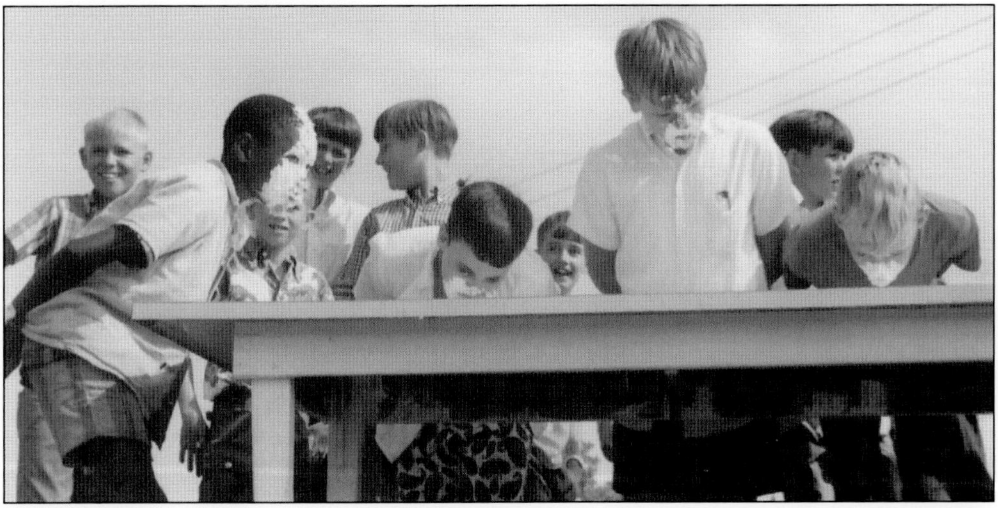

Fun and games at the Fourth of July celebration sometimes means getting pie in one's face. The 1968 pie-eating contest, pictured above, attracted a number of hungry participants. In 1989, children's games included sack races, and the lucky boys seen below were the first to cross the finish line. In the early years, other games included the greased pig and greasy pole contests, three-legged races, boxing matches, and rolling potatoes with one's nose.

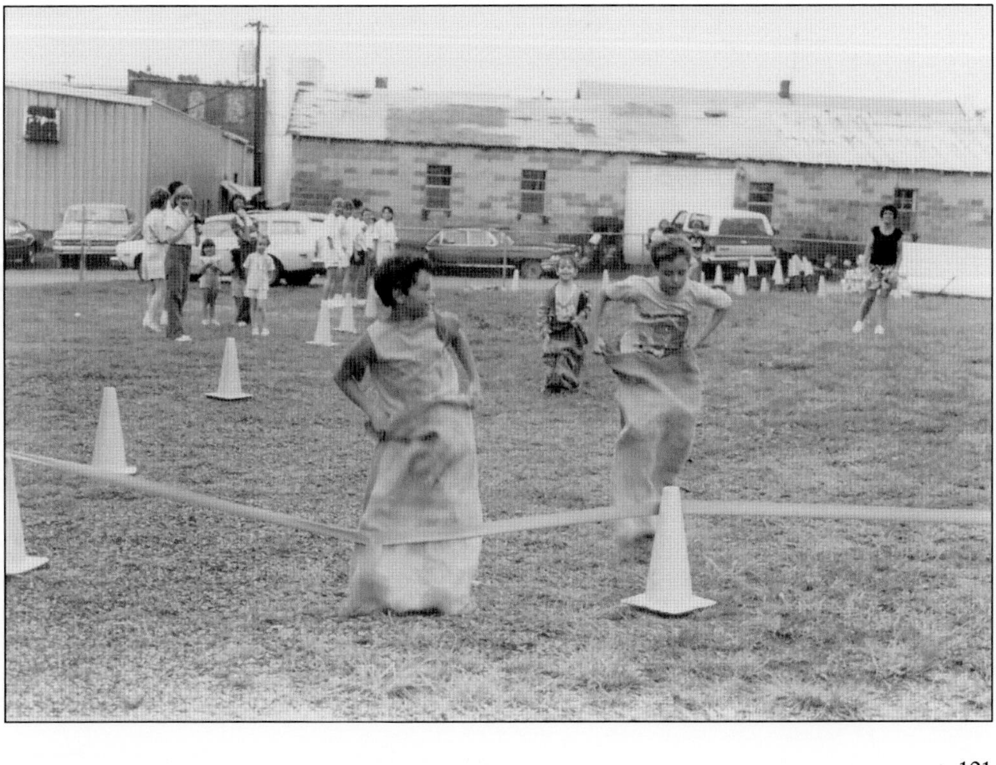

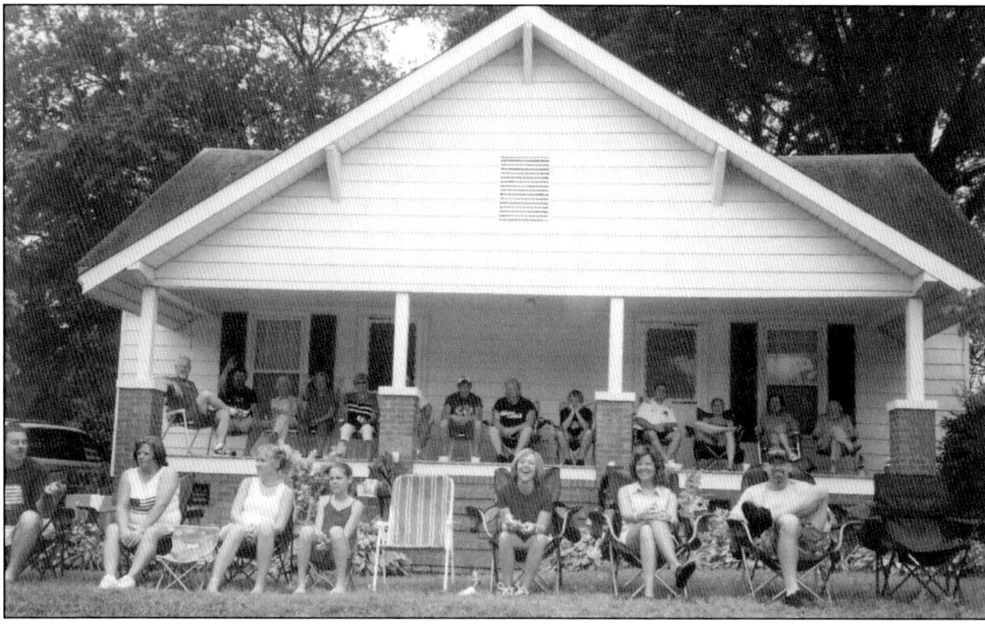

Families gather to watch the parades go by, participate in the festival rides and activities, and eat. The T.E. Arrowood family relaxes in their front yard to watch the parade. The Arrowood home is one of the early structures on Main Street, built about 1930.

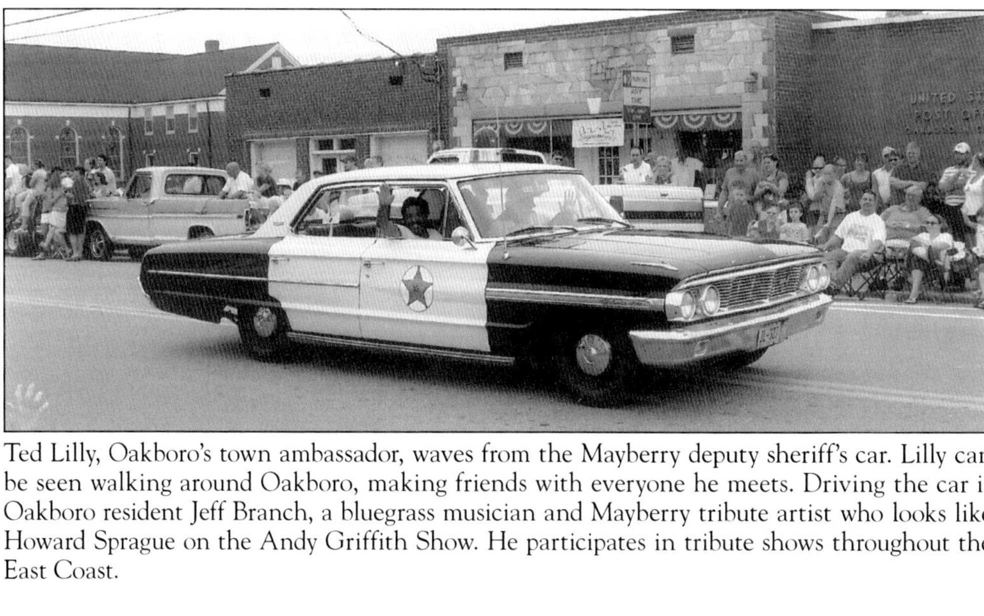

Ted Lilly, Oakboro's town ambassador, waves from the Mayberry deputy sheriff's car. Lilly can be seen walking around Oakboro, making friends with everyone he meets. Driving the car is Oakboro resident Jeff Branch, a bluegrass musician and Mayberry tribute artist who looks like Howard Sprague on the Andy Griffith Show. He participates in tribute shows throughout the East Coast.

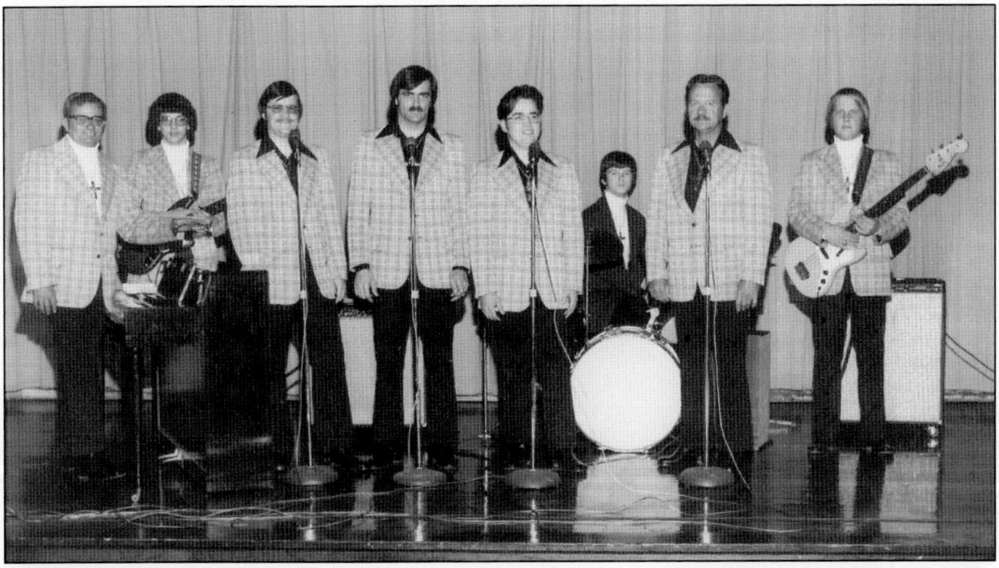

The Singing Towers have sung together for more than 38 years. Seen here in 1975, the band includes, from left to right, pianist Gene Conklin, rhythm guitarist Tony Hathcock, tenor Leonard Harvell, lead Julius Abernathy, baritone Danny Sprinkle, drummer Butch Lambert, bass singer Heath Hahn, and bassist Tony Hatley. They have traveled all over the southeast performing Christian concerts. (Courtesy of Heath Hahn.)

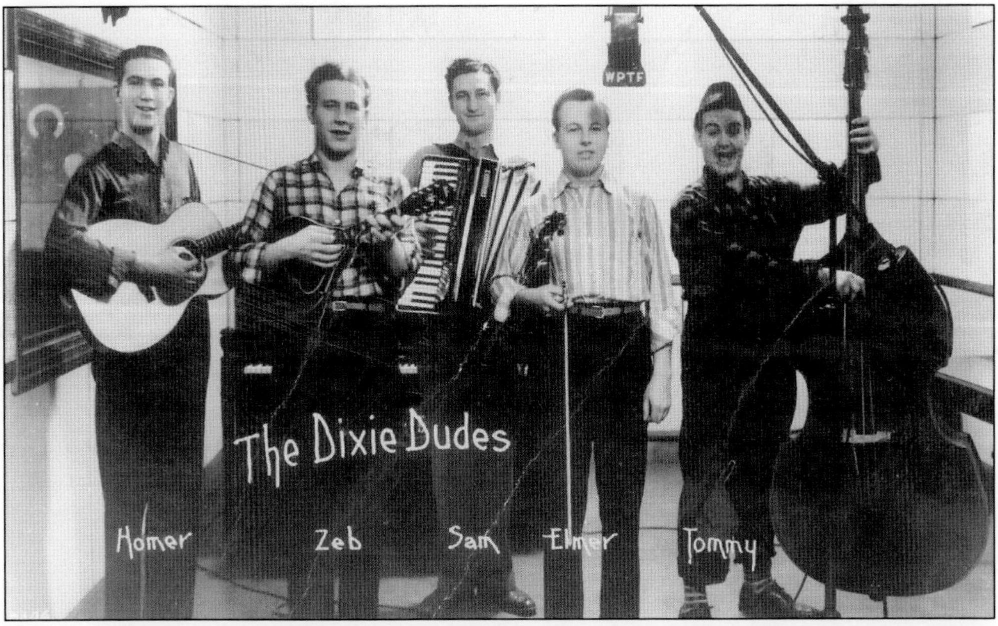

The Dixie Dudes from the Oakboro community are seen here performing in Raleigh at radio station WPTF. "Homer" is Homer Drye, who was also known as Homer Briarhopper. Guitarist "Zeb" is Jennings Robinson, Theodore Buford plays "Sam" on the accordion, Newell Hathcock is the fiddler "Elmer," and "Tommy" the bassist is Dee Page Erwin, who played with Ernest Tubb in Nashville. Hathcock hosted an annual bluegrass festival on his property just outside of Oakboro.

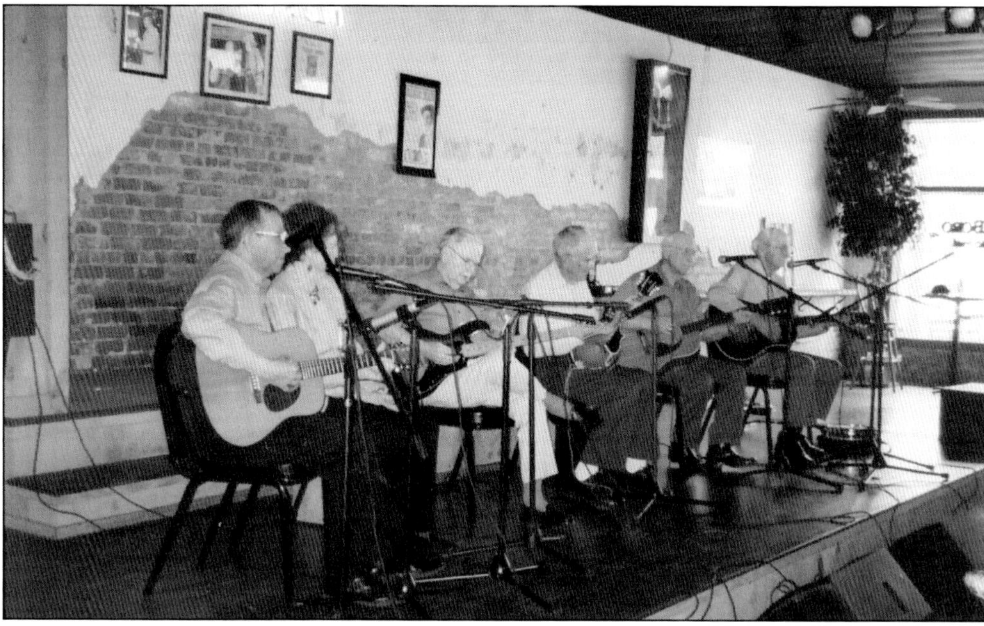

The Old House Band performed at various community events and traveled regularly to visit nursing homes. Seen here from left to right at the Oakboro Music Hall in 2006 are Johnny and Naomi Clontz, Lee Burris, Joe Morton, John D. Whitley, and Bill Lee. Other members of the band not pictured include L.B. Teeter, Felton Hinson, Maddie Little, Clint Joyner, and Ray Yow.

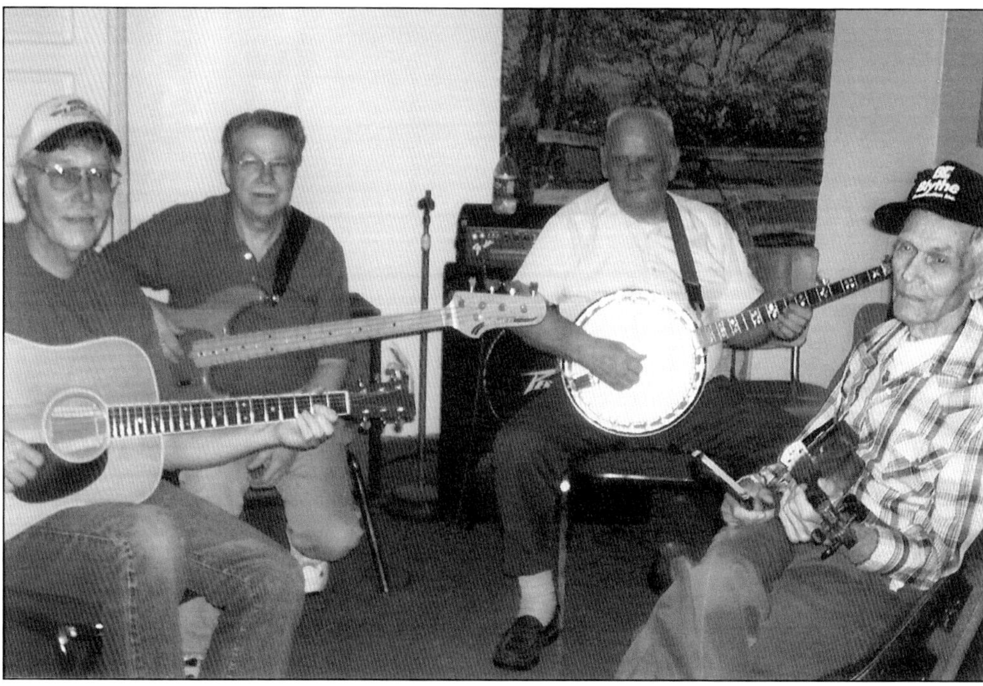

On Friday nights, from left to right, Bernard Barbee, Bob Hatley, Gene Helms, and Laurence Barbee gathered at a little cabin on Lawrence's property to play.

The bluegrass group the Jones Brothers and the Log Cabin Boys were popular in the 1960s and 1970s. Bruce and Lee Jones were the core of the group, which also included Richard Hollis, David Deese, and Larry Pyler, who grew up in Oakboro.

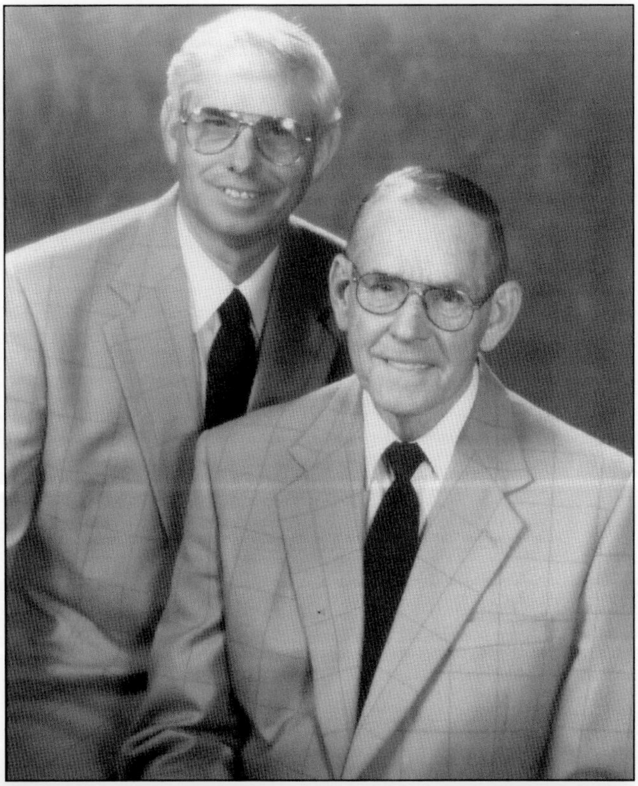

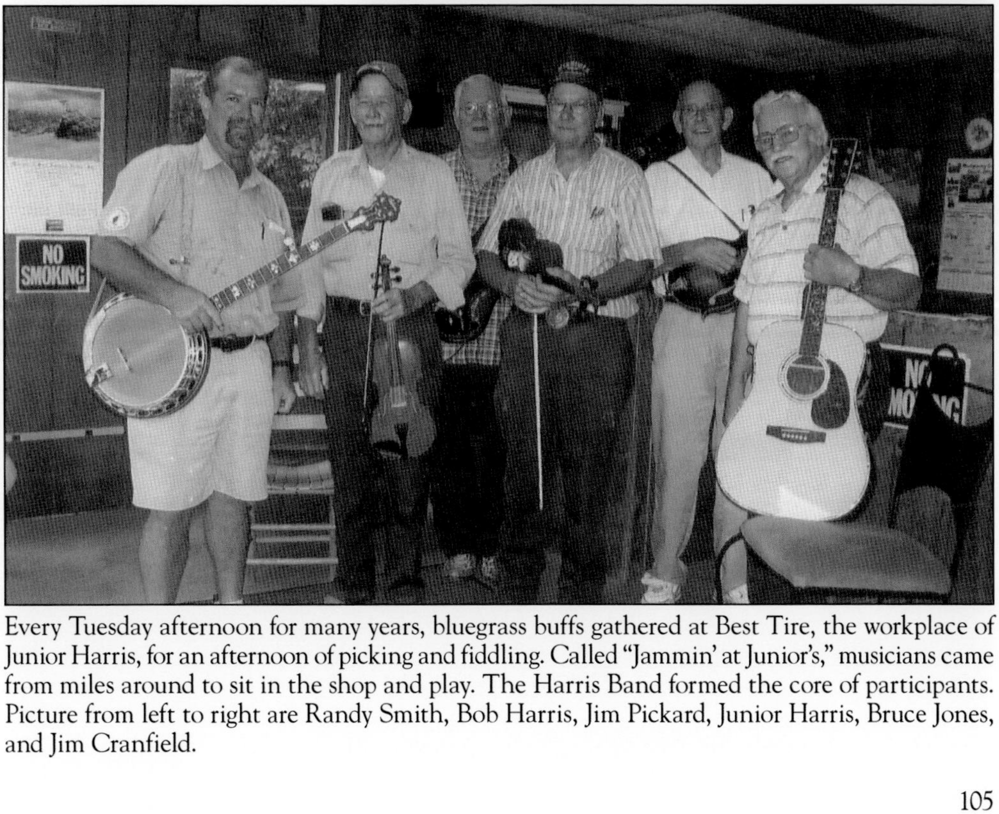

Every Tuesday afternoon for many years, bluegrass buffs gathered at Best Tire, the workplace of Junior Harris, for an afternoon of picking and fiddling. Called "Jammin' at Junior's," musicians came from miles around to sit in the shop and play. The Harris Band formed the core of participants. Picture from left to right are Randy Smith, Bob Harris, Jim Pickard, Junior Harris, Bruce Jones, and Jim Cranfield.

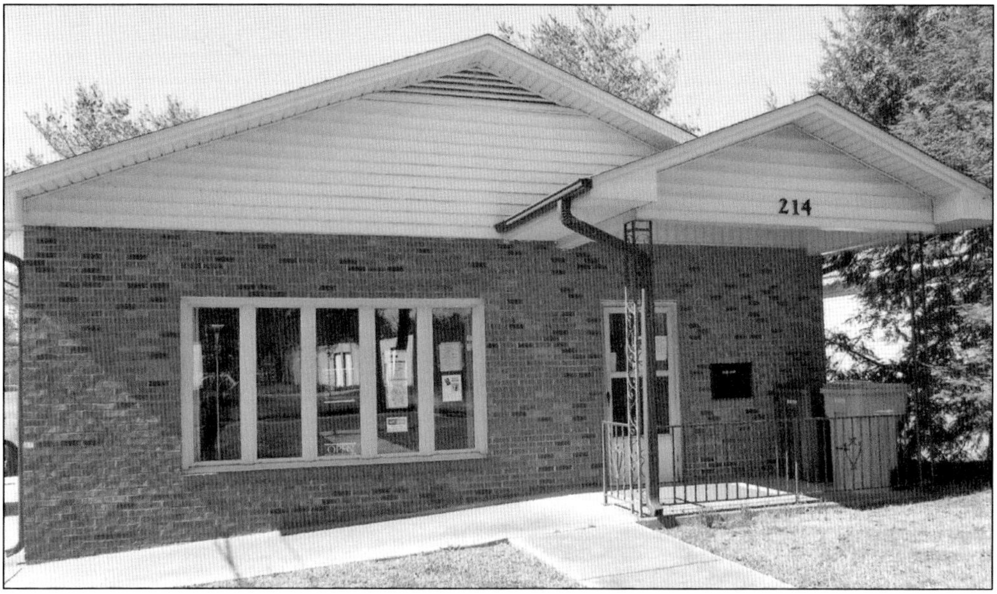

The Oakboro branch of the Stanly County Library was built by the vocational classes from West Stanly High School in 1979. The library enjoys a wide circulation and houses many different types of media for patrons. A comprehensive computer system permits patrons to access e-mail and surf the internet.

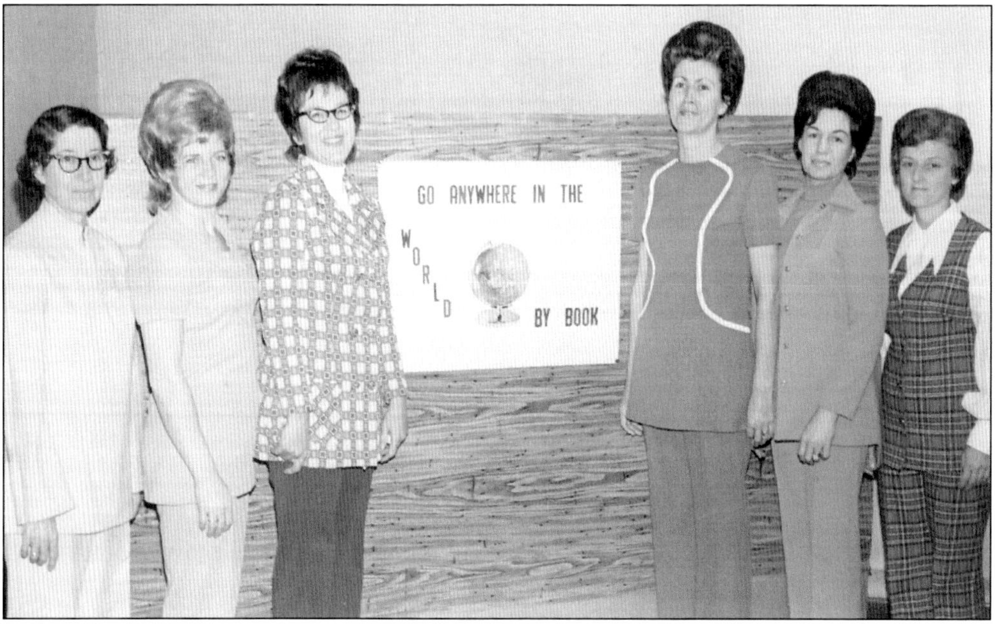

The Oakboro Library supporters worked hard to provide services in the interim before the county agreed to take on the responsibility for the facility. Members of the group from left to right are Hetty Baucom, Irene Kennedy, Bea Goodman, Juanita Carpenter, Shelby Davis, and Laverne Smith.

Arch Benton Huneycutt, the son of Civil War veteran Eli Monroe Huneycutt and Tempe J. Smith, taught in local schools before becoming licensed to preach in the Methodist Church. When his health declined, he sought solace in his family home, where he wrote poetry and songs in the shade of the oak trees and played his fiddle in the evenings. A collection of his work, *Rural Song*, was published in 1927. (Courtesy of Brooks Barnhardt.)

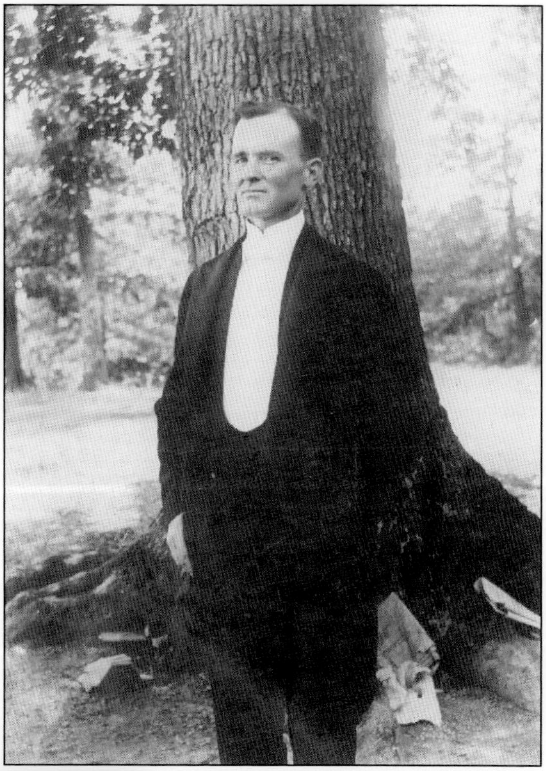

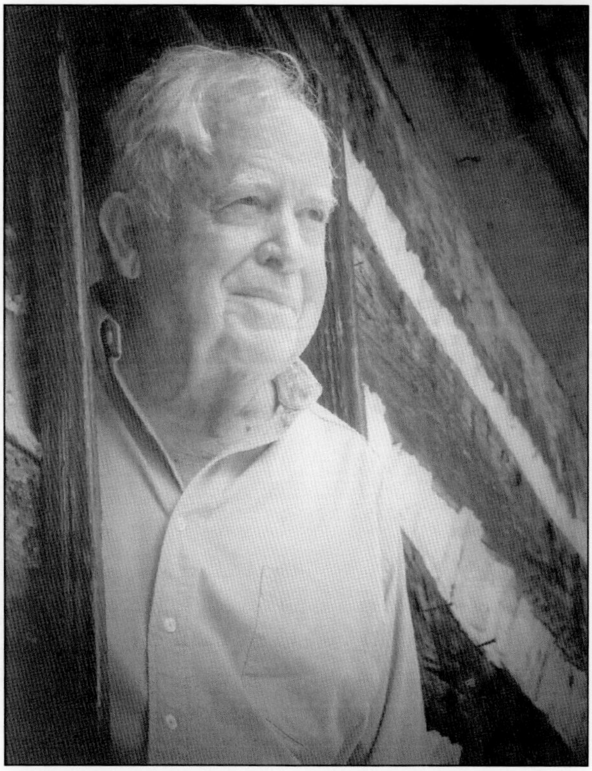

Fred T. Morgan was born in Big Lick and became an award-winning writer, working for the *Stanly News and Press* for 34 years. He is the author of four books on folklore of the Uwharries, as well as one about his tenure at the newspaper. Morgan also wrote prolifically in magazines such as *Our State*, a publication dedicated to North Carolina. (Courtesy of Brooks Barnhardt.)

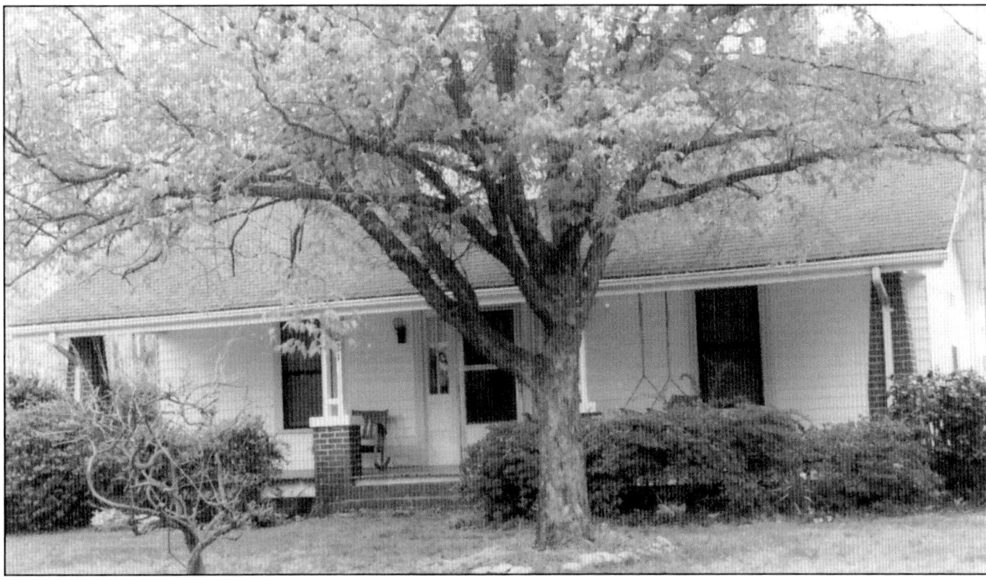

From about 1880 until 1920, the A.V. Thomas house was a one-room log schoolhouse. After it ceased to be used as a school, the owners added more rooms around the core and made it a home.

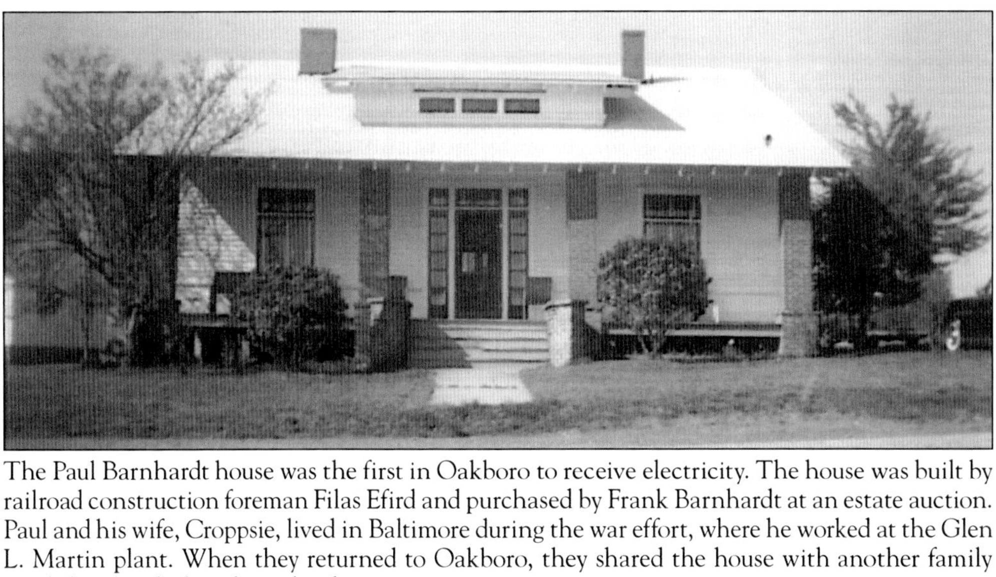

The Paul Barnhardt house was the first in Oakboro to receive electricity. The house was built by railroad construction foreman Filas Efird and purchased by Frank Barnhardt at an estate auction. Paul and his wife, Croppsie, lived in Baltimore during the war effort, where he worked at the Glen L. Martin plant. When they returned to Oakboro, they shared the house with another family until that family found another home.

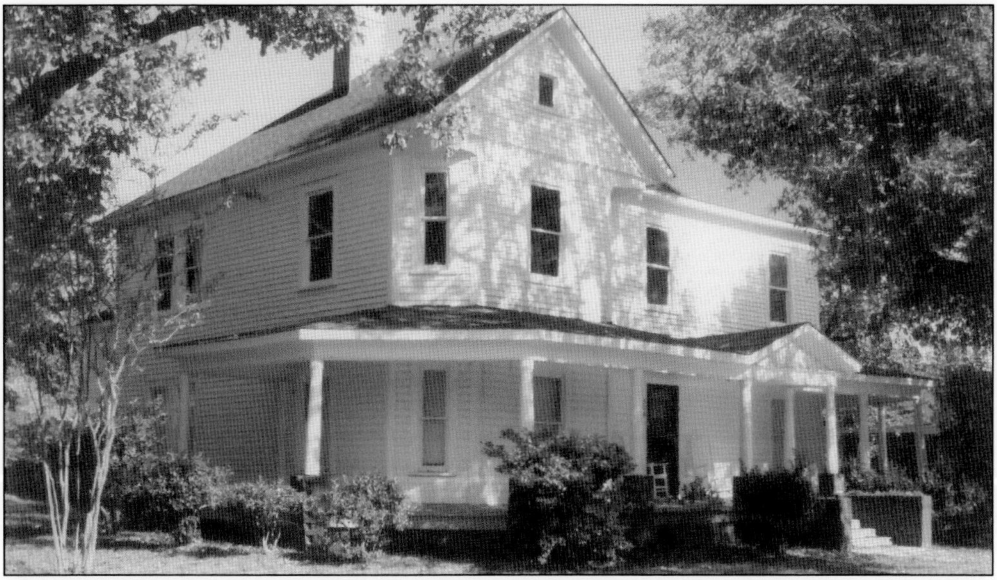

The Coble-Teeter house was built about 1925 by carpenter Jim Barbee. The two-story house has a hip roof and a wraparound porch. It was purchased in 1948 by Mattie (Love) Teeter and remained in the family until the death of its last owner, Mozelle Teeter, who bequeathed the property to the Oakboro Regional Historical Foundation.

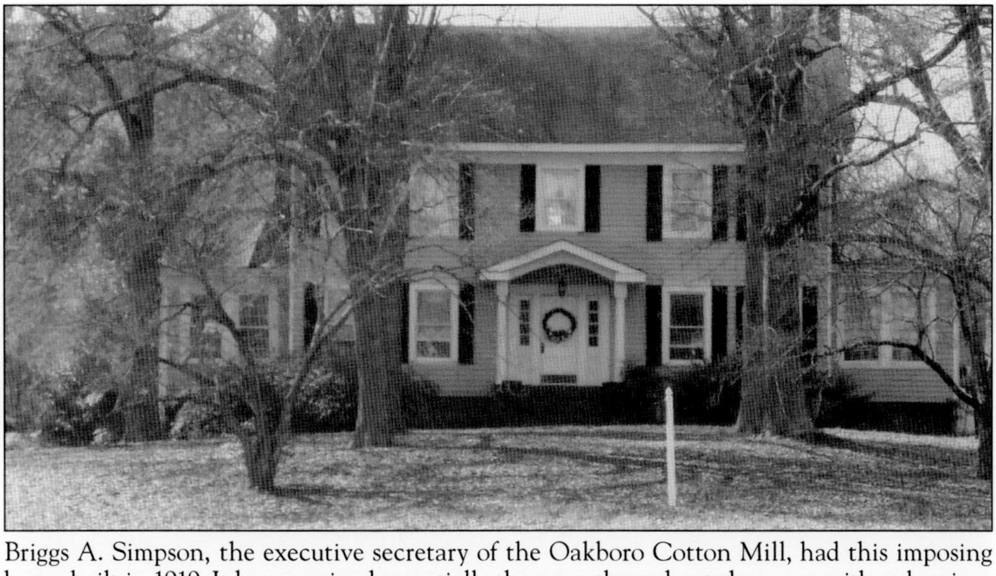

Briggs A. Simpson, the executive secretary of the Oakboro Cotton Mill, had this imposing house built in 1919. It has remained essentially the same throughout the years, with only minor modifications for convenience. Both the exterior and the interior exhibit elements of early Colonial Revival homes in the country. Owners Jim and Mary Williams maintain the unique character of the home.

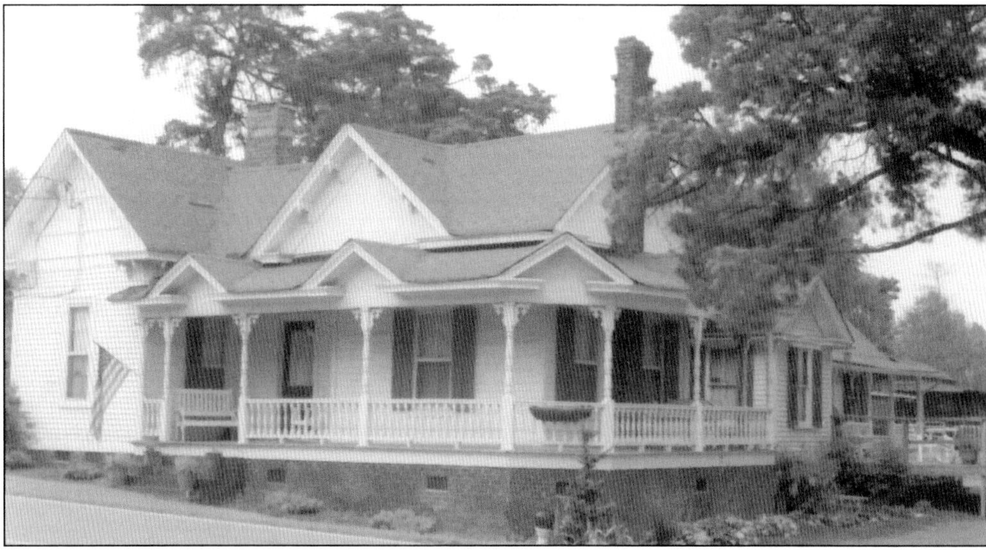

The W.A. "Billie" Cagle house was built in three stages between 1886 and 1901. Adorned with herringbone-pattern gables, hand-molded exterior brick chimneys, and lathe-turned posts with brackets on the wraparound porch, the house is said to be Stanly County's fanciest expression of the picturesque style.

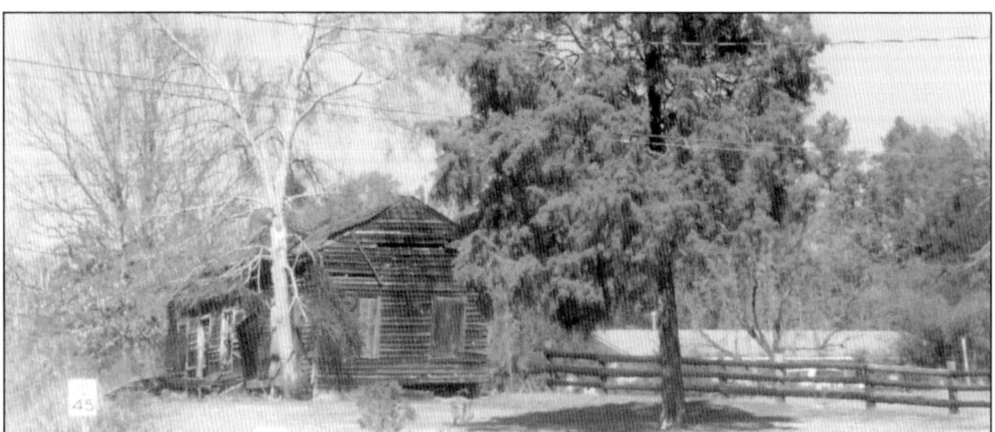

The Russell house was the family home of Cagle's wife, Mary Jane. Now falling down, the home was a two-room farmhouse with a slate-rock chimney. Local folklore claims this dwelling may have housed Jesse James for a brief time as he recruited members for his gang, but there is no real evidence to support it.

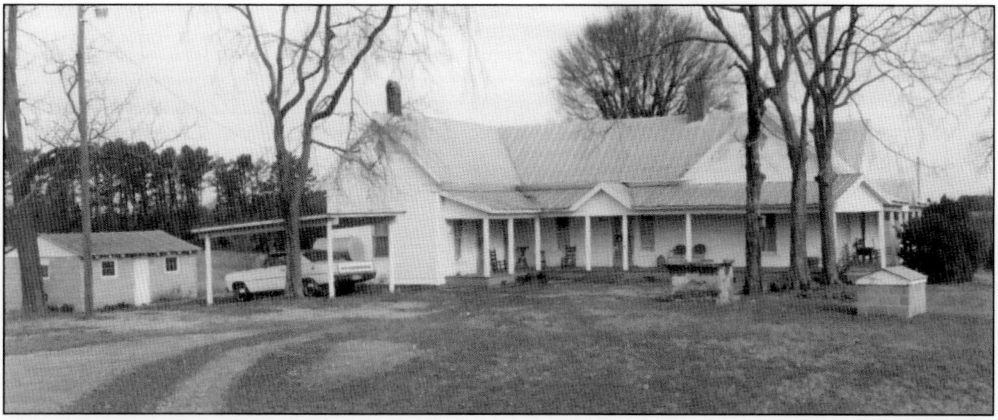

This late-Victorian farmhouse was built around 1900 and expanded in the early 1920s. Typical period elements include a wraparound porch, diamond-shaped louvers, and glass-panel entrance doors. The 125-acre non-mechanized farm was home to the Christopher Obediah Whitley family until it was demolished in the late 1990s.

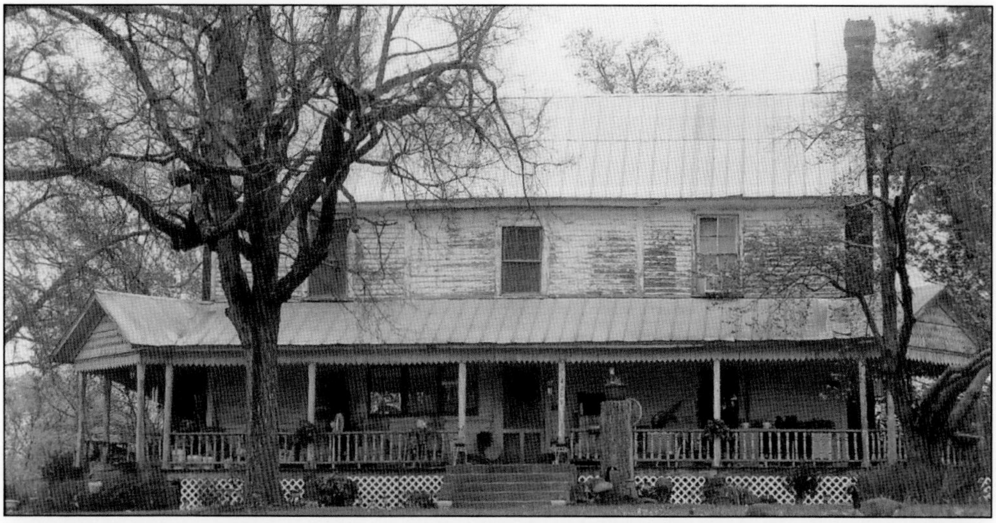

The Q.E.C. Coble farmhouse was built between 1915 and 1920. The two-story home is trimmed in Victorian style and has a brick chimney at each gable end. The second-story bedrooms have fireplaces, a rare feature in early-20th-century houses. Q.E.C. Coble, a significant landowner in Stanly and Union Counties, operated a mill on Rocky River a quarter-mile from his home.

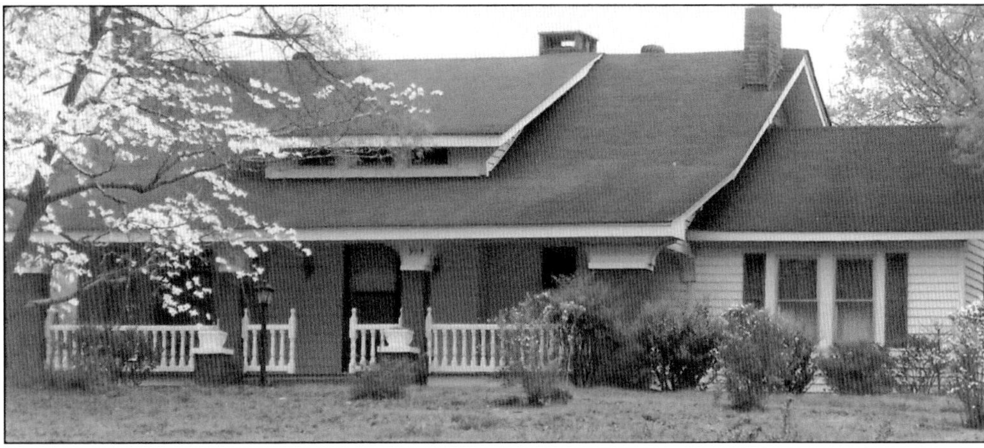

The Barger house, sitting on a hill on North Main Street, was the family home of druggist C.N. Barger and his wife and daughters. The house has gabled sides and a deep front porch. It was originally built by a member of the Furr family.

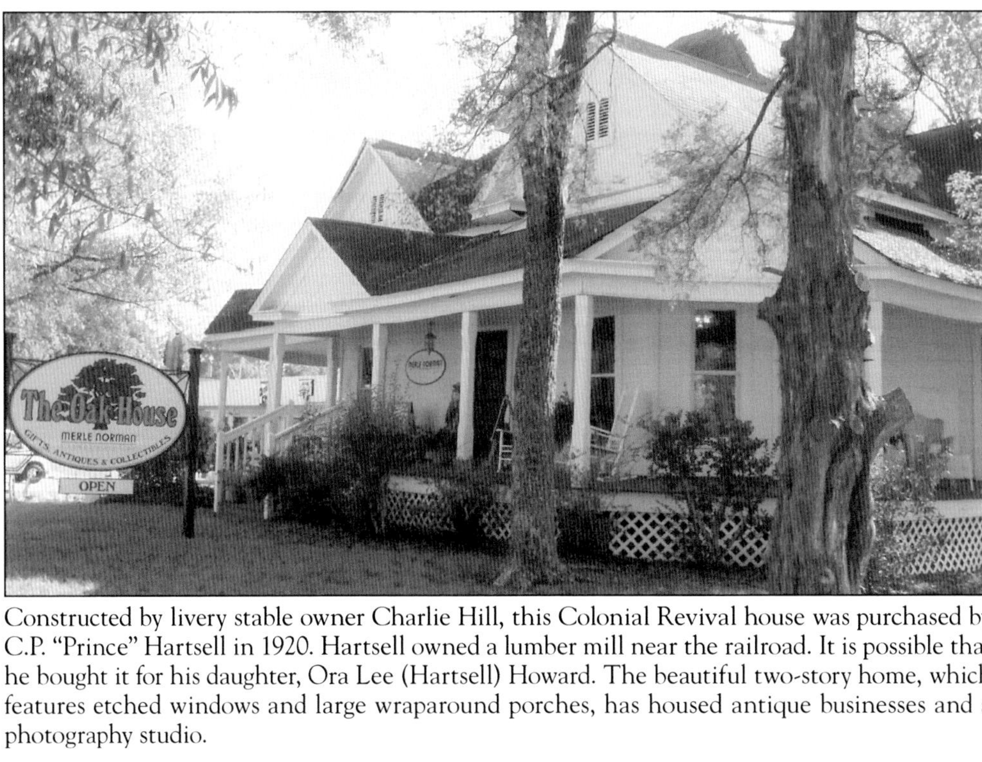

Constructed by livery stable owner Charlie Hill, this Colonial Revival house was purchased by C.P. "Prince" Hartsell in 1920. Hartsell owned a lumber mill near the railroad. It is possible that he bought it for his daughter, Ora Lee (Hartsell) Howard. The beautiful two-story home, which features etched windows and large wraparound porches, has housed antique businesses and a photography studio.

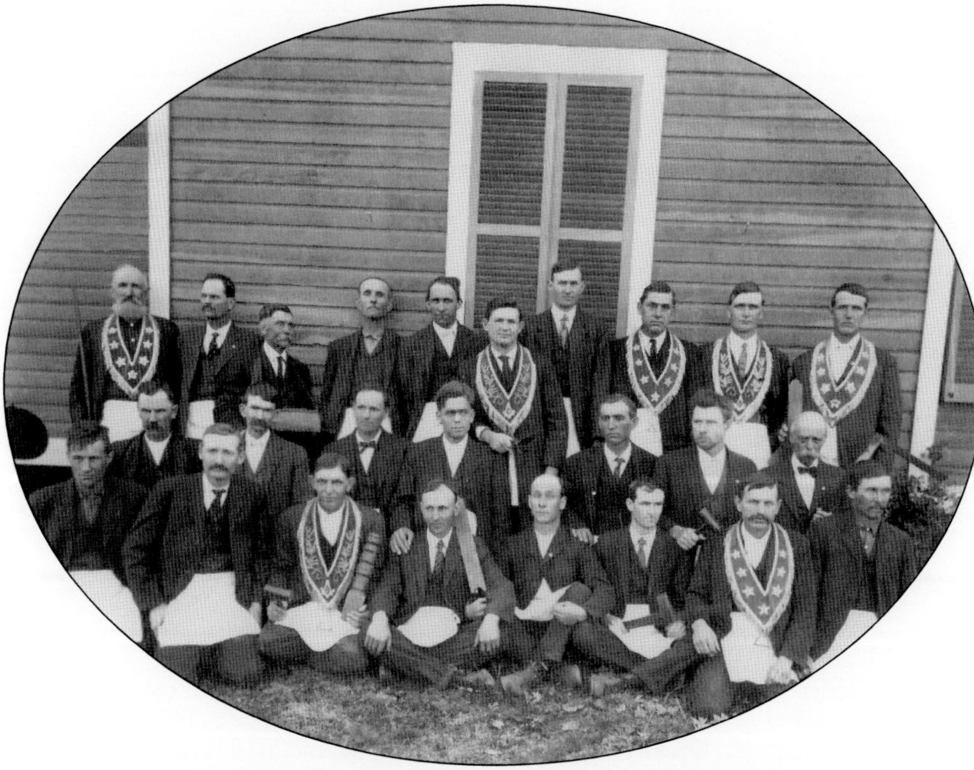

A group of influential men from the Big Lick and Oakboro areas formed the Big Lick Lodge of Ancient, Free, and Accepted Masons. One of the leaders of the group was Rev. C.J. Black (center), a Baptist minister and schoolmaster.

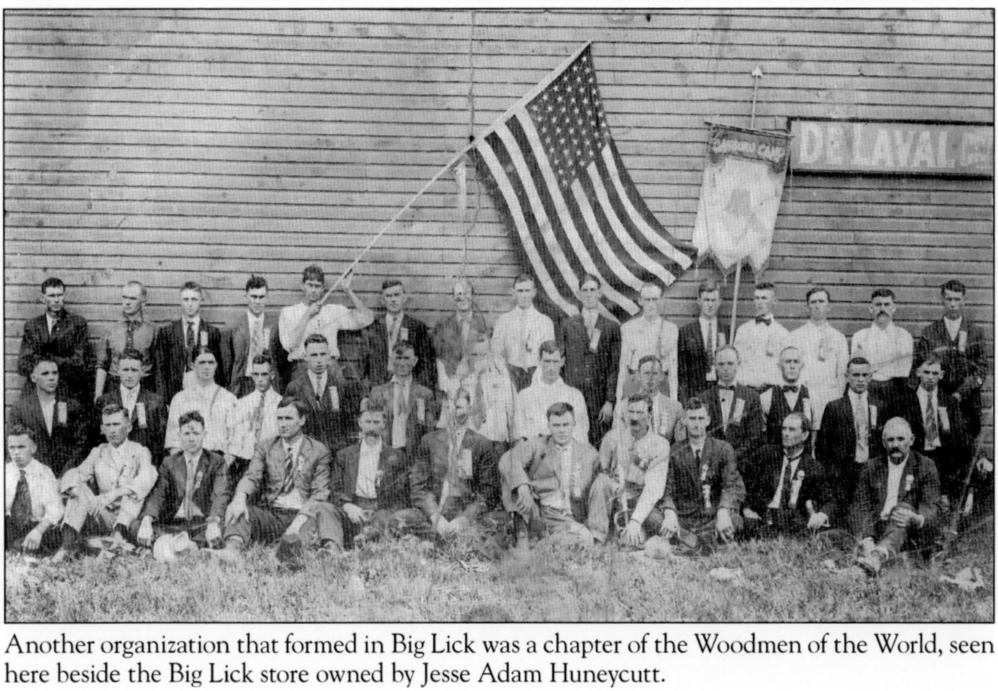

Another organization that formed in Big Lick was a chapter of the Woodmen of the World, seen here beside the Big Lick store owned by Jesse Adam Huneycutt.

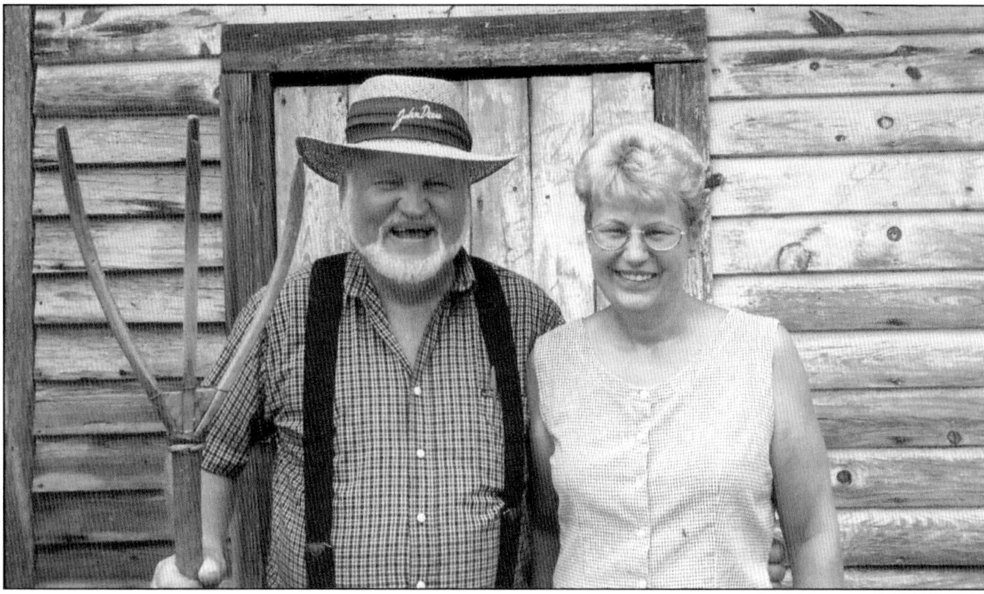

Ted Hinson has been an auctioneer for more than 50 years and has traveled across the South to buy and sell antiques and farm equipment. He and wife, Janice, opened Big Lick Festival Park to have a place in which antique dealers from all over the East Coast could show their wares. Hinson has appeared on national television in his jaunts on the antique trail. Big Lick Festival Park is now the home of Hinson's Auctions and the Big Lick Antique Festival Gun and Knife Show. The park also hosts nationally sanctioned tractor pulls, country flea markets, the annual Big Lick Bluegrass Festival, and a lumberjack competition. A born storyteller, Hinson wrote about the tale of the witch of Big Lick on his Internet site. Local legends abound about the Big Lick area. (Courtesy of Ted Hinson.)

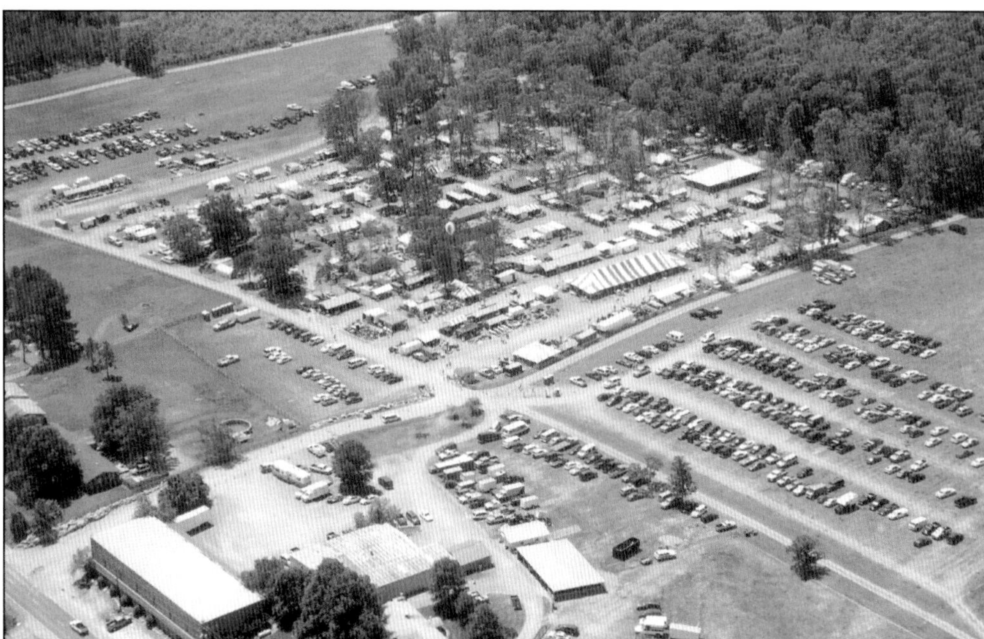

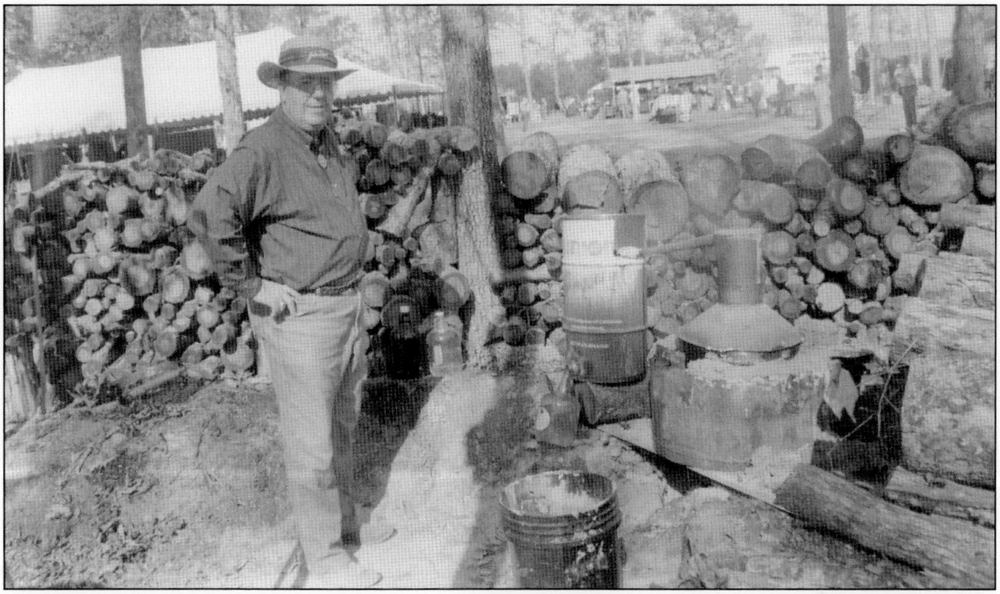

Each year at the Big Lick Festival Park, Gary Medlin demonstrates how to make moonshine. The western part of Stanly County held many moonshine operations, and Medlin demonstrates the equipment and methods of the craft to interested parties.

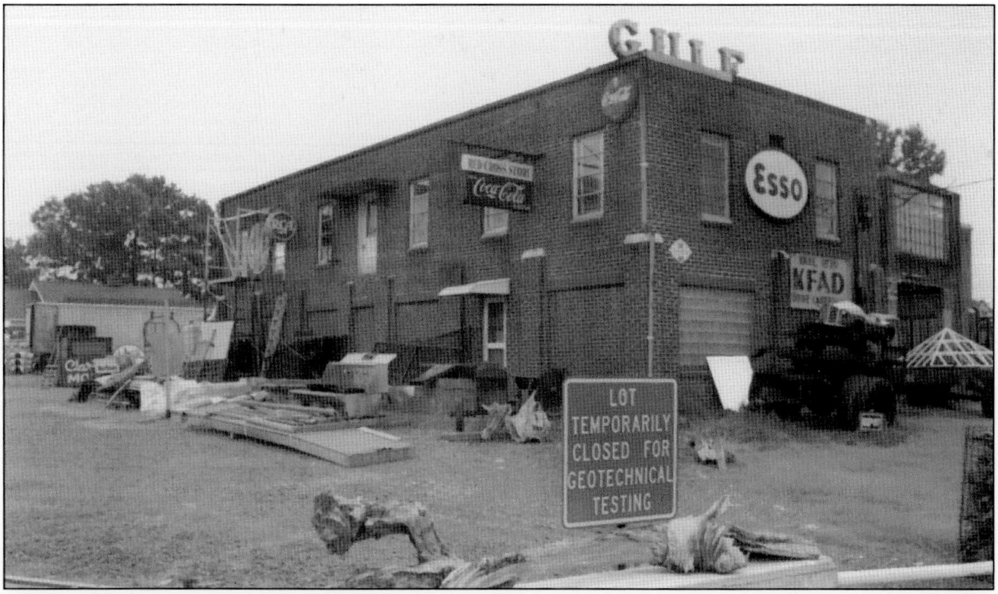

The building that houses Mr. Mike's Antique Shop, seen here, was in the right of way for the widening of Highway 24/27, so owner Mike Hinson moved it. This photograph was taken while testing was being done to determine the exact new location for the building. Hinson has appeared on the television show *American Pickers* and stocks many hard-to-find antiques and novelties.

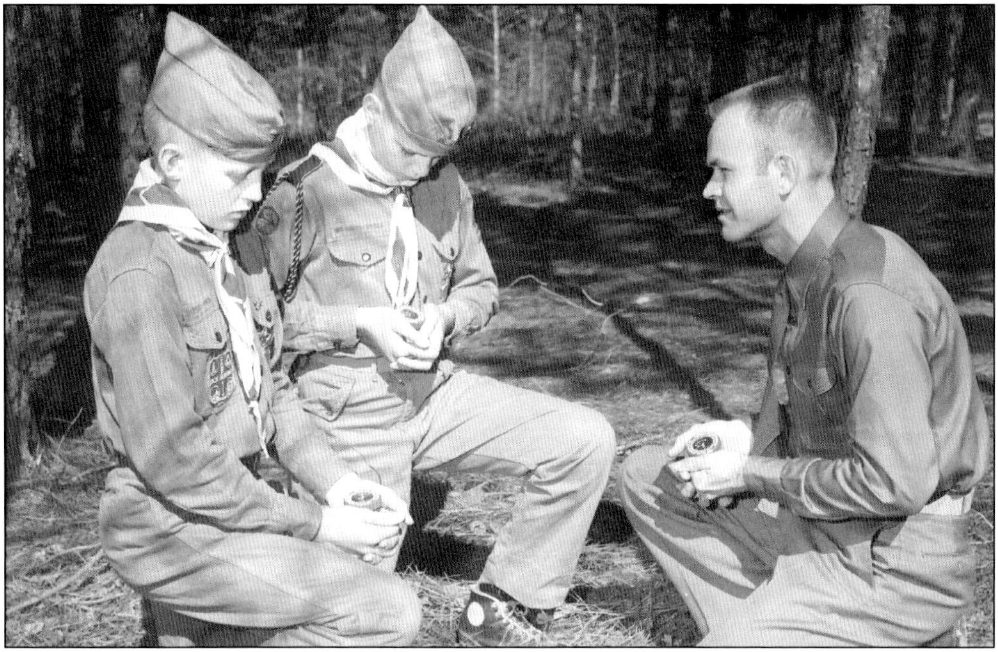

Oakboro Scouts Clyde Hatley (left) and Mackie McLendon (middle) are being taught how to read a compass by Melton Smith. Oakboro has a long tradition of scouting, which continues to this day. The various troops, made up of both boys and girls, meet in the Scout Hut on Seventh Street.

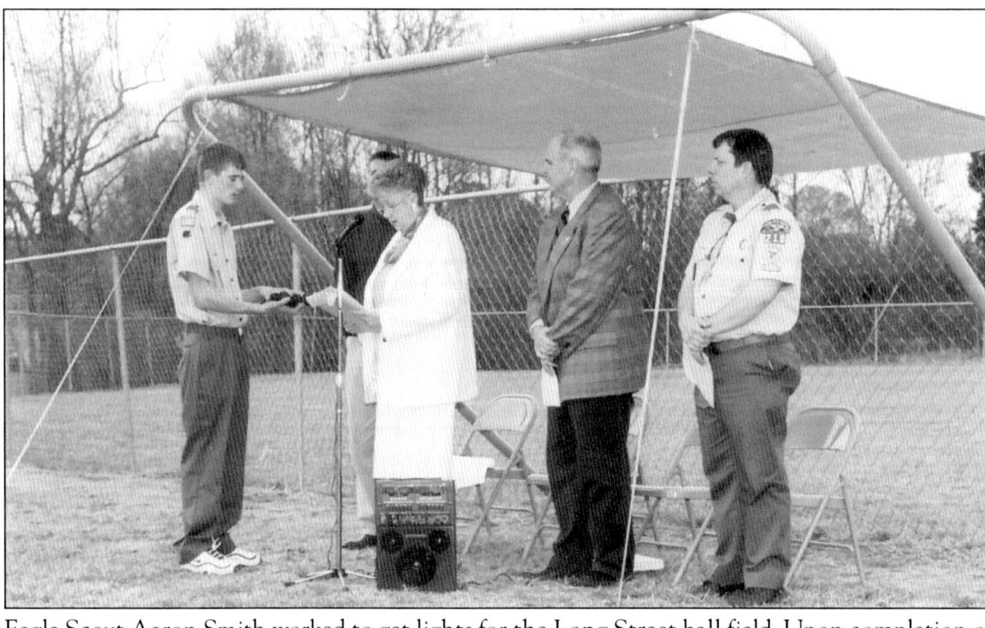

Eagle Scout Aaron Smith worked to get lights for the Long Street ball field. Upon completion of the project, he was presented with a US flag by Congressman Robin Hayes and a North Carolina State flag by Mayor Joyce Little. Smith was joined by his father, Randy, barely visible in the background, and scoutmaster Steve Teeter.

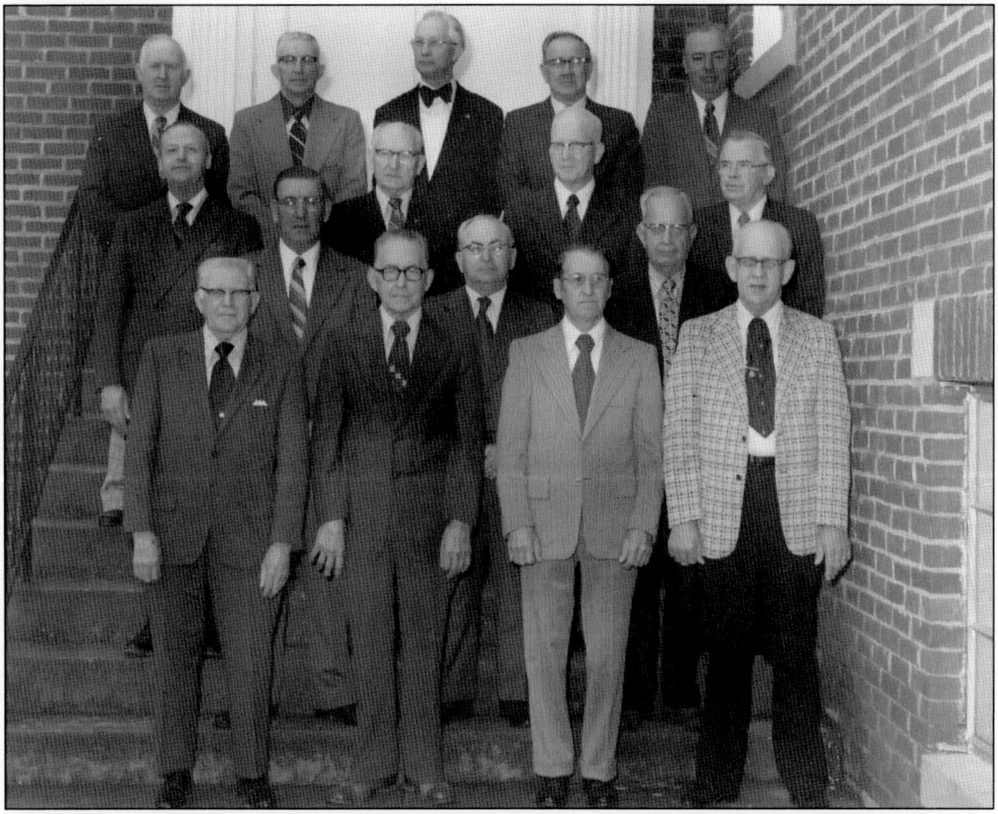

Among the 1970 men's Sunday school class of Oakboro First Baptist Church were influential leaders of the community. Pictured from left to right are (first row) Vann Coble, Claude Poplin, Silas Curlee, and T.E. Arrowood; (second row) Marvin Hatley, Frank Wallace, and Albert Rogers; (third row) J.D. Davis, Seymore Whitley, Raymond Drye, and Baylus Drye; (fourth row) Guy Rushing, Earl Crowell, Raymon C. Hatley, Crowell Smith, and Craig Huneycutt.

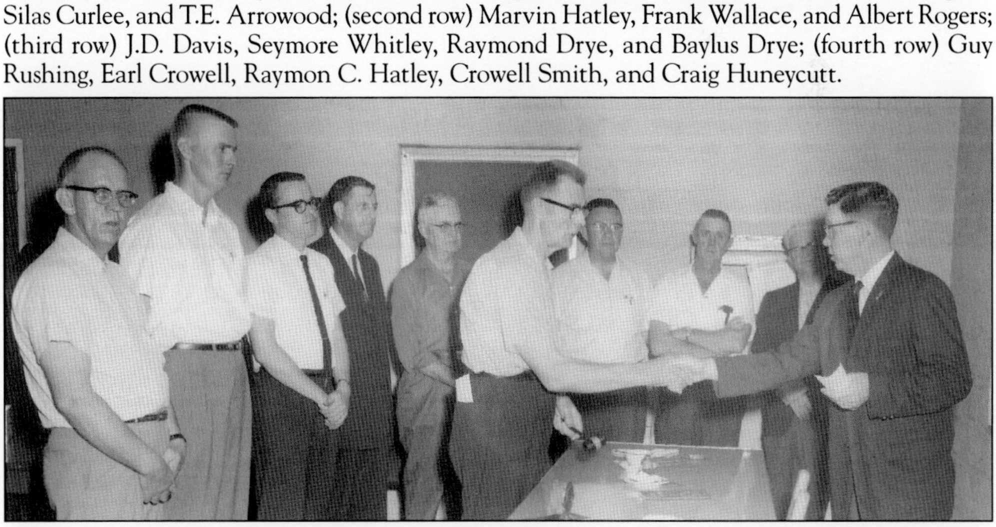

The Lions Club is one of a group of civic organizations established to serve Oakboro. In this photograph, Lyman Austin installs officers of the Lions Club for 1947. Others seen here are, from left to right, Eugene Arrowood, Harward Efird, Maurice Drye, Reverend Amos Kiser, Grover Harward, I.P. Efird (shaking hands), Maurice Smith, T.W. Coble, A.E. Howell, and Lyman Austin (shaking hands).

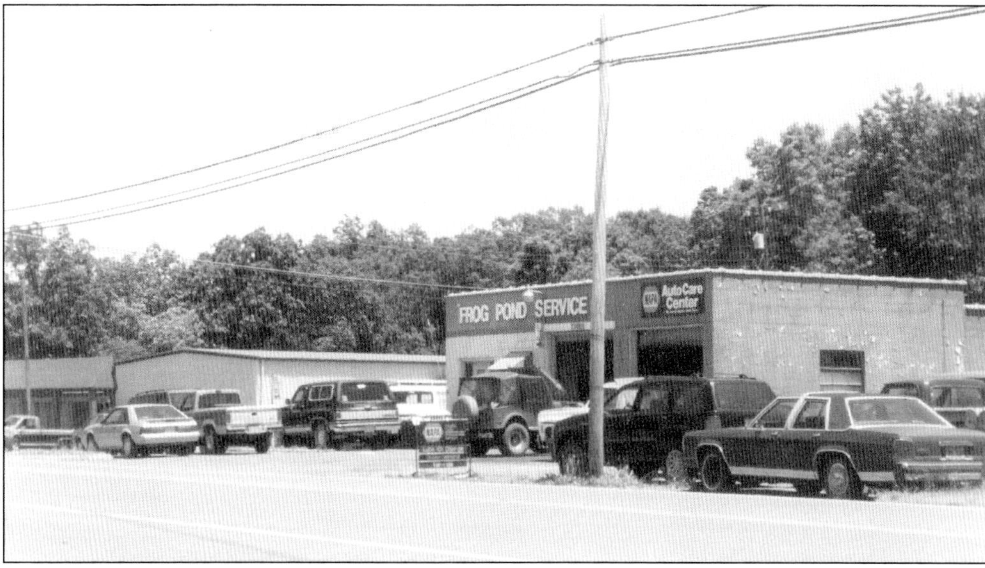

Frog Pond Service, established in the early 1950s, was operated by Futrell Clark and later by Hoyle Drake and Floyd Hinson. The building, situated on the south corner of Frog Pond Road and Highway 24/27, is currently owned and operated by Avera Whitley, offers automobile parts, and handles general repairs.

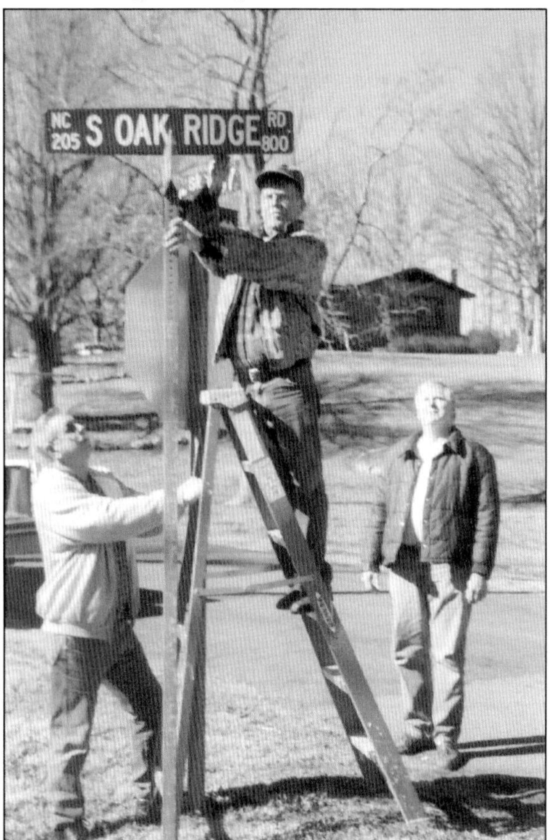

The area known as Red Cross is just four miles north of Oakboro, and its history is considered a part of the Oakboro area. In 2002, the community banded together and incorporated as the town of Red Cross, North Carolina. This photograph shows, from left to right, councilman Larry Wayne Smith, resident James Speight, and mayor Ray Quick installing street signs for the new town.

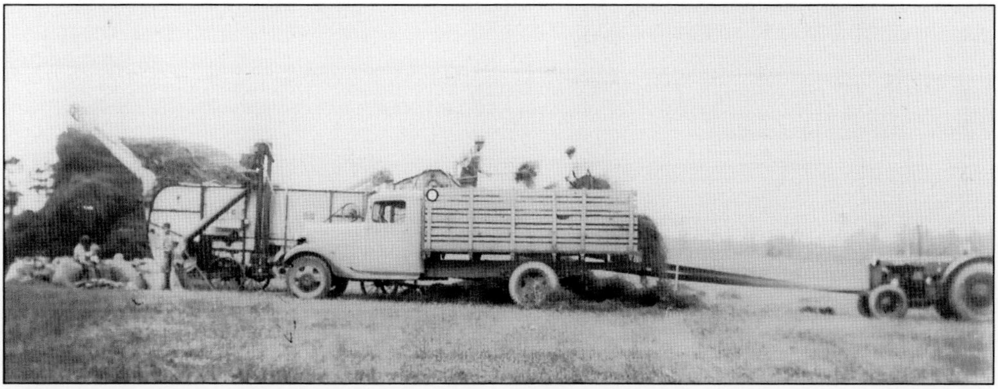

This truck is being loaded with lespedeza hay in a field on the Dan Hinson farm in Red Cross. Farming is still a big industry in the areas surrounding Oakboro; cotton is being planted again, and poultry farms have been profitable.

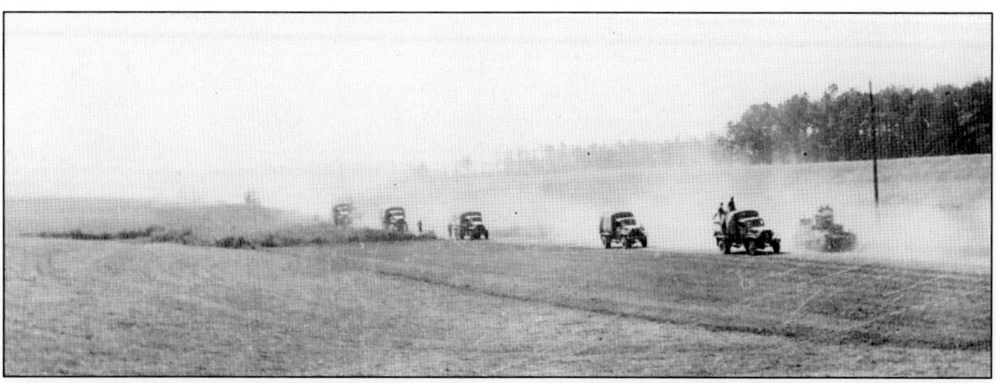

In 1941, the US Army held maneuvers in the area around Oakboro. This image, titled "Capturing Tanks," shows a line of tanks raising dust on a road north of town. General Patton is said to have been involved with the maneuvers. (Courtesy of SCHPM.)

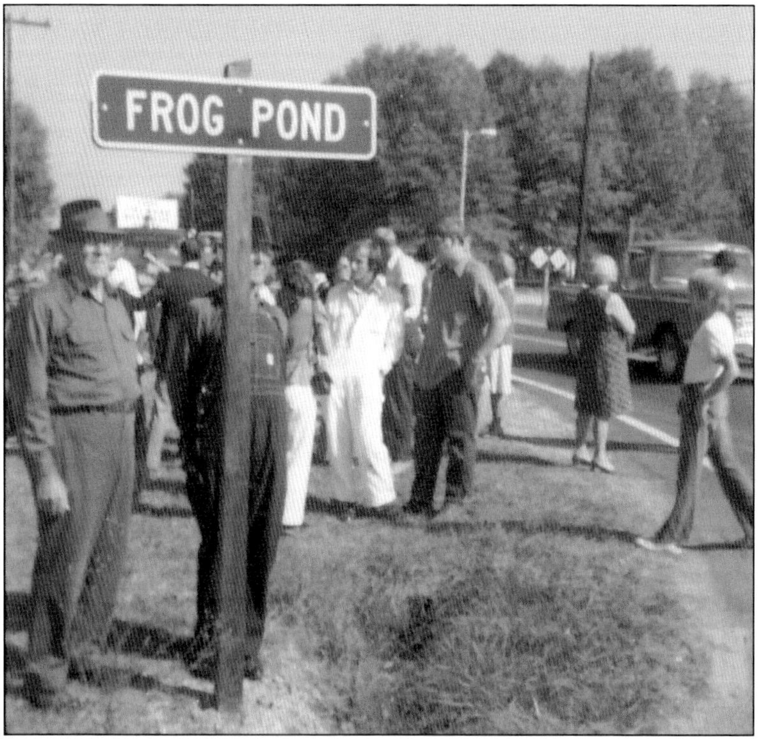

Ralph Burris (left) and an unidentified man stand by the new Frog Pond sign after debates concerning the renaming of the community of Frog Pond. The name remained unchanged. Frog Pond was saluted by the television show *Hee Haw* in the 1970s.

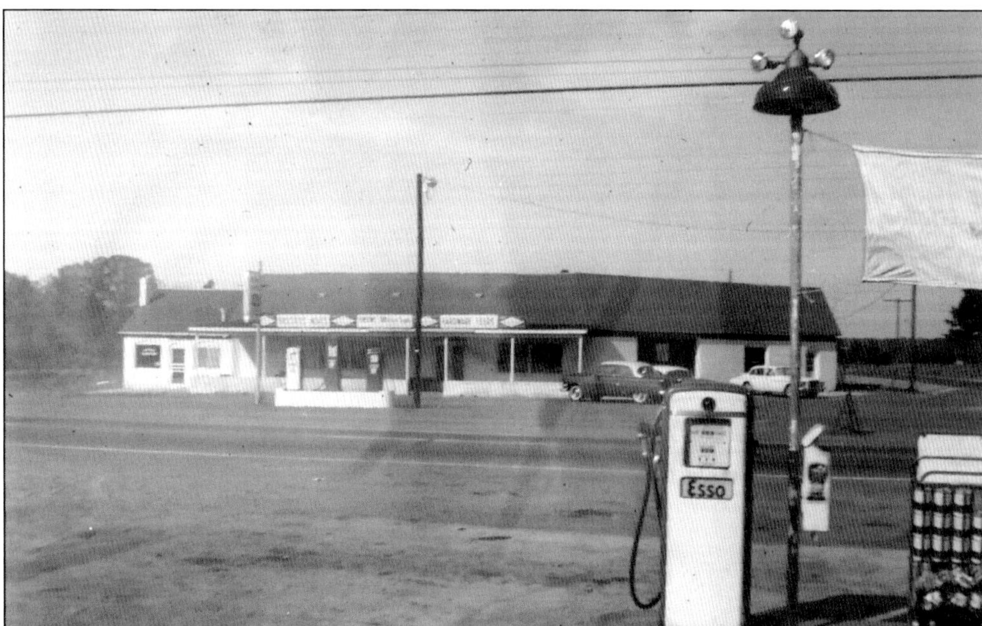

This photograph of the grocery store owned by Ellis Huneycutt at Frog Pond was taken in the 1960s. For many years, Gaddis Clark ran the section on the right as a garage. The small building to the left was Farrington Smith's bakery until Smith died, and then it housed Alberta Hinson's barbershop. The store closed around 1960.

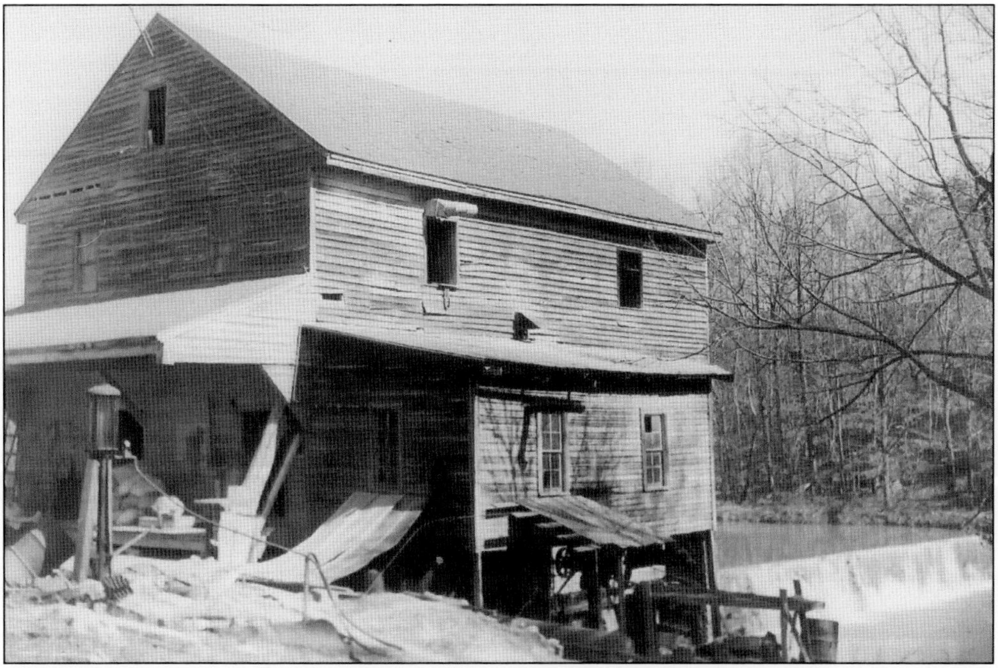

The Bridgeport Mill in the Frog Pond community was very active in the early 1900s. The old two-story wooden mill is seen here with the dam in the background. An old gas tank, a barrel, and a pile of tin are out front, and the water race is to the right. (Courtesy of SCHPM.)

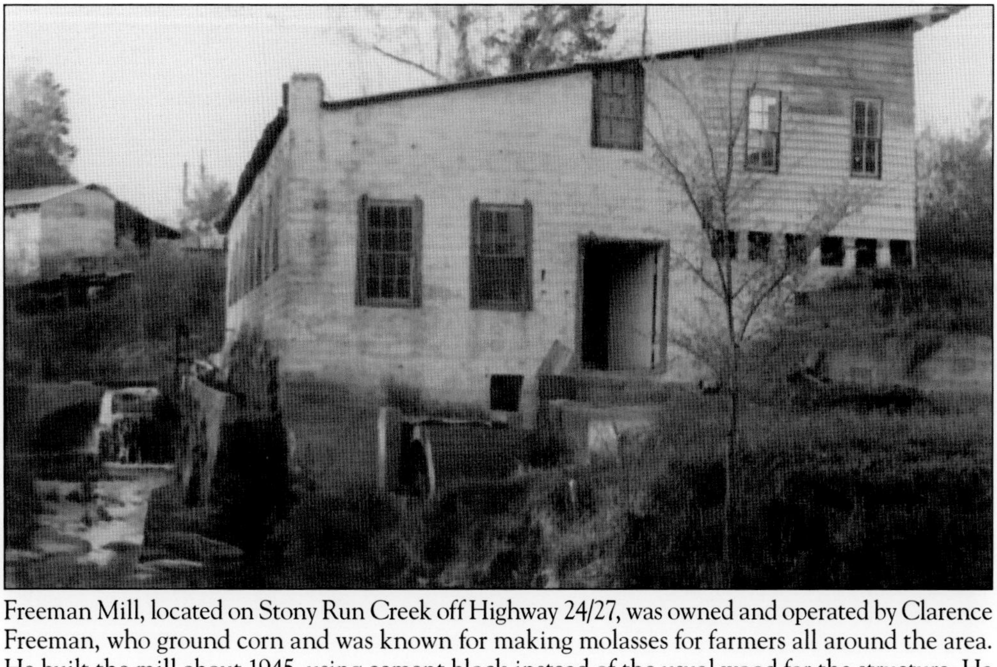

Freeman Mill, located on Stony Run Creek off Highway 24/27, was owned and operated by Clarence Freeman, who ground corn and was known for making molasses for farmers all around the area. He built the mill about 1945, using cement block instead of the usual wood for the structure. He also used recycled tractor tires for the mill's turbine wheels. (Courtesy of SCHPM.)

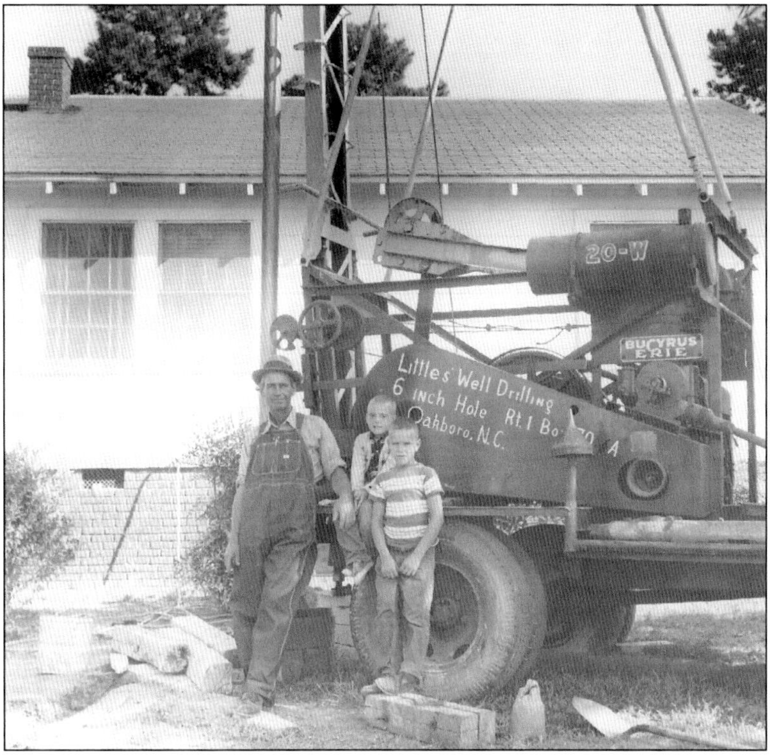

From left to right, Howard Little, ? Watkins, and Little's son Sylvester rest beside Little's well-digging machine in 1958. Little was kept busy in the 1950s and 1960s as the population of the area grew and people needed water for their new homes. (Courtesy of Eva Ann Howard and Jerry Carpenter.)

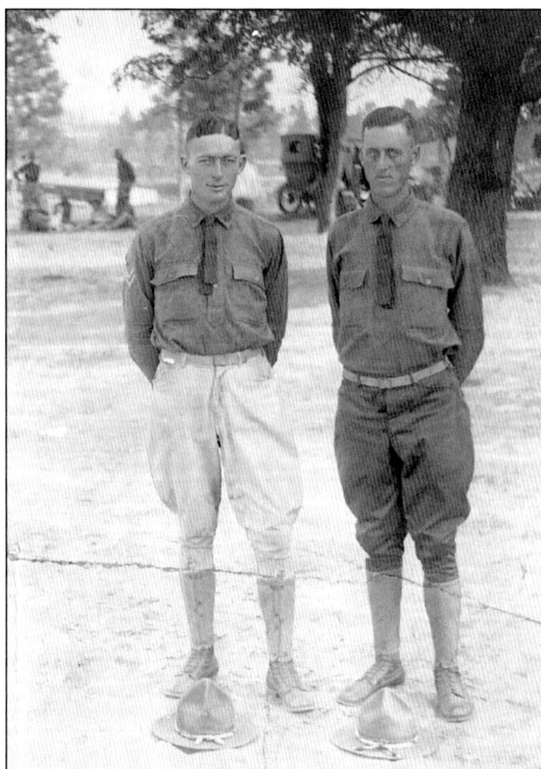

Brothers Charles Raymond Hathcock (left) and Thomas Burton Hathcock both served in World War I. During their tour of Europe, they were befriended by a French peasant couple who welcomed them into their home and treated them like family. The Hathcocks were a prominent family in the Mineral Springs community.

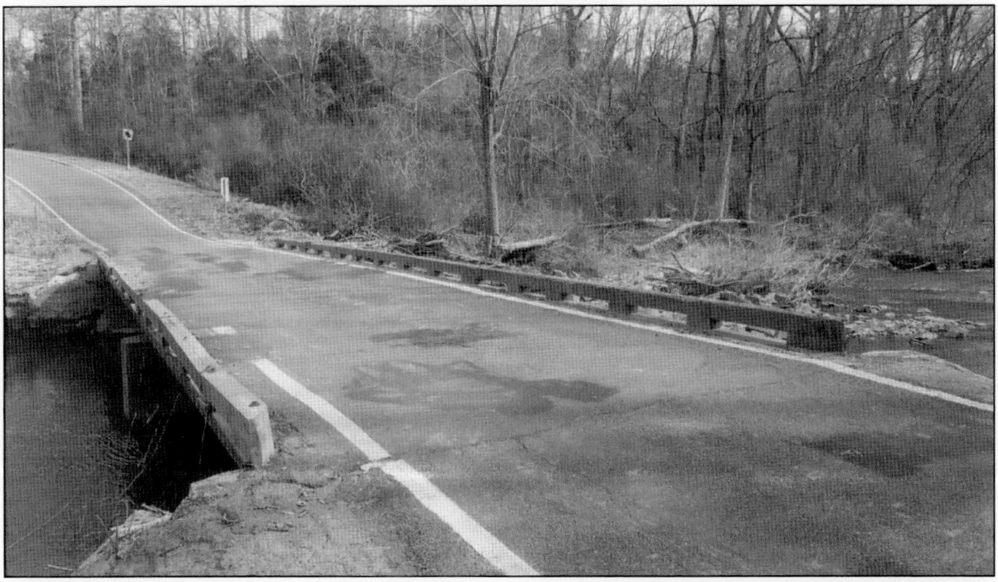

Western Stanly County has a number of low-water bridges. When heavy rains come, the creeks overflow, and these bridges become impassable. One such bridge goes over a little creek leading into Bear Creek at a place called Booger Hollar. Some say ghosts thrive there, others claim that a car parked on the bridge will roll backwards, and some have claimed to see strange lights appearing there at night.

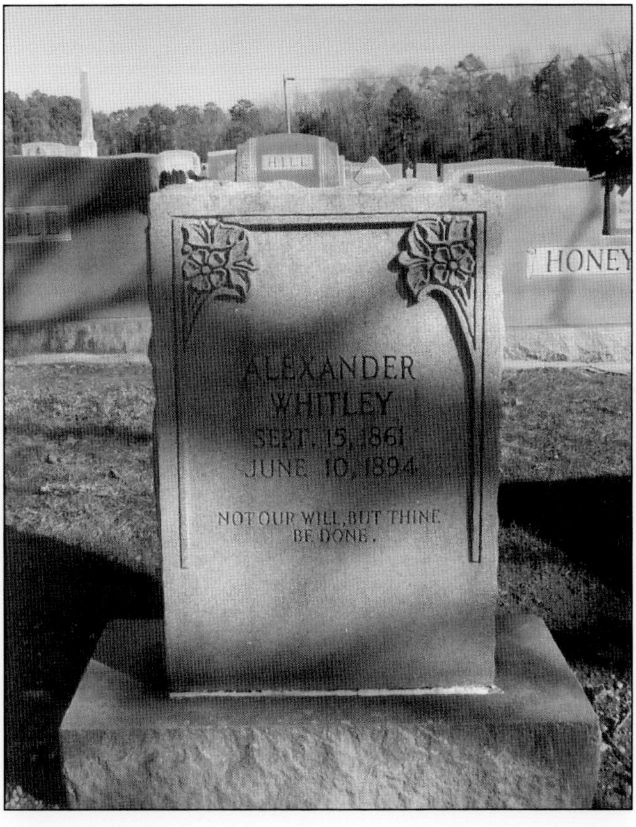

The legend of Alex Whitley has intrigued people for decades. David Almond wrote about the life and death of the infamous murderer in *The Lynching of Alex Whitley*. Local legend has it that after his death by hanging in Albemarle and his burial in a hasty grave there, his family snuck back, dug him up, and reburied him in this grave in the cemetery at Smith Grove Primitive Baptist Church.

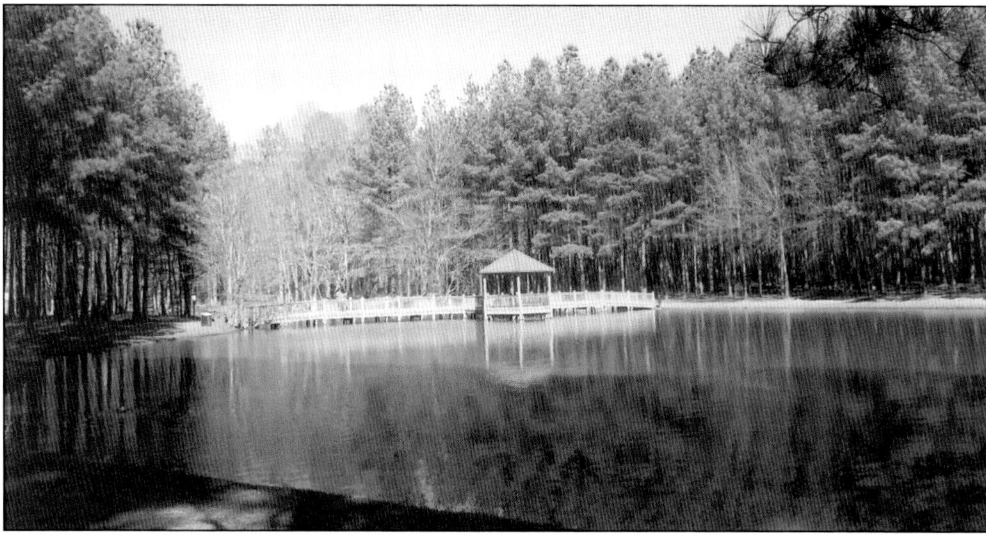

When the knitting mill closed, the company sold a portion of land to the Town of Oakboro for a district park. The park has been a huge success, with many residents using the facilities there. Work continues on creating an environment for folks who want to enjoy the outdoors. The park has also been a major asset in attracting visitors to the area.

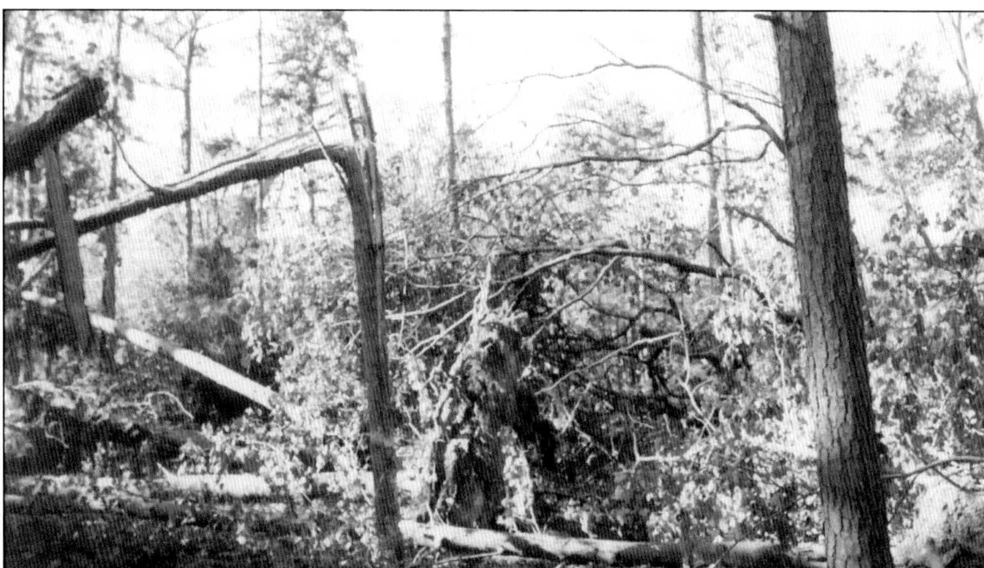

In the minds of locals, September 22, 1989, remains the day the hurricane hit. Hurricane Hugo, a storm as large as the state of Georgia, crashed its way into the Carolinas, destroying buildings, trees, and anything else in its way. The Oakboro area was hit hard, and hundreds of trees and sheds were downed or destroyed. (Courtesy of Jane Barnhardt.)

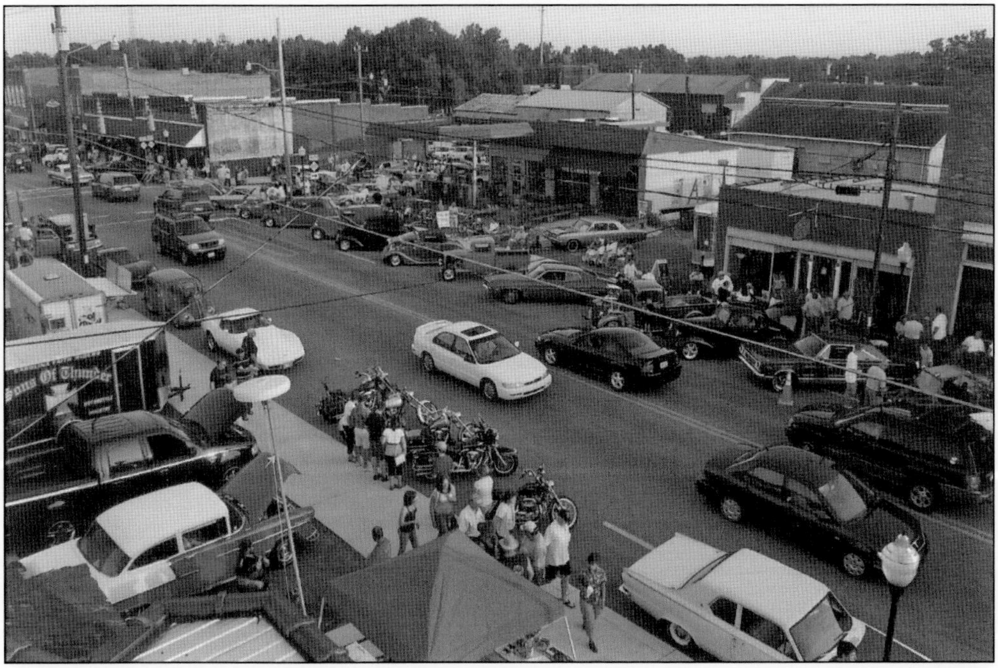

The town of Oakboro opens its doors and streets once a month to host a cruise-in. Owners of antique automobiles, muscle cars, and other vehicles line the streets to meet and talk to one another about their machines. On the fourth Friday of each month between April and October at about 9:00 p.m., the call goes out for the burnout—taking a vehicle to a designated place and spinning tires until they burn out or blow out. Thousands of folks attend the show and enjoy the restaurants and businesses in the town. (Courtesy of Greater Oakboro Business Association.)

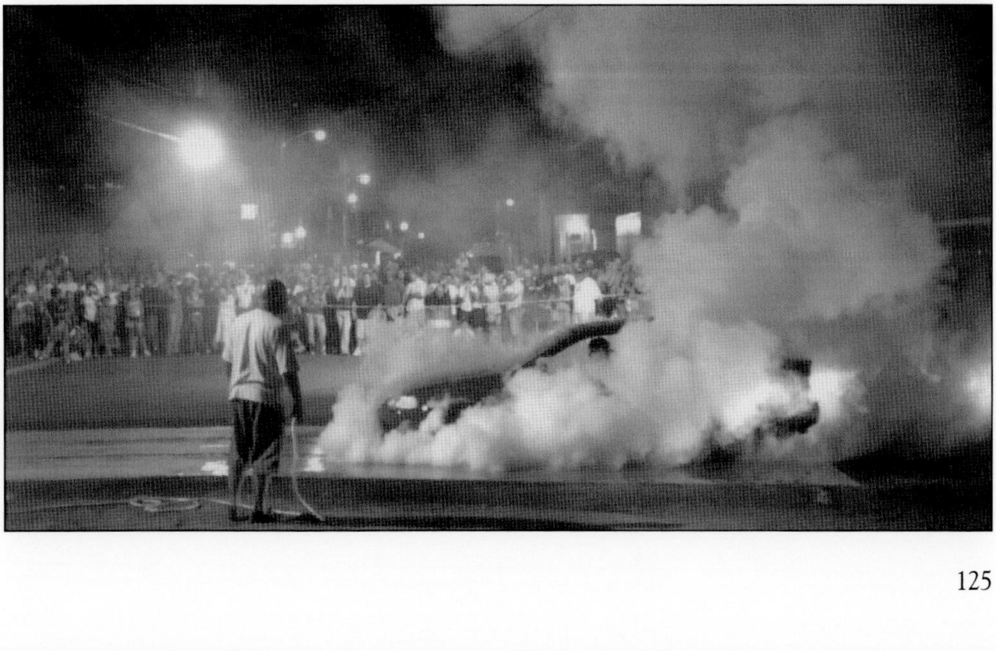

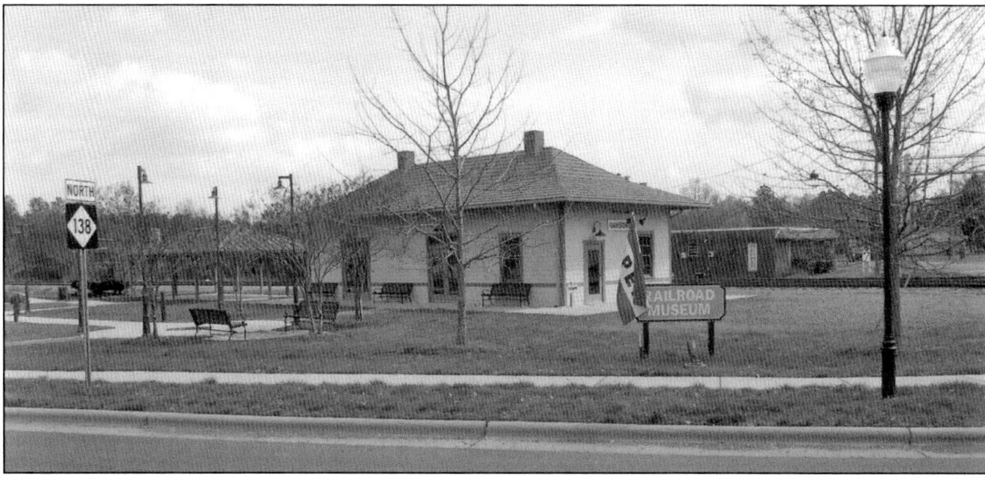

The Railroad Museum is a replica of the original Norfolk Southern depot and showcases artifacts from the beginning of the railroad to the present. Designed to honor and properly acknowledge people in the area who were instrumental in building the line, the museum houses the original Western Union telegraph key, desk, chairs, and adding machine. Also on display are items relating to the history of local workers. A Norfolk Southern caboose is permanently situated on tracks at the railroad museum. The symbolic railroad car brings attention to the history of the facility and provides an attraction for visitors. Plans are being made to restore the inside of the caboose to its original state.

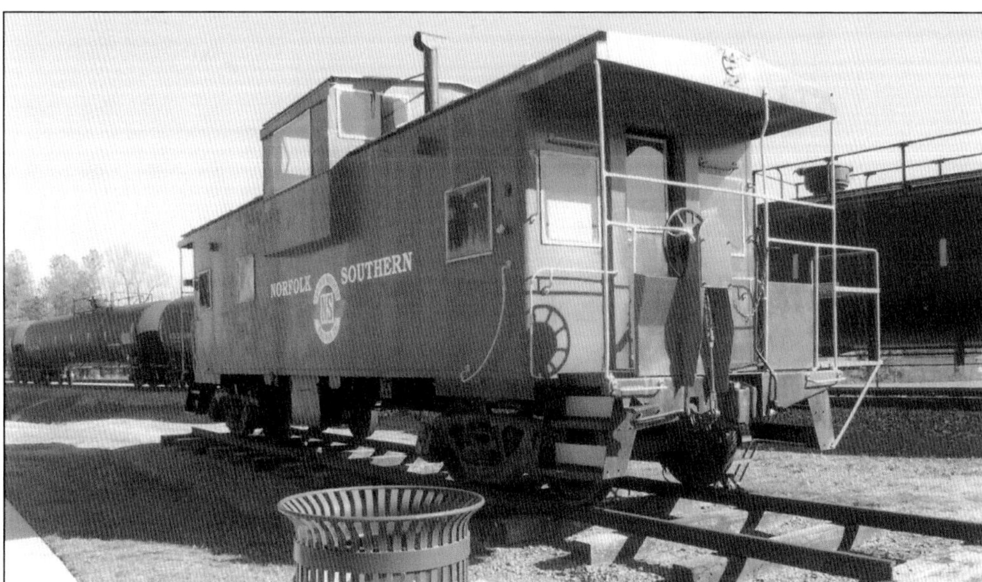

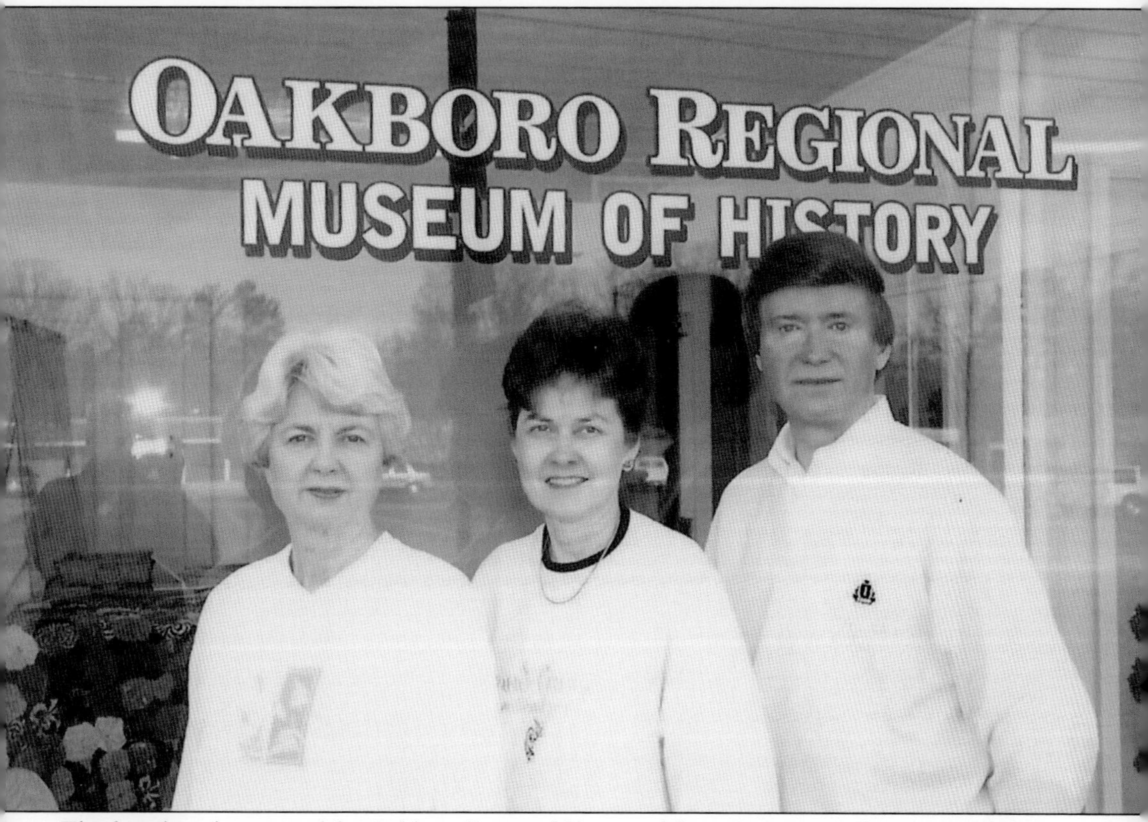

The founding directors of the Oakboro Regional Historical Foundation are to be commended for the work they have done in bringing a sense of history to the community. Pictured from left to right are Claudette B. Love, Jane H. Barnhardt, and Robert P. Barbee. Although each person has his or her own area of expertise, they worked in harmony and provided leadership in the effort to create a museum. Founded in 1999, the organization has grown tremendously. A museum was created, and other facilities have been acquired. Properties such as the Oakboro Presbyterian Church, the Railroad Museum, and the Coble-Teeter house have been added to its list of responsibilities. For this reason, the board of directors was expanded to include four additional members: Judy C. Tucker, Anabel W. Speight, Annabelle P. Morgan, and L. Douglas Burgess.

Discover Thousands of Local History Books Featuring Millions of Vintage Images

Arcadia Publishing, the leading local history publisher in the United States, is committed to making history accessible and meaningful through publishing books that celebrate and preserve the heritage of America's people and places.

Find more books like this at
www.arcadiapublishing.com

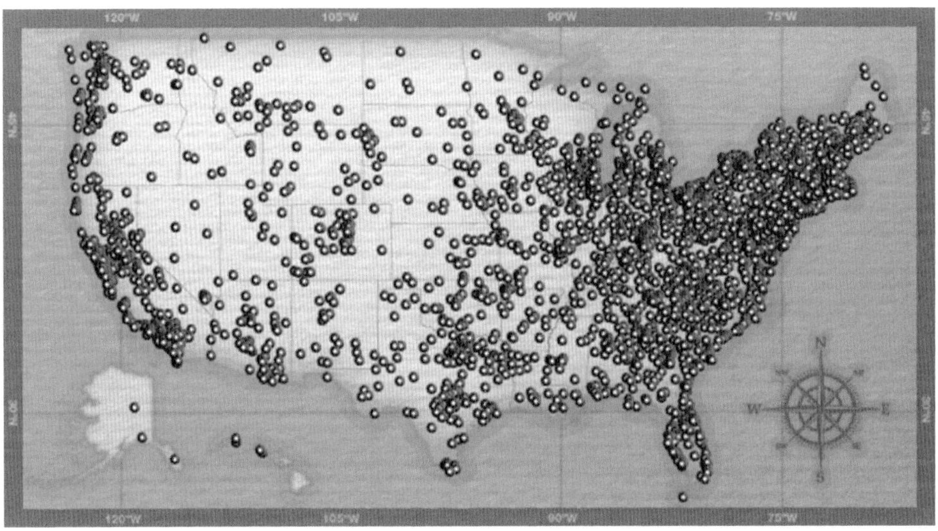

Search for your hometown history, your old stomping grounds, and even your favorite sports team.

Consistent with our mission to preserve history on a local level, this book was printed in South Carolina on American-made paper and manufactured entirely in the United States. Products carrying the accredited Forest Stewardship Council (FSC) label are printed on 100 percent FSC-certified paper.

MADE IN THE USA